WE OF THE
NEVER-NEVER

WE OF THE NEVER-NEVER

NEVER-NEVER

MRS AENEAS GUNN'S CLASSIC, TOGETHER WITH
THE LITTLE BLACK PRINCESS,
IN A SPECIAL, CONDENSED EDITION

Angus & Robertson Publishers

ANGUS & ROBERTSON PUBLISHERS
London • Sydney • Melbourne

We of the Never-Never first published 1908
The Little Black Princess first published 1905
This combined abridged edition first published by Angus &
Robertson Publishers, Australia, 1982

Reprinted 1982

Copyright Dr Harry A. Derham 1905, 1908

National Library of Australia
Cataloguing-in-publication data.
Gunn, Mrs Aeneas, 1870-1961.
  We of the Never-Never.
  Previously published as separate v.: London:
  Hutchinson, 1908 and London: A. Moring, 1905.
  Contents: We of the Never-Never—The little black princess.
  ISBN 0 207 14531 8.
  ISBN 0 207 14523 7 (pbk.).
  1. Northern Territory—Social life and customs—
  1901-1914. I. Title. II. Title: The little black princess.
  (Series: Australian classics (Angus & Robertson)).
994.2904'1'0924

Typeset in 10pt Baskerville by Hedges & Bell
Printed in Australia by Hedges & Bell

PUBLISHER'S NOTE

Before her marriage to Aeneas Gunn on 31 December 1901, Miss Jeannie Taylor had spent almost all her life in Melbourne. She had been a teacher during her working life there.

The newly married Mr and Mrs Gunn reached the remote Elsey cattle station in February 1902, and although Jeannie spent little more than a year there, she was able to learn a great deal about the local inhabitants and station life.

Mrs Gunn took a genuine interest in the Aborigines with whom she came in contact. It is obvious from some of the things she said and did, however, that she believed Aborigines should change their ways and copy the behaviour of the whites; but then, most Europeans of that day believed people of other races should copy the ways of the white man and did not recognise the importance of people retaining their racial identity. Mrs Gunn had sympathy and true affection for the Aborigines at a time when these attitudes were sadly lacking in other Europeans.

Although *The Little Black Princess* (1905) was published before *We of the Never-Never* (1908), the latter book has been placed first in this combined volume (with the exception of the last chapter which is now the Afterword), because it tells of the Gunns' trek to Elsey Station and of the many incidents which occurred during that journey and during their stay at the station. *The Little Black Princess* is the story of Bett-Bett, an eight-year-old Aboriginal princess who lived at Elsey Station and who developed a great affection for Mrs Gunn, her "Little Missus".

TO THE PUBLIC

IT is with the full consent of the bush-folk that this one year of their lives—the year 1902—is given to the world.

"Tell 'em anything you like," they said, one and all, unconsciously testifying to their single-heartedness. And in the telling I have striven to give that year as I found it.

At every turn the bush-folk have helped me; verifying statements and furnishing details required with minute exactness.

JEANNIE GUNN

Hawthorn
October, 1907

PRELUDE

WE—are just some of the bush-folk of the Never-Never.

Distinct in the foreground stand:

The Maluka, the Little Missus, the Sanguine Scot, the Head Stockman, the Dandy, the Quiet Stockman, the Fizzer, Mine Host, the Wag, Some of our Guests, a few black "boys" and lubras, a dog or two, Tam-o'-Shanter, Happy Dick, Sam Lee, and last but by no means least, Cheon—the ever-mirthful, irrepressible Cheon, who was crudely recorded on the station books as cook and gardener.

The background is filled in with an ever-moving company — a strange medley of Whites, Blacks and Chinese; of travellers, overlanders, and billabongers, who passed in and out of our lives, leaving behind them sometimes bright memories, sometimes sad, and sometimes little memory at all.

And All of Us, and many of this company, shared each other's lives for one bright, sunny year, away Behind the Back of Beyond, in the Land of the Never-Never; in that elusive land with an elusive name—a land of dangers and hardships and privations, yet loved as few lands are loved—a land that bewitches her people with strange spells and mysteries, until they call sweet bitter, and bitter sweet. Called the Never-Never, the Maluka loved to say, because they who have lived in it Never-Never voluntarily leave it. Sadly enough, there are too many who Never-Never do leave it. Others—the unfitted—will tell you that it is so called because they who succeed in getting out of it swear they will Never-Never return to it. But we who have lived in it, and loved it, and left it, know that our hearts can Never-Never rest away from it.

CAST OF CHARACTERS

as portrayed in the magnificent film *We of the Never-Never* produced by Adams Packer/Film Corporation of Western Australia.

The MISSUS
Jeannie (Mrs Aeneas) Gunn, the Maluka's wife (played by Angela Punch McGregor).

The MALUKA
Aeneas James Gunn, the Boss and husband to the Missus (played by Arthur Dignam).

BETT-BETT
An Aboriginal child, the Little Black Princess (played by Sibini Willi).

DAN
(the Head Stockman)
A bushman of the old type, bent on "educating the Missus" (played by Martin Vaughan).

MAC
(the Sanguine Scot)
The previous station manager, an incurable optimist and champion of the Missus (played by Tony Barry).

JACK
(the Quiet Stockman) A shy young
stockman, an expert with horses
(played by Lewis Fitz-Gerald).

The DANDY
A stockman, so known because of
his love for orderly surroundings
(played by John Jarratt).

CHEON
An invaluable Chinese cook, "the
jolliest old josser going"
(played by Cecil Parkee).

JACKEROO
An Aboriginal station hand
(played by Tommy Lewis).

MINE HOST
The proprietor of the pub
(played by Bob "Tex" Morton).

ROSY
A station lubra
(played by Mawuyul Yathalaway).

WE OF THE
NEVER-NEVER

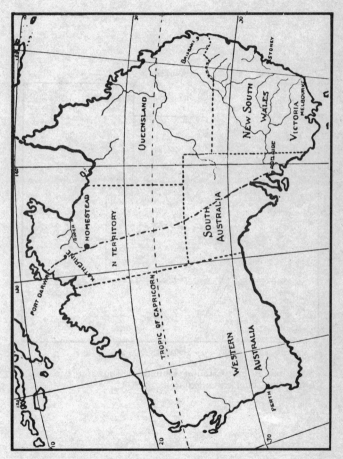

Overland route, Adelaide to Darwin

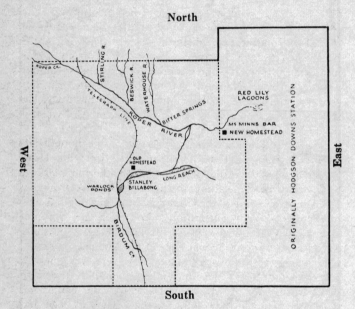

North

West

East

South

Scale map of Elsey Station. Dotted line shows area in 1902.
Outer line, later extended area.

Chapter 1

THE UNKNOWN WOMAN

TO begin somewhere near the beginning, the Maluka—better known at that time as the new Boss for the Elsey—and I, his "missus", were at Darwin in the Northern Territory, waiting for the train that was to take us just as far as it could—one hundred and fifty miles—on our way to the Never-Never. It was out of town just then, up-country somewhere, billabonging in true bush-whacker style, but was expected to return in a day or two, when it would be at our service.

Jack, the Quiet Stockman, was out at the homestead, "seeing to things" there. The Sanguine Scot, the Head Stockman, and the Dandy were in at the Katherine, marking time, as it were, awaiting instructions by wire from the Maluka, while some of the Company "put finishing touches" to their New Year celebrations. And everyone, with, of course, the exception of those in Darwin, was blissfully unconscious of even the existence of the Maluka's missus.

Knowing the Maluka by repute, however, everyone was agreed that the "Elsey had struck it lucky", until the telegraph wire, whispering the gossip of Darwin to the Katherine, whispered that the "new Boss for the Elsey had been and gone and married a missus just before leaving the South, and was bringing her along with him". Then the Sanguine Scot was filled with wrath, the Company with compassion, while the Dandy's consternation found relief in a dismayed "Heavens above!" (The Dandy, by the way, was only a dandy in his love of sweet, clean clothes and orderly surroundings. The heart of the man had not a touch of dandyism in it.) The Head Stockman was absent in his camp. Had he been present, much might have been said on the "advantages of having a woman about the place". The Wag, however, retained his usual flow of speech and spirits.

1

"Buck up, chaps!" he chuckled encouragingly. "They're not all snorters, you know. You might have the luck to strike one of the 'ministering angel' variety."

But the Sanguine Scot had been thinking rapidly, and, with characteristic hopefulness, felt he had the bull by the horns. "We'll just have to block her, chaps; that's all," he said. "A wire or two should do it"; and, inviting the Dandy "to come and lend a hand", led the way to the telegraph office; and presently there quivered into Darwin the first hint that a missus was not wanted at the Elsey.

"Would advise leaving wife behind till homestead can be repaired," it said; and, still confident of success, Mac felt that "ought to do the trick". "If it doesn't," he added, "we'll give her something stronger."

We, in Darwin, having exhausted the sight-seeing resources of the little town, were wishing "something interesting would happen", when the message was handed to the Maluka.

"This may do as a stopgap," he said, opening it, adding as he read it. "It looks brimful of possibilities for interested onlookers, seeing it advises leaving the wife behind." The Maluka spoke from experience, having been himself an interested onlooker "down south", when it had been suggested there that the wife should be left behind while he spied out the land; for, although the Maluka knew most of the Territory, he had not yet been to the Elsey Cattle Station.

Preferring to be "the interested onlooker" myself this time, when we went to the telegraph office it was the Maluka who wired: "Wife coming, secure buggy"; and in an incredibly short space of time the answer came back: "No buggy obtainable."

Darwin looked interested. "Mac hasn't wasted much time in making enquiries," it said.

"Or in apologies or explanations," the Maluka added shortly, and sent in reply:

"Wife can ride, secure suitable mount."

But the Sanguine Scot's fighting blood was up, and almost immediately the wire rapped out:

"No side-saddle obtainable. Stock horses all flash"; and the onlookers started in astonishment.

"Mac's in deadly earnest this time," they said, and the Maluka, with a quiet "So am I", went back to the telegraph.

Now, in the Territory, everybody knows everybody else, but particularly the telegraph people; and it often happens that when telegrams of general interest are passing through, they are accompanied by confidential asides—little scraps of harmless gossip not intended for the departmental books. Therefore it was whispered in the tail of the last message that the Katherine was watching the fight with interest, was inclined to "reckon the missus was a goer", and that public sympathy was with the stockman—the Katherine had its women-folk and was thankful; but the Katherine knew that although a woman in a settlement only rules her husband's home, the wife of station-manager holds the peace and comfort of the stockmen in the hollow of her hand.

"Stock horses all flash," the Sanguine Scot said, and then went out and apologised to an old bay horse. "We had to settle her hash somehow, Roper, old chap," he said, stroking the beautiful neck, adding tenderly as the grand old head nosed into him: "You silly old fool! You'd carry her like a lamb if I let you."

Then the Maluka's reply came, and Mac whistled in amazement. "By George!" he said to those near him, "she *is* a goer, a regular goer"; and after much careful thought wired an inane suggestion about waiting until after the Wet.

Darwin laughed outright, and an emphatic: "Wife determined, coming Tuesday's train", from the Maluka was followed by a complete breakdown at the Katherine.

Then Darwin came in twos and threes to discuss the situation, and while the men offered every form of service and encouragement, the women-folk spoke of a woman "going bush" as "sheer madness". "Besides, no woman travels during the Wet," they said, and the Maluka "hoped she would prove the exception".

"But she'll be bored to death if she does reach the homestead alive," they prophesied; and I told them they were not very complimentary to the Maluka.

3

"You don't understand," they hastened to explain. "He'll be camping out most of his time, miles away from the homestead," and I said, "So will I."

"So you think," they corrected. "But you'll find that a woman alone in a camp of men is decidedly out of place"; and I felt severely snubbed.

The Maluka suggested that he might yet succeed in persuading some suitable woman to come out with us, a maid or companion; but the opposition, wagging wise heads, pursed incredulous lips, as it declared that "no one but a fool would go out there for either love or money". A prophecy that came true, for eventually we went "bush" womanless.

The Maluka's eyes twinkled as he listened. "Does the cap fit, little 'un?" he asked; but the womenfolk told him that it was not a matter for joking.

"Do you know that there is not another white woman within a hundred-mile radius?" they asked; and the Maluka pointed out that it was not all disadvantage for a woman to be alone in a world of men. "The men who form her world are generally better and truer men, because the woman in their midst is dependent on them alone, for companionship, and love, and protecting care," he assured them.

"Men are selfish brutes," the opposition declared, rather irrelevantly, looking pointedly at the Maluka.

He smiled with as much deference as he could command. "Also," he said, "a woman alone in a world of men rarely complains of their selfishness"; and I hastened to his assistance. "Particularly when those men are chivalrous bushmen," I began; then hesitated, for, since reading the telegrams, my ideas of bush chivalry needed readjustment.

"Particularly when those men are chivalrous bushmen," the Maluka agreed, with the merry twinkle in his eyes; for he perfectly understood the cause of the sudden breakdown. Then he added gravely: "For the average bushman will face fire and flood, hunger and even death itself, to help the frail or weak ones who come into his life; although he'll strive to the utmost to keep the Unknown Woman out of his environments, particuarly when those environments are a hundred miles from anywhere."

The opposition looked incredulous. "Hunger and death!"

4

it said. "Fiddlesticks!" "It would just serve them right if she went"; and the menfolk pointed out that this was, now, hardly flattering to the missus.

The Maluka passed the interruption by without comment. "The Unknown Woman is brimful of possibilities to a bushman," he went on; "for although she *may* be all womanly strength and tenderness, she may also be anything, from a weak timid fool to a self-righteous shrew, bristling with virtue and indignation. Still," he added earnestly, as the opposition began to murmur, "when a woman does come into our lives, whatever type she may be, she lacks nothing in the way of chivalry, and it rests with herself whether she remains an outsider or becomes just One of Us. Just One of Us," he repeated, unconsciously pleading hard for the bushman and his greatest need—"not a goddess on a pedestal, but just a comrade to share our joys and sorrows with."

The opposition wavered. "If it wasn't for those telegrams," it said. But Darwin, seeing the telegrams in a new light, took up the cudgels for the bushmen.

"Poor beggars," it said, "you can't blame them. When you come to think of it, the Unknown Woman *is* brimful of possibilities." Even then, at the Katherine, the possibilities of the Unknown Woman were being tersely summed up by the Wag.

"You'll sometimes get ten different sorts rolled into one," he said finally, after a long dissertation. "But, generally speaking, there's just three sorts of 'em. There's Snorters—the Goers, you know—the sort that go rampaging round, looking for insults, and naturally finding them; and then there's fools; and *they're* mostly screeching when they're not smirking—the uncertain-coy-and-hard-to-please variety, you know," he chuckled. "And then," he added seriously, "there's the right sort, the sort you tell things to. They're A1 all through the piece."

The Sanguine Scot was confident, though, that they were all alike, and none of 'em were wanted; but one of the Company suggested "if she was little, she'd do. The little 'uns are all right," he said.

But public opinion deciding that "the sort that go messing

5

round where they know they're not wanted are always big and muscular and Snorters", the Sanguine Scot was encouraged in his determination to "block her somehow".

"I'll block her yet; see if I don't," he said confidently. "After all these years on their own, the boys don't want a woman messing round the place." And when he set out for the railway along the north track, to face the "escorting trick", he repeated his assurances. "I'll block her, chaps, never fear," he said; and glowering at a "quiet" horse that had been sent by the lady at the Telegraph, added savagely, "and I'll begin by losing that brute first turn out".

Chapter 2

THE LAND OF PLENTY OF TIME

FROM sun-up to sundown on Tuesday, the train glided quietly forward on its way towards the Never-Never; and from sun-up to sundown the Maluka and I experienced the kindly consideration that it always shows to travellers; it boiled a billy for us at its furnace; loitered through the pleasantest valleys; smiled indulgently, and slackened speed whenever we made merry with the blacks, by pelting them with chunks of watermelon; and generally waited on us hand and foot, the Man-in-Charge pointing out the beauty spots and places of interest, and making tea for us at frequent intervals.

It was a delightful train—just a simple-hearted, chivalrous, weather-beaten, old bush-whacker, at the service of the entire Territory. "There's nothing the least bit officious or stand-offish about it," I was saying, when the Man-in-Charge came in with the first billy of tea.

"Of course not!" he said, unhooking cups from various crooked-up fingers. "It's a Territorian, you see."

"And had all the false veneer of civilisation peeled off long ago," the Maluka said, adding with a sly look at my discarded gloves and gossamer. "It's wonderful how quietly the Territory does its work."

The Man-in-Charge smiled openly as he poured out the tea, proving thereby his kinship with all other Territorians; and as the train came to a standstill, swung off and slipped some letters into a box nailed to an old tree-trunk.

At the far end of the train, away from the engine, the passengers' car had been placed, and as in front of it a long, long line of low-stacked sinuous trucks slipped along in the rear of the engine, all was open view before us; and all day long, as the engine trudged onwards—hands in pockets, so to speak, and whistling merrily as it trudged—I stood beside the Maluka on the little platform in front of the passengers' car, drinking in my first deep, intoxicating draught of the glories of the tropical bush.

There were no fences to shut us in; and as the train zig-zagged through jungle and forest and river-valley — stopping now and then to drink deeply at magnificent rivers ablaze with water-lilies — it almost seemed as though it were some kindly mammoth creature, wandering at will through the bush.

Here and there, kangaroos and other wild creatures of the bush loped out of our way and, sitting up, looked curiously after us; again and again little groups of blacks hailed us, scrambling after watermelon and tobacco with shouts of delight; and, invariably, on nearing the tiny settlements along the railway, we drove before us white fleeing flocks of goats.

At every settlement we stopped and passed the time of day and, giving out mail-bags, moved on again into the forest. Now and again, stockmen rode out of the timber and received mail-bags, and once a great burly bushman, a staunch old friend of the Maluka's, boarded the train, and greeted him with a hearty hand-shake.

"Hullo! old chap!" he called in welcome, as he mounted the steps of the little platform. "I've come to inspect your latest investment"; but catching sight of the "latest investment", he broke into a deafening roar.

"Good Lord!" he shouted, looking down upon me from his great height, "is that all there is of her? They're expecting one of the prize-fighting variety down there," and he jerked his head towards the Never-Never. Then he congratulated the Maluka on the size of his missus.

"Gimme the little 'uns," he said, nearly wringing my hand off in his approval. "You can't beat 'em for pluck."

Until sundown we jogged quietly on, meandering through further pleasant places and meetings; drinking tea and chatting with the Man-in-Charge between whiles, extracting a maximum of pleasure from a minimum rate of speed; for travelling in the Territory has not yet passed that ideal stage where the travelling itself — the actual going — is all pleasantness.

8

As we approached Pine Creek I confided to the menfolk that I was feeling a little nervous. "Supposing that telegraphing bush-whacker decides to shoot me off-hand on my arrival," I said; and the Man-in-Charge said amiably: "It'll be brought in as justifiable homicide; that's all." Then reconnoitring from the platform, he "feared" we were "about to be boycotted".

There certainly were very few men on the station, and the Man-in-Charge, recognising one of them as the landlord of the Playford, assured us there was nothing to fear from that quarter. "You see, you represent business to him," he explained.

Everyone but the landlord seemed to have urgent business in the office or at the far end of the platform, but it was quickly evident that there was nothing to fear from him; for, finding himself alone to do the honours of the Creek, he greeted us with an amused: "She doesn't look up to sample sent by telegram"; and I felt every meeting would be, at least, unconventional. Then we heard that as Mac had "only just arrived from the Katherine, he couldn't leave his horses until they were fixed up"; but the landlord's eyes having wandered back to the "Goer", he winked deliberately at the Maluka before inviting us to "step across to the pub".

The Pub seemed utterly deserted, and with another wink the landlord explained the silence by saying that "a cyclone of some sort" had swept most of his "regulars" away; and then he went shouting through the echoing passages for a "boy" to "fetch along tea".

Before the tea appeared, an angry Scots voice crept to us through thin partitions, saying: "It's not a fit place for a woman, and, besides, nobody wants her!" And in a little while we heard the same voice inquire for "the Boss".

"The telegraphing bush-whacker," I said, and invited the Maluka to come and see me defy him. But when I found myself face to face with over six feet of brawny, quizzing, wrathful-looking Scotsman, all my courage slipped away and, edging closer to the Maluka, I held out my hand to the bushman, murmuring lamely: "How do you do?"

Instantly a change came over the rugged, bearded face. At the sight of the "Goer" reduced to a meek five feet, all the wrath died out of it, and with twitching lips and twinkling eyes Mac answered mechanically, "Quite well, thank you," and then coughed in embarrassment.

That was all; no fierce blocking, no defying. And with the cough, the absurdity of the whole affair, striking us simultaneously, left us grinning like a trio of Cheshire cats.

It was a most eloquent grinning, making all spoken apology or explanation unnecessary; and by the time it had faded away we thoroughly understood each other, being drawn together by a mutual love of the ridiculous. Only a mutual love of the ridiculous, yet not so slender a basis for a lifelong friendship as appears, and by no means an uncommon one "out bush".

"Does the station pay for the telegrams, or the loser?" the landlord asked in an aside, as we went in to supper; and after supper the preparations began for the morrow's start.

The Sanguine Scot, anxious to make amends for the telegrams, was full of suggestions for smoothing out the difficulties of the road. Like many men of his type, whatever he did he did it with all his heart and soul—hating, loving, avenging, or forgiving with equal energy; and he now applied himself to helping the Maluka to "make things easy for her", as zealously as he had striven to "block her somehow".

Sorting out pack-bags, he put one aside, with a "We'll have to spare that for her duds. It won't do for her to be short. She'll have enough to put up with without that." But when I thanked him, and said I could manage nicely with only one, as I would not need much on the road, he and the Maluka sat down and stared at each other in dismay. "That's for everything you'll need till the waggons come," they explained; "your road kit goes in your swag."

The waggons went Inside once a year—"after the Wet", and would arrive at the homestead early in June. As it was then only the middle of January, I too sat down and stared in dismay at the solitary pack-bag to the great, heaped-up pile that had been sorted out as indispensable.

"You'll have to cull your herd a bit, that's all," Mac said; and needlework was pointed out as a luxury. Then books were "cut out", after that the house linen was looked to, and as I hesitated over the number of pillowcases we could manage with, Mac cried triumphantly: "You won't need those anyway, for there's no pillows."

The Maluka thought he had prepared me for everything in the way of roughness; but in a flash we knew that I had yet to learn what a bushman means by rough.

As the pillowcases fell to the ground, Mac was at a loss to account for my consternation. "What's gone wrong?" he exclaimed in concern. Mac was often an unconscious humorist.

But the Maluka came with his ever-ready sympathy. "Poor little 'un," he said gently, "there's little else but chivalry and a bite of tucker for a woman out bush."

Then a light broke in on Mac. "Is it only the pillows?" he said. "I thought something had gone wrong." Then his eyes began to twinkle. "There's stacks of pillows in Darwin," he said meaningly.

It was exactly the moral fillip I needed, and in another minute we were cheerfully "culling our herd" again.

Exposed to Mac's scorn, the simplest comforts became foolish luxuries. "A couple of changes of everything is stacks," he said encouragingly, clearing a space for packing. "There's heaps of soap and water at the station, and things dry here before you can waltz round twice."

Hopefulness is always infectious, and before Mac's cheery optimism the pile of necessities grew rapidly smaller. Indeed, with such visions of soap and water and waltzing washer-women, a couple of changes of everything appeared absurd luxury. But even optimism can have disadvantages; for in our enthusiasm we forgot that a couple of cambric blouses, a cotton dress or two, and a change of skirts, are hardly equal to the strain of nearly five months' constant wear and washing.

The pillowcases went in, however. Mac settled that difficulty by saying that "all hands could be put on to pluck birds. The place is stiff with 'em," he explained, showing what a simple matter it would be, after all. The Maluka, turning out two cushions, a large and a smaller one, simplified matters even more. "A bird in the hand, you know," he said, finding room for them in the swag.

Before all the arrangements were completed, others of the

11

Creek had begun to thaw, and were "lending a hand" here and there. The question of horses coming up, I confided in the helpers that I was relieved to hear that the Telegraph had sent a quiet horse. "I am *really* afraid of buck-jumpers, you know," I said, and the Creek, looking sideways at Mac, became incoherent.

"Oh, look here!" he spluttered. "I say! Oh, look here! It really was too bad!" Then, after an awkward pause, he blurted out, "I don't know what you'll think, but the brute strayed first camp and—he's lost, saddle and all."

The Maluka shot him a swift, questioning glance; but poor Mac looked so unhappy that we assured him "we'd manage somehow". Perhaps we could tame one of the flash buck-jumpers, the Maluka suggested. But Mac said it "wouldn't be as bad as that", and, making full confession, placed old Roper at our service.

By morning, however, a magnificent chestnut, "Flash", well broken into the side-saddle, had been conjured up from somewhere by the Creek. But two of the pack-horses had strayed, and by the time they were found the morning had slipped away, and it was too late to start until after dinner. Then after dinner a terrific thunderstorm broke over the settlement and, as the rain fell in torrents, Mac thought it looked "like a case of tomorrow all right".

Naturally, I felt impatient at the delay, but was told by the Creek that "there was no hurry"! "Tomorrow's still untouched," Mac explained. "This is the Land of Plenty of Time; Plenty of Time and Wait a While. You'll be doing a bit of waiting before you've done with it."

"If this rain goes on, she'll be doing a bit of waiting at the Fergusson; unless she learns the horse's tail trick," the Creek put in. On enquiry, it proved that the "horse's tail" trick meant swimming a horse through the flood, and hanging on to its tail until it fought a way across; and I felt I would prefer "waiting a bit".

The rain did go on and, roaring over the roof, made conversation difficult. The bushmen called it a "bit of a storm"; but every square inch of the heavens seemed occupied by lightning and thunderbolts.

"Nothing to what we can do sometimes," everyone agreed.

"*We* do things in style up here — often run half a dozen storms at once. You see, when you are weather-bound, you might as well have something worth looking at."

The storm lasted nearly three hours, and when it cleared Mac went over to the Telegraph, where some confidential chatting must have taken place; for when he returned he told us that the Dandy was starting out for the homestead next day to "fix things up a bit". The Head Stockman, however, waited back for orders.

The morning dawned bright and clear, and Mac advised "making a dash for the Fergusson". "We might just get through before this rain comes down the valley," he said.

The Creek was most enthusiastic with its help, bustling about with packbags and surcingles, and generally "mixing things".

When the time came to say goodbye it showed signs of breaking down; but mastering its grief with a mightily audible effort, it wished us "good luck", and stood watching as we rode out of the little settlement.

Every time we looked back it raised its hat; and as we rode at the head of our orderly little cavalcade of pack horses, with Jackaroo, the black "boy", bringing up the rear, we flattered ourselves on the dignity of our departure. Mac called it "style", and the Maluka was hoping that the Creek was properly impressed, when Flash unexpectedly headed off for his late home. An exciting scrimmage ensued, and the procession was broken into fragments.

The Creek flew to the rescue and, when order was finally restored, the woman, who had defied the Sanguine Scot and his telegrams, entered the forest that fringes the Never-Never, sitting meekly upon a led horse.

Chapter 3

THE HORSE'S TAIL TRICK

BUSH chivalry demanding that a woman's discomfiture should be ignored, Mac kept his eyes on the horizon for the first quarter of a mile, and talked volubly of the prospects of the Wet and the resources of the Territory; but when Flash was released and, after a short tussle, settled down into a free, swinging amble, he offered congratulations in his own whimsical way.

"He's like the rest of us," he said, with a sly, sidelong look at the Maluka, "perfectly reconciled to his fate."

Although it was only sixty-five miles to the Katherine, it took us exactly three days to travel the distance. Mac called it a "tip-top record for the Wet", and the Maluka agreed with him; for in the Territory it is not the number of miles that counts, but what is met with in those miles.

During the first afternoon we met so many amiable-looking watercourses that the Sanguine Scot grew more and more hopeful about crossing the Fergusson that night.

"We'll just do it if we push on," he said, after a critical look at the Cullen, then little more than a sweet, shady stream. "Our luck's dead in. She's only just moving. Yesterday's rain hasn't come down the valleys yet."

We pushed on in the moonlight; but when we reached the Fergusson two hours later, we found our luck was "dead out", for "she" was up and running a banker.

Mac's hopes sank below zero. "Now we've done it," he said ruefully, looking down at the swirling torrent. "It's a case of 'wait-a-while' after all."

But the Maluka's hopes always died hard. "There's still the Government yacht," he said, going to a huge iron punt that lay far above high-water mark. Mac called it a forlorn hope, and it looked it, as it lay deeply sunk in the muddy bank.

It was an immense affair, weighing over half a ton, and

14

provided by a thoughtful government for the transit of travellers "stuck up" by the river when in flood. An army of roughriders might have launched it; but as bushmen generally travel in single file, it lay a silent reproach to the wisdom of governments.

Some jester had chalked on its side "H.M.S. Immovable"; and after tugging valiantly at it for nearly half an hour, the Maluka and Mac and Jackaroo proved the truth of the bushman's irony.

There was no choice but a camp on the wrong side of the river, and after "dratting things" in general, and the Cullen in particular, Mac bowed to the inevitable and began to unpack the team, stacking packbags and saddles up on the rocks off the wet grass.

By the time the billy was boiling he was trying hard to be cheerful, but without much success. "Oh well," he said, as we settled down round the fire, "this is the Land of Plenty of Time, that's one comfort. Another whole week starts next Sunday"; then relapsing altogether, he said gloomily, "We'll be spending it here, too, by the look of things."

"Unless the missus feels equal to the horse's tail trick," the Maluka suggested.

The missus felt equal to anything *but* the tail trick and said so; and conversation flagged for a while as each tried to hit upon some way out of the difficulty.

Suddenly Mac gave his thigh a prodigious slap. "I've struck it!" he shouted and, pointing to a thick wire rope, just visible in the moonlight as it stretched across the river from flood bank to flood bank, added hesitatingly: "We send mailbags—and—valuables over on that, when the river's up."

It was impossible to mistake his meaning, or the Maluka's exclamation of relief, or that neither man doubted for a moment that the woman was willing to be flung across a deep, swirling river on a swaying wire; and as many a man has appeared brave because he has lacked the courage to own to his cowardice, so I said airily that "anything was better than going back", and found the men exchanging glances.

"No one's going back," the Maluka said quietly; and then I learned that the Wet does not "do things by half". "Once they

15

began to move the flood waters must have come down the valley in tidal waves," the Maluka explained. "The Cullen we've just left will probably be a roaring torrent by now."

"We're stuck between two rivers; that's what's happened," Mac added savagely. "Might have guessed that miserable little Cullen was up to her old sneaking ways." And to explain Mac's former "dratting", the Maluka said, "It's a way the rivers have up here. They entice travellers over with smiles and promises and, before they can get back, call down the flood waters and shut them in."

"I'm glad I thought of the wire," Mac added cheerfully, and slipped into reminiscences of the Wet, drawing the Maluka also into experiences. And as they drifted from one experience to another, forced camps for days on stony outcrops in the midst of seas of water were touched on lightly as hardly worth mentioning; while "eating yourself out of tucker, and getting down to water-rats and bandicoots", compared favourably with a day or two spent in trees or on stockyard fences. As for crossing a river on a stout wire rope! After the first few reminiscences, and an incident or two in connection with "doing the horse's tail trick", that appeared an exceedingly safe and pleasant way of overcoming the difficulty, and it became very evident why women do not travel "during the Wet".

"The river's still rising," Mac announced by way of good-morning. "We'll have to bustle up and get across or the water'll be over the wire, and then we'll be done for."

Bustle as we would, however, "getting across" was a tedious business. It took nearly an hour's bustling and urging and galloping before the horses could be persuaded to attempt the swim, and then only after old Roper had been partly dragged and partly hauled through the backwash by the amphibious Jackaroo.

Another half-hour slipped by in sending the horses' hobbles across on the pulley that ran on the wire, and in the hobbling out of the horses. Then, with Jackaroo on one side of the river, and the Maluka and Mac on the other, swags, saddles, pack-bags, and camp baggage went over one by one; and it was well past midday before all was finished.

Then my turn came. A surcingle—one of the long thick

straps that keep all firm on a pack-horse—was buckled through the pulley, and the Maluka crossed first, just to test its safety. It was safe enough; but as he was dragged through the water most of the way, the pleasantness of "getting across" on the wire proved a myth.

Mac shortened the strap, and then sat me in it, like a child in a swing. "Your lighter weight will run clear of the water," he said, with his usual optimism. "It's only a matter of holding on and keeping cool"; and as the Maluka began to haul he added final instructions. "Hang on like grim death, and keep cool whatever happens," he said.

I promised to obey, and all went well until I reached mid-stream. Then, the wire beginning to sag threateningly towards the water, Mac flung his whole weight on to his end of it and, to his horror, I shot up into the air like a sky-rocket.

"Hang on! Keep cool!" Mac yelled, in a frenzy of apprehension, as he swung on his end of the wire, Jackaroo became convulsed with laughter, but the Maluka pulled hard, and I was soon on the right side of the river, declaring that I preferred experiences when they were over. Later on, Mac accounted for his terror with another unconscious flash of humour. "You never can count on a woman keeping cool when the unexpected happens," he said.

We offered to haul him over. "It's only a matter of holding on and keeping cool," we said; but he preferred to swim.

"It's a pity you didn't think of telegraphing this performance," I shouted across the floods; but, in his relief, Mac was equal to the occasion.

"I'm glad I didn't," he shouted back gallantly, with a sweeping flourish of his hat; "it might have blocked you from coming." The bushman was learning a new accomplishment.

All afternoon we were supposed to be "making a dash" for the Edith, a river twelve miles further on; but there was nothing very dashing about our pace. The air was stifling, swelteringly hot, and the flies maddening in their persistence. The horses developed puffs, and when we were not being half-drowned in torrents of rain we were being parboiled in steamy atmosphere. The track was as tracks usually are "during the Wet", and for four hours we laboured on, slipping and slithering over the greasy track, varying the monotony now and then with a floundering scramble through a boggy creek crossing. Our appearance was about as dashing as our pace; and draggled, wet through, and perspiring, and out of conceit with primitive travelling—having spent the afternoon combining a minimum rate of travelling with a maximum of discomfort—we arrived at the Edith an hour after sundown to find her a wide eddying stream.

"Won't be more than a ducking," Mac said cheerfully. "Couldn't be much wetter than we are," and the Maluka taking the reins from my horse, we rode into the stream, Mac keeping behind, "to pick her up in case she floats off," he said, thinking he was putting courage into me.

It wasn't as bad as it looked; and after a little stumbling and plunging and drifting the horses were clambering out up the opposite bank, and by next sundown—after scrambling through a few more rivers—we found ourselves looking down at the flooded Katherine, flowing below in the valley of a rocky gorge.

Sixty-five miles in three days, against sixty miles an hour of the express trains of the world. "Speed's the thing," cries the world, and speeds on, gaining little but speed; and we bush-folk travel our sixty miles and gain all that is worth gaining—excepting speed.

"Hand-over-hand this time," Mac said, looking up at the telegraph wire that stretched far overhead. "There's no pulley here. Hand-over-hand, or the horse's tail trick."

But Mine Host of the "Pub" had seen us, and running down the opposite side of the gorge, launched a boat at the river's brink; then pulling upstream for about a hundred yards or so in the backwash, faced about, and raced down and across the swift-flowing current with long, sweeping strokes; and as we rode down the steep, winding track to meet him, Mac became jocular and, reminding us that the gauntlet of the Katherine had yet to be run, also reminded us that the sympathies of the Katherine were with the stockmen; adding with a chuckle, as Mine Host bore down on us: "You don't even represent business here; no woman ever does."

Then the boat grounded, and Mine Host sprang ashore—another burly six-foot bushman—and greeted us with a flashing smile and a laughing "There's not much of her left". And then, stepping with quiet unconcern into over two feet of water, pushed the boat against a jutting ledge for my convenience. "Wet feet don't count," he laughed, with another of his flashing smiles when remonstrated with, and Mac chuckled in an aside, "Didn't I tell you a woman doesn't represent business here?"

Chapter 4

THE "PUB"

THE swim being beyond the horses, they were left hobbled out on the north bank, to wait for the river to fall; and after another swift race down and across stream, Mine Host landed everyone safely on the south side of the flood, and soon we were clambering up the steep track that led from the river to the "Pub".

Coming up from the river, the Katherine Settlement appeared to consist solely of the "Pub" and its accompanying store; but beyond the "Pub", which, by the way, seemed to be hanging on to its own verandah posts for support, we found an elongated, three-roomed building nestling under deep verandahs, and half-hidden beneath a grove of lofty scarlet-flowering poincianas.

"The Cottage is always set apart for distinguished visitors," Mine Host said, bidding us welcome with another smile, but never a hint that he was placing his own private quarters at our disposal. Like all bushmen, he could be delicately reticent when conferring a favour; but a forgotten razor-strop betrayed him later on.

In the meantime we discovered the remainder of the Settlement from the Cottage verandah, spying out the Police Station as it lurked in ambush just round the first bend in a winding bush track—apparently keeping one eye on the "Pub"; and then we caught a gleam of white roofs away beyond further bends in the track, where the Overland Telegraph "Department" stood on a little rise, aloof from the "Pub" and the Police, shut away from the world, yet attending to its affairs and, incidentally, to those of the bush-folk; a tiny settlement, with a tiny permanent population of four men and two women—women who found their homes all-sufficient, and rarely left them, although the menfolk were here, there, and everywhere.

All around and within the Settlement was bush; and beyond the bush, stretching away and away on every side of it, those hundreds of thousands of square miles that constitute the Never-Never—miles sending out and absorbing again from day to day the floating population of the Katherine.

Before supper the Telegraph Department and the Police Station called on the Cottage to present compliments. Then the Wag came with his welcome. "Didn't expect you to-day," he drawled, with unmistakable double meaning in his drawl. "You've come sooner than we expected. Must have had luck with the rivers"; and Mac became enthusiastic. "Luck!" he cried. "Luck! Skinned through everything by the skin of our teeth. No one else'll get through these rivers under a week." And they didn't.

Remembering the telegrams, the Wag shot a swift, quizzing glance at him; but it took more than a glance to disconcert Mac once his mind was made up, and he met it unmoved, and entered into a vivid description of the "passage of the Fergusson", which filled in our time until supper.

After supper the Cottage returned the calls, and then, rain coming down in torrents, the Telegraph, the Police, the Cottage, and the "Pub" retired to rest, wondering what the morrow would bring forth.

The morrow brought forth more rain, and the certainty that, as the river was still rising, the swim would be beyond the horses for several days yet; and because of this uncertainty, the Katherine bestirred itself to honour its tethered guests.

For a day the Katherine "took its bearings", and keen, scrutinising glances summed up the Unknown Woman, looking her through and through until she was no longer an Unknown Woman, while the Maluka looked on interested. He knew the bush-folk well, and that their instinct would be unerring, and left the missus to slip into whichever niche in their lives they thought fit to place her. And as she slipped into a niche built up of strong, staunch comradeship, the black community considered that they, too, had fathomed the missus; and it became history in the camp that the

21

Maluka had stolen her from a powerful Chief of the Whites, and deeming it wise to disappear with her until the affair had blown over, had put many flooded rivers between him and his pursuers. "Would any woman have flung herself across rivers on wires, speeding on without rest or pause, unless afraid of pursuit?" the camp asked in committee, and the most sceptical were silenced.

Then followed other days of pleasant intercourse; for, once sure of its welcome, bushmen are lavish with their friendship. And as we roamed about the tiny settlement, the Wag and others vied with the Maluka, Mine Host, and Mac in "making things pleasant for the missus"; relating experiences for her entertainment; and showing all there was to be shown.

Neither the Head Stockman nor the little bushman, however, had made any offers of friendship, Dan having gone out to the station immediately after interviewing the Maluka, while the little bushman spent most of his time getting out of the way of the missus whenever she appeared on his horizon.

"A Tam-o'-Shanter fleeing from the furies of a too fertile imagination," the Maluka laughed after a particularly comical dash for cover.

The fourth day, the flood having fallen, it was decided that it would be well to cross the horses in the rear of a boat.

As the flood was three or four hundred yards wide and many feet deep, a swim was impossible without help, and every horse was to be supported or guided, or dragged over in the rear of the boat, with a halter held by a man in the stern.

It was no child's play. Every inch of the way had its difficulties. The poor brutes knew the swim was beyond them; and as the boat, pulling steadily on, dragged them from the shallows into the deeper water, they plunged and snorted in fear, until they found themselves swimming, and were obliged to give all their attention to keeping themselves afloat.

Some required little assistance when once off their feet; just a slow, steady pull from the oars, and a taut enough halter to lean on in the tight places. But others rolled over like logs when the full force of the current struck them, threatening to drag the boat under, as it and the horse raced away down stream with the oarsmen straining their utmost.

It was hard enough work for the oarsmen; but the seat of honour was in the stern of the boat, and no man filled it better than Little Tam. Alert and full of resource, with one hand on the tiller, he leaned over the boat, lengthening or shortening rope for the halter, and regulating the speed of the oarsmen with unerring judgment; giving a staunch swimmer time and a short rope to lean on, or literally dragging the faint-hearted across at full speed; careful only of one thing: to keep the head above water.

There were ten horses in all to cross, and at the end of two hours' hard pulling there was only one left to come—old Roper.

Mac took the halter into his own hands—there was no one else worthy—and, slipping into the stern of the boat, spoke first to the horse and then to the oarsmen; and as the boat glided forward, the noble, trusting, old horse—confident that his long-tried human friend would set no impossible task—came quietly through the shallows, sniffing questionings at the half-submerged bushes.

"Give him time!" Mac called. "Let him think it out," as step by step Roper followed, the halter running slack on the water. When almost out of his depth, he paused just a moment, then, obeying the tightening rope, drifted himself to the flood and struck firmly and bravely out.

Staunchly he and Mac dealt with the current; taking time and approaching it quietly, meeting it with taut rope and unflinching nerve, drifting for a few breaths to judge its force; then, nothing daunted, they battled forward, stroke after stroke, and won across without once pulling the boat out of its course.

Only Roper could have done it; and when the splendid neck and shoulders appeared above water as he touched bottom, on the submerged track, he was greeted with a cheer and a hearty, unanimous "Bravo! old chap!" Then Mac returned thanks with a grateful look and, leaping ashore, looked over the beautiful, wet, shining limbs, declaring he could have "done it on his own", if required.

Once assured that we were anxious for a start, the Katherine set about speeding the parting guests with gifts of farewell. The Wag brought fresh tomatoes and a cucumber; The Telegraph sent eggs; the Police a freshly baked cake; the Chinese cook baked bread, and Mine Host came with a few potatoes and a flat-iron. To the surprise of the Katherine, I received the potatoes without enthusiasm, not having been long enough in the Territory to know their rare value, and, besides, I was puzzling over the flat-iron.

"What's it for?" I asked, and the Wag shouted in mock amazement: "For? To iron duds with, of course," as Mine Host assured us it was of no use to him beyond keeping a door open.

Still puzzled, I said I thought there would not be any need to iron "duds" until we reached the homestead, and the Maluka said quietly: "It's for the homestead. There will be nothing like that there."

Mac exploded with an impetuous, "Good Heavens! What *does* she expect? First pillows and now irons!"

Gradually realising that down South we have little idea of what "rough" means to a bushman, I had from day to day been modifying my ideas of a station home from a mansion to a commodious wooden cottage, plainly but comfortably furnished. The Cottage had confirmed this idea, but Mac soon settled the question beyond all doubt.

"Look here!" he said emphatically. "Before she leaves this place she'll just *have* to grasp things a bit better," and sitting down on a swag he talked rapidly for ten minutes, taking a queer delight in making everything sound as bad as possible, "knocking the stiffening out of the missus", as he phrased it, and certainly bringing the "commodious station home" about her ears, which was just as well, perhaps.

After a few scathing remarks on the homestead in general, which he called "one of those down-at-the-heels, anything'll-do sort of places", he described The House. "It's mostly verandahs and promises," he said, "but one room is finished. *We* call it The House, but you'll probably call it a Hut, even though it has got doors and calico windows framed and on hinges."

Then followed an inventory of the furniture. "There's one

fairly steady, good-sized table — at least it doesn't fall over, unless someone leans on it; then there's a bed with a wire mattress, but nothing else on it; and there's a chair or two up to your weight (the Boss'll either have to stand up or lie down), and I don't know that there's much else excepting plenty of cups and plates — they're enamel, fortunately, so you won't have much trouble with the servants breaking things. Of course, there's a Christmas card and a few works of art on the walls for you to look at when you're tired of looking at yourself in the glass. Glass! There's a looking-glass — goodness knows how it got there! You ought to be thankful for that and the wire mattress. You won't find many of them out bush."

I humbly acknowledged thankfulness, and felt deeply grateful to Mine Host when, with ready thoughtfulness, he brought a couple of china cups and stood them among the baggage — the heart of Mine Host was as warm and sincere as his flashing smiles. I learned, in time, to be indifferent to china cups, but that flat-iron became one of my most cherished possessions.

The commodious station home destroyed, the Katherine bestirred itself further in the speeding of its guests. The Telegraph came with the offer of their buggy, and then the Police offered theirs; but Mine Host, harnessing two nuggety little horses into his buckboard, drove round to the store, declaring a buckboard was the "only thing for the road". "You won't feel the journey at all in it," he said, and drove us round the settlement to prove how pleasant and easy travelling could be in the Wet.

"No buggy obtainable," murmured the Maluka, reviewing the three offers. But the Sanguine Scot was quite unabashed and answered coolly: "You forgot those telegrams were sent to that other woman — the goer, you know — there *was* no buggy obtainable for *her*. By George; wasn't she a snorter? I knew I'd block her somehow," and then he added with a gallant bow and a flourish: "You can see for yourselves, chaps, that she didn't come."

The buckboard only being decided on, the Katherine advised getting out to the five-mile overnight, declaring it "would take all day to get away from the Settlement in the

25

morning"; and a little before sundown Mac set out with the pack teams and loose horses, leaving us to follow in the buckboard at sun-up; and just before the Katherine "turned in" for the night, the Maluka went to the office to settle accounts with Mine Host.

In five minutes he was back, standing among the poincianas, and then after a little while of silence he said gently, "Mac was right. A woman does not represent business here." Mine Host had indignantly refused payment for a woman's board and lodging.

"I had to pay, though," the Maluka laughed, with one of his quick changes of humour. "But, then, I'm only a man."

Chapter 5

WELCOME HOME!

WHEN we arrived at the five-mile in the morning we found Mac "packed up" and ready for the start and, passing the reins to him, the Maluka said, "You know the road best"; and Mac, being what he called a "bit of a Jehu," we set off in great style — across country, apparently — missing trees by a hair's breadth, and bumping over the ant-hills, boulders, and broken boughs that lay half-hidden in the long grass.

After being nearly bumped out of the buckboard several times, I asked if there wasn't any track anywhere; and Mac once again exploded with astonishment.

"We're on the track," he shouted. "Good Heavens! do you mean to say you can't see it on ahead there?" and he pointed towards what looked like thickly timbered country, plentifully strewn with further boulders and boughs and ant-hills, and as I shook my head, he shrugged his shoulders hopelessly. "And we're on the main transcontinental route from Adelaide to Port Darwin," he said.

"Any track anywhere!" he mimicked presently, as we lurched, and heaved, and bumped along. "What'll she say when we get into the long-grass country?"

"Long here!" he ejaculated, when I thought the grass we were driving through was fairly long (it was about three feet). "Just you wait!"

I waited submissively, if bouncing about a buckboard over thirty miles of obstacles can be called waiting, and next day we "got into the long-grass country"; miles of grass, waving level with and above our heads — grass ten feet high and more, shutting out everything but grass.

The Maluka was riding a little behind, at the head of the pack-team, to relieve the buckboard horses; but we could see neither him nor the team, and Mac looked triumphantly round as the staunch little horses pushed on through the forest of grass that swirled and bent and swished and reeled all about the buckboard.

"Didn't I tell you?" he said. "This is what we call long grass"; and he asked if I could "see any track now". "It's as plain as a pikestaff," he declared, trying to show what he called a "clear break all the way". "Oh, I'm a dead homer all right," he shouted, after further going, as we came out at the "King" crossing.

"Now for it! Hang on!" he warned, and we went down the steep bank at a hand gallop; and as the horses rushed into the swift-flowing stream, he said unconcernedly: "I wonder how deep this is," adding, as the buckboard lifted and swerved when the current struck it: "By George! They're off their feet," and leaning over the splashboard lashed at the undaunted little beasts until they raced up the opposite bank.

"That's the style!" he shouted in triumph, as they drew up, panting and dripping, well over the rise from the crossing. "Close thing, though! Did you get your feet wet?"

"Did you get your feet wet!" That was all, when I was expecting every form of concern imaginable. For a moment I felt indignant at Mac's recklessness and lack of concern, and said severely, "You shouldn't take such risks."

But Mac was blissfully unconscious of the severity. "Risks!" he said. "Why, it wasn't wide enough for anything to happen, bar a ducking. If you rush it, the horses are pushed across before they know they're off their feet."

"Bar a ducking, indeed!" But Mac was out of the buckboard, shouting back, "Hold hard there! It's a swim," and continued shouting directions until the horses were across with comparatively dry packbags. Then he and the Maluka shook hands and congratulated each other on being on the right side of everything.

"No more rivers!" the Maluka said.

"Clear run home, bar a deluge," Mac added gathering up the reins. "We'll strike the front gate to-night."

All afternoon we followed the telegraph line, and there the track was really well defined; then at sundown Mac drew up, and with a flourish of hats he and the Maluka bade the missus "Welcome Home!" All around and about was bush,

28

and only bush, that, and the telegraph line, and Mac, touching on one of the slender galvanised iron poles, explained the welcome. "This is the front gate!" he said; "another forty-five miles and we'll be knocking at the front door." And they called the Elsey "a nice little place"! Perhaps it was when compared with runs of six million acres.

The camp was pitched just inside the "front gate", near a wide-spreading sheet of water, "Easter's Billabong," and at supper time the conversation turned on bush cookery.

"Never tasted Johnny cakes!" Mac said. "Your education hasn't begun yet. We'll have some for breakfast; I'm real slap-up at Johnny cakes!" and rummaging in a pack-bag, he produced flour, cream of tartar, soda and a mixing dish, and set to work at once.

"I'm real slap-up at Johnny cakes! No mistake!" he assured us, as he knelt on the ground, big and burly, in front of the mixing dish, kneading enthusiastically at his mixture. "Look at that!" as air bubbles appeared all over the light, spongy dough. "Didn't I tell you I knew a thing or two about cooking?" and cutting off the nuggety-looking chunks, he buried them in the hot ashes.

When they were cooked, crisp and brown, he displayed them with just pride. "Well!" he said, "Who's slap-up at Johnny cakes?" and standing them on end in the mixing dish he rigged up tents—a deluge being expected—and carried them into his own for safety.

During the night the deluge came, and the billabong, walking up its flood banks, ran about the borders of our camp, sending so many exploring little rivulets through Mac's tent, that he was obliged to pass most of the night perched on a pyramid of pack-bags and saddles.

Unfortunately, in the confusion and darkness, the dish of Johnny cakes became the base of the pyramid, and was consequently missing at breakfast time. After a long hunt Mac recovered it and stood looking dejectedly at the ruins of his cookery—a heap of flat, stodgy-looking slabs, "Must have been sitting on 'em all night," he said, "and there's no other bread for breakfast."

There was no doubt that we must eat them or go without bread of any kind; but as we sat tugging at the gluey guttapercha-like substance, Mac's sense of humour revived, "Didn't I tell you I was slap-up at Johnny cakes?" he chuckled, adding with further infinitely more humorous chuckles: "You mightn't think it; but I really am." Then he pointed to Jackaroo, who was watching in bewilderment, while the Maluka hunted for the crispest crust, not for himself, but the woman. "White fellow big fellow fool all right! eh, Jackaroo?" he asked, and Jackaroo openly agreed with him.

Finding the black soil flats impassable after the deluge, Mac left the tracks, having decided to stick to the ridges all day; and all that had gone before was smoothness in comparison with what was in store.

All day the buckboard rocked and bumped through the timber, and the Maluka, riding behind, from time to time pointed out the advantages of travelling across country, as we bounced about the buckboard like rubber balls: "There's so little chance of getting stiff with sitting still," he said; and when I expressed fears for the springs, Mac reassured me by saying a buckboard had none, excepting those under the seat.

If Mac was a "bit of a Jehu", he certainly was a "dead homer", for after miles of scrub and grass and timber, we came out at our evening camp at the Bitter Springs, the head waters of the Roper River, to find the Head Stockman there, with his faithful, tawny-coloured shadow, "Old Sool'em", beside him.

Dog and man greeted us sedately, and soon Dan had a billy boiling for tea, and a blazing fire; and accepted an invitation to join us at supper and "bring something in the way of bread along with him".

With a commonplace remark about the trip out, he placed a crisp, newly-baked damper on the tea-towel that acted as supper cloth; but when we all agreed that he was "real slap-up at damper making", he scented a joke and shot a quick, questioning glance around; then deciding that it was wiser not to laugh at all than to laugh in the wrong place, he only said, he was "not a bad hand at the damper trick". Dan liked his jokes well labelled when dealing with the Unknown Woman.

He was a bushman of the old type, one of the men of the droving days; full of old theories, old faiths, and old prejudices, and clinging always to old habits and methods. Year by year as the bush had receded and shrunk before the railways, he had receded with it, keeping always just behind the Back of Beyond, droving, bullock-punching, stock-keeping, and unconsciously opening up the way for that very civilisation that was driving him further and further back. In the forty years since his boyhood, railways had driven him out of Victoria, New South Wales, and Queensland, and were now threatening even the Never-Never, and Dan was beginning to fear that they would not leave "enough bush to bury a man in".

Enough bush to bury a man in! That is all these men of the droving days have ever asked of their nation; and yet without them the pioneers would have been tied hand and foot, and because of them Australia is what it is.

"Had a good trip out?" Dan asked, feeling safe on that subject, and appeared to listen to the details of the road with interest; but all the time the shrewd hazel eyes were upon me, drawing rapid conclusions, and I began to feel absurdly anxious to know their verdict. That was not to come before bedtime; and only those who knew the life of the stations in the Never-Never know how much was depending on the stockmen's verdict.

Dan had his own methods of dealing with the Unknown Woman. Forty years out-bush had convinced him that "most of 'em were the right sort", but it had also convinced him that "you had to take 'em all differently", and he always felt his way carefully, watching and waiting, ready to open out at the first touch of fellowship and understanding, but just as ready to withdraw into himself at the faintest approach to a snub.

By the time supper was over he had risked a joke or two, and taking heart by their reception, launched boldly into the conversation, chuckling with delight as the Maluka and Mac amused themselves by examining the missus on bushcraft.

"She'll need a deal of educating before we let her out alone," he said, after a particularly bad failure, with the first touch of that air of proprietorship that was to become his

31

favourite attitude towards his missus.

"It's only common sense; you'll soon get used to it," Mac said in encouragement, giving us one of his delightful backhanders. Then in all seriousness Dan suggested teaching her some of the signs of water at hand, right off, "in case she does get lost any time", and also seriously, the Maluka and Mac "thought it would be as well, perhaps".

Then the townsman's self-satisfied arrogance came to the surface. "You needn't bother about me," I said, confident I had as much common sense as any bushman. "If ever I do get lost, I'll just catch a cow and milk it."

Knowing nothing of the wild, scared cattle of the fenceless runs of the Never-Never, I was prepared for anything rather than the roar of delight that greeted the example of town "common sense".

"Missus! missus!" the Maluka cried, as soon as he could speak, "you'll need a deal of educating"; and while Mac gasped, "Oh I say! Look here!" Dan, with tears in his eyes, chuckled: "She'll have a drouth on by the time she runs one down"—Dan always called a thirst a drouth. "Oh, Lord!" he said, picturing the scene in his mind's eye, 'I'll catch a cow and milk it,' she says."

Then, dancing with fun, the hazel eyes looked round the company, and as Dan rose, preparatory to turning in, we felt we were about to hear their verdict. When it came it was characteristic of the man in uniqueness of wording:

"She's the dead finish!" he said, wiping his eyes on his shirt sleeve. "Reckoned she was the minute I heard her talking about slap-up dampers"; and in some indescribable way we knew he had paid the woman who was just entering his life the highest compliment in his power.

At breakfast Dan expressed surprise because there was no milk, and the pleasantry being well received, he considered the moment ripe for one of his pet theories.

"She'll do for this place!" he said, wagging his head wisely. "I've been forty years out-bush, and I've known eight or ten women in that time, so I ought to know something about it. Anyway, the one that could see jokes suited best." And, as we packed up and set out for the last lap of our journey he was still rambling about his theory. "Yes," he said, "you can dodge most things out bush; but you can't dodge jokes for long. They'll run you down sooner or later." Then, finding the missus had thrown away a "good cup of tea just because a few flies had got into it", he became grave, and doubted whether "the missus'll do after all", until reassured by the Maluka that "she'll be fishing them out with the indifference of a Stoic in a week or two"; and I was.

When within a few miles of the homestead, the buckboard took a sharp turn round a patch of scrub, and before anyone realised what was happening we were in the midst of a mob of pack-horses, and face to face with the Quiet Stockman—a strong, erect, young Scot, who carried his six foot two of bone and muscle with the lithe ease of a bushman.

"Hallo!" Mac shouted, pulling up. Then, with the air of a showman introducing some rare exhibit, added: "This is the missus, Jack."

Jack touched his hat and moved uneasily in his saddle, answering Mac's questions in monosyllables. Then the Maluka came up, and Mac, taking pity on the embarrassed bushman, suggested "getting along", and we left him sitting rigidly on his horse, trying to collect his scattered senses.

"That was unrehearsed," Mac chuckled, as we drove on. "He's clearing out! Reckon he didn't set out exactly hoping to meet us, though. Tam's a lady's man in comparison", but loyal to his comrade above his amusement, he added warmly: "You can't beat Jack by much, though, when it comes to sticking to a pal," unconscious that he was prophesying of the years to come, when the missus had become one of those pals.

"There's only the Dandy left now," Mac went on, as we spun along an ever more definite track, "and he'll be all right as soon as he gets used to it. Never knew such a chap for finding something decent in everybody he strikes." Naturally I hoped he would "find something decent in me", having learned what it meant to the stockmen to have a woman pitchforked into their daily lives, when those lives were to be lived side by side, in camp, or in saddle, or the homestead.

Mac hesitated a moment, and then out flashed one of his happy inspirations. "Don't you bother about the Dandy," he said; "bushmen have a sixth sense, and know a pal when they see one."

"Of course!" Mac added, as an afterthought, "It's not often they find a pal in a woman"; and I add to-day that when they do, that woman is to be envied by her friends.

"Eyes front!" Mac shouted suddenly, and in a moment the homestead was in sight, and the front gate forty-five miles behind us. "If ever you *do* reach the homestead alive," the Darwin ladies had said; and now *they* were three hundred miles away from us to the north-west.

"Sam's spotted us!" Mac smiled as we skimmed on, and a slim little Chinaman ran across between the buildings. "We'd better do the thing in style," and whipping up the horses, he whirled them through the open slip-rails, past the stockyards, away across the grassy homestead enclosure, and pulled up with a rattle of hoofs and wheels at the head of a little avenue of buildings.

The Dandy, fresh and spotless, appeared in a doorway; black boys sprang up like a crop of mushrooms and took charge of the buckboard; Dan rattled in with the pack-teams, and horses were jangling hobbles and rattling harness all about us, as I found myself standing in the shadow of a queer, unfinished building, with the Maluka and Mac surrounded by a mob of leaping, bounding dogs, flourishing, as best they could, another "Welcome Home!"

"Well?" Mac asked, beating off dogs at every turn. "Is it a House or a Hut?"

"A Betwixt and Between," we decided; and then the Dandy was presented. And the steady grey eyes, apparently finding "something decent" in the missus, with a welcoming smile and ready tact he said:

"I'm sure we're all real glad to see *you*." Just the tiniest emphasis on the word "you", but that, and the quick, bright look that accompanied the emphasis, told as nothing else could, that it was "that other woman" that had not been wanted. Unconventional, of course, but when the welcome is conventional out-bush, it is unworthy of the name of welcome.

The Maluka knew this well, but before he could speak, Mac had seized a little half-grown dog—the most persistent of all the leaping dogs—by her tightly curled-up tail, and setting her down at my feet, said: "And this is Tiddle'ums," adding, with another flourishing bow, "a present from a Brither Scot," while Tiddle'ums in no way resented the indignity. Having a tail that curled tightly over her back like a cup handle, she expected to be lifted up by it.

Then one after the other Mac presented the station dogs: Quart-pot, Drover, Tuppence, Misery, Buller, and a dozen others; and as I bowed gravely to each in turn Dan chuckled in appreciation "She'll do! Told you she was the dead finish."

Then, the introductions over, the Maluka said: "And now I suppose she may consider herself just 'One of us'."

Chapter 6

MOSTLY VERANDAHS AND PROMISES

THE homestead, standing half-way up the slope that rose from the billabong, had, after all, little of that "down-at-heels, anything'll-do" appearance that Mac had so scathingly described. No one could call it a "commodious station home", and it was even patched up and shabby; but for all that, neat and cared for. An orderly little array of one-roomed buildings, mostly built of sawn slabs, and ranged round a broad oblong space with a precision that suggested the idea of a section of a street cut out from some neat compact little village.

The cook's quarters, kitchens, men's quarters, store, meat-house, and waggon-house, facing each other on either side of this oblong space, formed a short avenue—the main thoroughfare of the homestead—the centre of which was occupied by an immense wood-heap, the favourite gossiping place of some of the old blackfellows, while across the western end of it, and looking down upon it, but a little aloof from the rest of the buildings, stood the House, or, rather, as much of it as had been rebuilt after the cyclone of 1897. As befitted their social positions, the forge and blackboys' "humpy" kept a respectful distance well round the south-eastern corner of this thoroughfare; but, for some unknown reason, the fowl-roosts had been erected over Sam Lee's sleeping quarters. That comprised this tiny homestead of a million and a quarter acres, with the Katherine Settlement a hundred miles to the north of it; one neighbour ninety miles to the east; another, a hundred and five to the south; and others about two hundred miles to the west.

Unfortunately, Mac's description of the House had been only too correct. With the exception of the one roughly finished room at its eastern end, it was "mostly verandahs and promises".

After the cyclone had wrecked the building, scattering timber and sheets of iron in all directions, everything had lain exactly where it had fallen for some weeks, at the mercy of the wind and weather. At the end of those weeks a travelling Chinese carpenter arrived at the station with such excellent common-sense ideas of what a bush homestead should be, that he had been engaged to rebuild it.

His plans showed a wide-roofed building, built upon two-foot piles, with two large centre rooms opening into each other and surrounded by a deep verandah on every side; while two small rooms, a bathroom and an office, were to nestle each under one of the eastern corners of this deep twelve-foot verandah. Without a doubt, excellent common-sense ideas; but, unfortunately, much larger than the supply of timber. Rough-hewn posts for the two-foot piles and verandah supports could be had for the cutting and therefore did not give out; but the man used joists and uprights with such reckless extravagance, that by the time the skeleton of the building was up, the completion of the contract was impossible. With philosophical indifference, however, he finished one room completely; left a second a mere outline of uprights and tye-beams; apparently forgot all about the bathroom and office; covered the whole roof, including verandahs, with corrugated iron; surveyed his work with a certain amount of stolid satisfaction; then announcing that "wood bin finissem", applied for his cheque and departed; and from that day nothing further had been done to the House, which stood before us "mostly verandahs and promises".

Although Mac's description of the House had been apt, he had sadly underrated the furniture. There were *four* chairs, all "up" to my weight, while two of them were up to the Maluka's. The cane was all gone, certainly, but had been replaced with greenhide seats (not green in colour, of course; only green in experience, never having seen a tan-pit). In addition to the chairs, the dining table, the four-poster bed, the wire mattress, and the looking-glass, there was a solid deal side table, made from the side of a packing case, with four solid legs and a solid shelf underneath; also a remarkably steady washstand that had no ware of any description, and a remarkably unsteady chest of four drawers, one of which refused to open, while the other three refused to shut. Further, the dining table was more than "fairly" steady, three of its legs being perfectly sound, and it therefore only *threatened* to fall over when leaned upon. And lastly, although most of the plates and all the cups were enamelware, there was almost a complete dinner service in china. The teapot, however, was tin, and, as Mac said, as "big as a house".

As for the walls, not only were the "works of art" there, but they themselves were uniquely dotted from ceiling to floor with the muddy imprints of dogs' feet — not left there by a Pegasus breed of winged dogs, but made by the muddy feet of the station dogs, as they pattered over the timber when it lay awaiting the carpenter, and no one had seen any necessity to remove them. Outside the verandahs, and all around the house, was what was to be known later as the garden, a grassy stretch of hillocky ground, well scratched and beaten down by dogs, goats and fowls; fenceless itself, being part of the grassy acres which were themselves fenced round to form the homestead enclosure. Just inside this enclosure, forming, in fact, the south-western barrier of it, stood the "billabong", then a spreading sheet of water; along its banks flourished the vegetable garden; outside the enclosure, towards the south-east, lay a grassy plain a mile across, and to the north-west were the stock-yards and house paddock — a paddock of five square miles, and the only fenced area on the run; while everywhere to the northwards, and all through the paddock, were dotted "white-ant" hills, all shapes and sizes, forming brick-red turrets among the green scrub and timber.

"Well!" Mac said, after we had completed a survey, "I said it wasn't a fit place for a woman, didn't I?"

But the Head Stockman was in one of his argumentative moods. "Any place is a fit place for a woman," he said, "provided the woman is fitted for the place. The right man in the right place, you know. Square people shouldn't try to get into round holes."

"The woman's *square* enough," the Maluka interrupted;

and Mac added, "And so is the *hole*," with a scornful emphasis on the word "hole".

Dan chuckled and surveyed the queer-looking building with new interest.

"It reminds me of a banyan tree with corrugated iron foliage," he said, adding as he went into details: "In a dim light the finished room would pass for the trunk of the tree and the uprights for the supports of the branches."

But the Maluka thought it looked more like a section of a mangrove swamp, piles and all.

"It looks very like a house nearly finished," I said severely; for, because of the verandah and many promises, I was again hopeful for something approaching that commodious station home. "A few able-bodied men could finish the dining room in a couple of days, and make a mansion of the rest of the building in a week or so."

But the able-bodied men had a different tale to tell.

"Steady! Go slow, missus!" they cried. "It may *look* like a house very nearly finished, but out-bush, we have to catch our hares before we cook them."

"*We* begin at the very beginning of things in the Never-Never," the Maluka explained. "Timber grows in trees in these parts, and has to be coaxed out with a saw."

"It's a bad habit it's got into," Dan chuckled; then pointing vaguely towards the thickly wooded long Reach, that lay a mile to the south of the homestead, beyond the grassy plain, he "supposed the dining room was down there just now, with the rest of the House".

With fast-ebbing hopes I looked in dismay at the distant forest undulating along the skyline, and the Maluka said sympathetically, "It's only too true, little 'un".

But Dan disapproved of spoken sympathy under trying circumstances. "It keeps 'em from toeing the line," he believed; and fearing I was on the point of showing the white feather, he broke in with: "We'll have to keep her toeing the line, boss," and then pointed out that "things might be worse". "In some countries there are no trees to cut down," he said.

"That's the style," he added, when I began to laugh in spite

39

of my disappointment. "We'll soon get you educated up to it."

But already the Sanguine Scot had found the bright side of the situation, and reminded us that we were in the Land of Plenty of Time. "There's time enough for everything in the Never-Never," he said. "She'll have many a pleasant ride along the Reach choosing trees for timber. Catching the hare's often the best part of the fun."

Mac's cheery optimism always carried all before it. Pleasant rides through shady forest-ways seemed a fair recompense for a little delay; and my spirits went up with a bound, to be dashed down again the next moment by Dan.

"We haven't got to the beginning of things yet," he interrupted, following up the line of thought the Maluka had at first suggested. "Before any trees are cut down, we'll have to dig a saw-pit and find a pit-sawyer." Dan was not a pessimist; he only liked to dig down to the root of things, besides objecting to sugar-coated pills as being a hindrance to education.

But the Dandy had joined the group, and being practical, suggested "trying to get hold of Little Johnny", declaring that "he would make things hum in no time".

Mac happened to know that Johnny was Inside somewhere on a job, and it was arranged that Dan should go into the Katherine at once for nails and "things", and to see if the telegraph people could find out Johnny's whereabouts down the line, and send him along.

But preparations for a week's journey take time out-bush, owing to that necessity of beginning at the beginning of things. Fresh horses were mustered, a mob of bullocks rounded up for a killer, swags and pack-bags packed; and just as all was in readiness for the start, the Quiet Stockman came in, bringing a small mob of colts with him.

"I'm leaving," he announced in the Quarters; then, feeling some explanation was necessary, added, "I *was* thinking of it before this happened." Strictly speaking, this may be true, although he omitted to say that he had abandoned the idea for some little time.

No one was surprised, and no one thought of asking *what* had happened, for Jack had always steered clear of women, as he termed it. Not that he feared or disliked them, but because he considered that they had nothing in common with men. "They're such terrors for asking questions," he said once, when pressed for an opinion, adding as an after-thought, "They never seem to learn much either," in his own quiet way summing up the average woman's conversation with a shy bushman: a long string of purposeless questions, followed by inane remarks on the answers.

"I'm leaving!" Jack had said, and later met the Maluka, unshaken in his resolve. There was that in the Maluka, however, that Jack had not calculated on—a something that drew all men to him, and made Dan speak of him in after-years as the "best boss ever I struck"; and although the interview only lasted a few minutes, and the Maluka spoke only of the work of the station, yet in those few minutes the Quiet Stockman changed his mind, and the notice was never given.

"I'm staying on," was all he said on returning to the Quarters; and quick decisions being unusual with Jack, everyone felt interested.

"Going to give her a chance?" Dan asked with a grin, and Jack looked uncomfortable.

"I've only seen the boss," he said.

Dan nodded with approval. "You've got some sense left, then," he said, "if you know a good boss when you see one."

Jack agreed in monosyllables; but when Dan settled down to argue out the advantages of having a woman about the place, he looked doubtful; but having nothing to say on the subject, said nothing; and when Dan left for the Katherine next morning he was still unconvinced.

Dan set out for the north track soon after sun-up, assuring us that he'd get hold of Johnny somehow; and before sun-down a traveller crossed the Creek before the billabong at the south track, and turned into the homestead enclosure.

We were vaguely chatting on all and sundry matters, as we sat under the verandah that faced the billabong when the traveller came into sight.

"Horse traveller!" Mac said, lazily shading his eyes, and then sprang to his feet with a yell. "Talk of luck!" he shouted. "You'll do, missus! Here's Johnny himself."

It was Johnny, sure enough; but Johnny had a cheque in

41

his pocket, and was yearning to see the "chaps at the Katherine"; and, after a good look through the House and store, decided that he really would have to go in the Settlement for—tools and "things".

"I'll be back in a week, missus," he said next morning, as he gathered his reins together before mounting, "and then we shan't be long. Three days in and three out, you know, bar accidents and a day's spell at the Katherine," he explained glibly. But the "chaps at the Katherine" proved too entertaining for Johnny, and a fortnight passed before we saw him again.

Chapter 7

GETTING THE MISSUS EDUCATED

THE Quiet Stockman was a Scotsman, and, like many Scotsmen, a strange contradiction of shy reserve and quiet, dignified self-assurance. Having made up his mind on women in general, he saw no reason for changing it; and as he went about his work, thoroughly and systematically avoided me. There was no slinking round corners, though; Jack couldn't slink. He had always looked the whole world in the face with his honest blue eyes, and could never do otherwise. He only took care that our paths did not cross more often than was absolutely necessary; but when they did, his Scots dignity asserted itself, and he said what had to be said with quiet self-possession, although he invariably moved away as soon as possible.

"It's just Jack's way," the Sanguine Scot said, anxious that his fellow Scot should not be misunderstood. "He'll be all there if ever you need him. He only draws the line at conversations."

But when I mounted the stockyard fence one morning to see the breaking-in of the colts, he looked as though he "drew the line" at that, too.

Fortunately for Jack's peace of mind, horse-breaking was not the only novelty at the homestead. Only a couple of changes of everything, in a tropical climate, meant an unbroken cycle of washing days, while apart from that, Sam Lee was full of surprises and the lubras' methods of house-cleaning were novel in the extreme.

Sam was bland, amiable, and inscrutable, and obedient to irritation; and the lubras were apt, and merry, and open-hearted, and wayward beyond comprehension. Sam did exactly as he was told, and the lubras did exactly as they thought fit, and the results were equally disconcerting.

Sam was asked for a glass of milk, and the lubras were told

to scrub the floor. Sam brought the milk immediately, and the lubras, after scrubbing two or three isolated patches on the floor, went off on some frolic of their own.

At afternoon tea there was no milk served. "There was none," Sam explained blandly. The missus had drunk it all. "Missus bin finissem milk all about," he said. When the lubras were brought back, *they* said *they* had "knocked up longa scrub", and finished the floor under protest.

The Maluka offered assistance, but I thought I ought to manage them myself, and set the lubras to clean and strip some feathers for a pillow — the Maluka had been busy with a shot-gun — and suggested to Sam that he might spend some of his spare time shooting birds.

The lubras worked steadily for a quarter of an hour at the feathers; then a dog-fight demanded all their attention, the feathers were left to the mercy of the winds, and were never gathered together. At sundown Sam fired into a colony of martins that Mac considered the luck of the homestead. Right into their midst he fired, as they slept in long, graceful garlands — one beside the other along the branches of a gum tree, each with its head snugly tucked away out of sight.

"Missus want feather!" Sam said, with his unfathomable smile, when Mac flared out at him, and again the missus appeared the culprit.

The Maluka advised making the orders a little clearer, and Sam was told to use more discretion in his obedience and, smiling and apologetic, promised to obey.

The lubras also promised to be more painstaking, reserving only the right to rest if they should "knock up longa work".

The Maluka, Mac and the Dandy looked on in amusement while the missus wrestled with the servant question; and even the Quiet Stockman grinned sympathetically at times, unconsciously becoming interested in a woman who was too occupied to ask questions.

For five days I "wrastled"; and the only comfort I had was in Bertie's Nellie, a gentle-faced old lubra — almost sweet-faced. She undoubtedly did her best and, showing signs of friendship, was invaluable in "rounding up" the other lubras when they showed signs of "knocking up".

On the morning of the sixth day Sam surpassed himself in obedience. I had hinted that breakfast should be a little earlier, adding timidly that he might use a little more ingenuity in the breakfast menu, and at the first grey streak of dawn breakfast was announced, and, dressing hurriedly, we sat down to what Sam called "Pumppee-King pie" with raisins and mince. The expression on Sam's face was celestial. No other word could describe it. There was also an underlying expression of triumph which made me suspicious of his apparent ingenuousness, and as the lubras had done little else but make faces at themselves in the looking-glass for two days (I was beginning to hate that looking-glass), I appealed to the Maluka for assistance.

He took Sam in hand, and the triumph slipped away from beneath the stolid face, and a certain amount of discrimination crept into his obedience from henceforth.

Then the Sanguine Scot said that he would "tackle the lubras for her", and in half an hour everywhere was swept and garnished, and the lubras were meek and submissive.

"You'll need to rule them with a rod of iron," Mac said, secretly pleased with his success. But there was one drawback to his methods, for next day, with the exception of Nellie, there were no lubras to rule with or without a rod of iron.

Jimmy, the water-carrier and general director of the wood-heap gossip, explained that they had gone off with the camp lubras for a day's recreation: "Him knock up longa all about work," he said, with an apologetic smile. Jimmy was either apologetic or condescending.

Nellie rounded them up when they returned, and the Maluka suggested, as a way out of the difficulty, that I should try to make myself more attractive than the camp lubras.

I went down to the Creek at once to carry out the Maluka's suggestion, and succeeded so well that I was soon the centre of a delightful dusky group, squatting on its haunches, and deep in the fascinations of teaching an outsider its language. The uncouth mispronunciations tickled the old men beyond description, and they kept me gurgling at difficult gutturals, until, convulsed at the contortion of everyday words and phrases, they echoed Dan's opinion in queer pidgin-English that the "missus needed a deal of education". Jimmy gradually became loftily condescending, and as for old Nellie, she had never enjoyed anything quite so much.

Undoubtedly I made myself attractive to the blackfellow mind; for, besides having proved unexpected entertainment, I had made everyone feel mightily superior to the missus. That power of inspiring others with a sense of superiority is an excellent trait to possess when dealing with a blackfellow, for there were more than enough helpers next day, and the work was done quickly and well, so as to leave plenty of time for merrymaking.

The Maluka and Mac were full of congratulations. "You've got the job well in hand now," Mac said, unconscious that he was about to throw everything into disorder again.

For six years Mac had been in charge of the station and, when he heard that the Maluka was coming north to represent the owners, he had decided to give bullock-punching a turn as a change from stock-keeping. Sanguine that "there was a good thing in it", he had bought a bullock waggon and team while in at the Katherine, and secured "loading" for Inside. Under these circumstances it was difficult to understand why he had been so determined in his blocking, the only reason he could ever be cajoled into giving being "that he was off the escorting trick, and, besides, the other chaps had to be thought of ".

He was now about to go to "see to things", taking Bertie, his right-hand boy, with him, but leaving Nellie with me. Bertie had expressed himself quite agreeable to the arrangement, but at the eleventh hour refused to go without Nellie; and Nellie, preferring the now fascinating homestead to the company of her lord and master, refused to go with him, and Mac was at his wits' end.

It was impossible to carry her off by force, so two days were spent in shrill ear-splitting arguments—the threads of Nellie's argument being that Bertie could easily "catch nuzzer lubra", and that the missus "must have one goodfellow lubra on the staff".

Mac, always chivalrous, said he would manage somehow without Bertie, rather than "upset things": but the Maluka would not agree, and finally Nellie consented to go, on condition that she would be left at the homestead when the waggons went through.

"Oh, well," Mac said in good-bye. "All's well that ends well," and he pointed to Nellie, safely stowed away in a grove of dogs that half filled the back of the buckboard.

But all had not ended for us. So many lubras put themselves on the homestead staff to fill the place left vacant by Nellie that the one room was filled to overflowing while the work was being done, and the Maluka was obliged to come to the rescue once more. He reduced the house staff to two, allowing a shadow or two extra in the persons of a few old blackfellows and a piccaninny or two, sending the rejected to camp.

In the morning there was a free fight in camp between the staff and some of the rejected lubras; the rejected, led by Jimmy's lubra—another Nellie—declaring the Maluka had meant two different lubras each day.

Again there was much ear-splitting argument, but finally a compromise was agreed on. Two lubras were to sit down permanently, while as many as wished might help with the washing and watering. Then the staff and the shadows settled down on the verandah beside me to watch while I evolved dresses for two lubras out of next to nothing in the way of material, and as I sewed, the Maluka, with some travellers who were "in" to help him, set to work to evolve a garden, also out of next to nothing in the way of material.

Hopeless as it looked, oblong beds were soon marked out at each of the four corners of the verandah, and beyond the beds a broad path was made to run right round the House. "The wilderness shall blossom like the rose," the Maluka said, planting seeds of a vigorous-growing flowering bean at one of the corner posts.

The travellers were deeply interested in the servant wrestle, and when the Staff was eventually clothed, and the rejected green with envy, decided that the "whole difficulty was solved, bar Sam".

Sam, however, was about to solve his part of the difficulty to everyone's satisfaction. A master as particular over the men's table as his own was not a master after Sam's heart, so he came to the Maluka, and announced, in the peculiar manner of Chinese cooks, that he was about to write for a new cook for the station, who would probably arrive within six weeks, when Sam, having installed him to our satisfaction, would, with our permission, leave our service.

The permission was graciously given, and as Sam retired we longed to tell him to engage someone renowned for his disobedience. We fancied later that our willingness piqued Sam, for after giving notice he bestirred himself to such an extent that one of our visitors tried to secure his services for himself, convinced we were throwing away a treasure.

Being within four miles of the Overland Telegraph — that backbone of the overland route—rarely a week was to pass without someone coming in, and at times our travellers came in twos and threes; and as each brought news of that world outside our tiny circle, carrying in perhaps an extra mail for us, or one out for us, they formed a strong link in the chain that bound us to the Outside.

Two hundred and fifty guests was the tally for that year, and earliest among them came a telegraph operator, who—as is the way with telegraph operators out-bush—invited us to "ride across to the wire for a shake hands with Outside"; and within an hour we came in sight of the telegraph wire as our horses mounted the stony ridge that overlooks the Warloch ponds, when the wire was forgotten for a moment in the kaleidoscope of moving, ever-changing colour that met our eyes.

Two wide-spreading, limpid ponds, the Warlochs lay before us, veiled in a glory of golden-flecked heliotrope and purple water-lilies, and floating deep-green leaves, with here and there gleaming little seas of water, opening out among the lilies, and standing knee-deep in the margins a rustling fringe of light reeds and giant bulrushes. All round the ponds stood dark groves of pandanus palms, and among and beyond the palms, tall grasses and forest trees, with here and there a spreading coolibah festooned from summit to trunk with brilliant crimson strands of mistletoe, and here and there a gaunt dead old giant of the forest, and everywhere above and beyond the timber deep sunny blue and flooding sunshine.

But the operator, being unpoetical, had ridden on to the "wire", and presently was "shinning up" one of its slender galvanised iron posts as a preliminary to the "handshake"; for, tapping the line being part of the routine of a telegraph operator in the Territory, "shinning up posts" is one of his necessary accomplishments.

In town, dust and haste and littered papers and nerve-racking bustle seem indispensable to the sending of a telegram; but when the bush-folk "shake hands" with Outside all is sunshine and restfulness, soft beauty and leisurely peace. With the murmuring bush about us, in clear space kept always cleared beneath those quivering wires, we stood all dressed in white, first looking up at the operator as, clinging to his pole, he tapped the line, and then looking down at him as he knelt at our feet with his tiny transmitter beside him clicking out our message to the south folk. And as we stood, with our horses' bridles over our arms and the horses nibbling at the sweet grasses, in touch with the world in spite of our isolation, a gorgeous butterfly rested for a brief space on the tiny instrument, with gently swaying purple wings, and away in the great world men were sending telegrams amid clatter and dust, unconscious of that tiny group of bush-folk, or that Nature, who does all things well, can beautify even the sending of a telegram.

In the heart of the bush, we stood, yet listening to the chatter of the townsfolk, for, business over, the little clicking instrument was gossiping cheerfully with us — the telegraph wire in the Territory being such a friendly wire. Daily it gathers gossip, and daily whispers it up and down the line, and daily news and gossip fly hither and thither; who's Inside, who has gone out, whom to expect, where the mailman is, the newest arrival in Darwin, and the latest rainfall at Powell's Creek.

Daily the telegraph people hear all the news of the Territory, and in due course give the news to the public, when the travellers gathering it, carry it out to the bush-folk, scattering it broadcast, until everybody knows everyone else, and all his business, and where it has taken him; and because of that knowledge, and in spite of those hundreds of thousands of square miles of bushland, the people of the

Territory are held together in one great brotherhood.

Among various items of news the little instrument told us that Dan was "packing up for the return trip"; and in a day or two he came in, bringing a packet of garden seeds and a china teapot from Mine Host, southern letters from the telegraph, and, from Little Johnny, news that he was getting "tools together and would be along in no time".

Being in one of his whimsical moods, Dan withheld congratulations.

"I've been thinking things over, boss," he said, assuming his most philosophical manner, "and I reckon any more rooms'll only interfere with getting the missus educated."

Later on he used the servant question to hang his argument on. "Just proves what I was saying," he said. "If the cleaning of one room causes all this trouble and worry, where'll she be when she's got four to look after? What with white ants, and blue mould, and mildew, and wrastling with lubras, there won't be one minute to spare for education."

He also professed disapproval of the Maluka's devices for making the homestead more habitable. "If this goes on we'll never learn her nothing but loafin'," he declared, when he found that a couple of yards of canvas and a few sticks had become a comfortable lounge chair. "Too much luxury!" he said, and he sat down on his own heels to show how he scorned luxuries.

"Don't you let 'em spoil your chances of education, missus. You were in luck when you struck this place; never saw luck to equal it. And if it holds good, something'll happen to stop you from ever having a house, so as to get you properly educated."

My luck "held good" for the time being; for when Johnny came along in a few days he announced, in answer to a very warm welcome, that "something had gone wrong at No. 3 Well", and that "he'd promised to see to it at once".

"Oh, Johnny!" I cried reproachfully, but the next moment was "toeing the line" even to the Head Stockman's satisfaction; for with a look of surprise Johnny had added: "I—I thought you'd reckon that travellers' water for the Dry came before your rooms." Out-bush we deal in hard facts.

"Thought I'd reckon!" I said, appalled to think my comfort

should even be spoken of when men's lives were in question. "Of course I do; I didn't understand, that was all."

"We haven't finished her education yet," Dan explained, and the Maluka added, "But she's learning."

Johnny looked perplexed. "Oh, well! That's all right, then," he said, rather ambiguously. "I'll be back as soon as possible, and then we shan't be long."

Two days later he left the homestead bound for the well, and as he disappeared into the ti-tree that bordered the south track, most of us agreed that "luck was out". Only Dan professed to think differently. "It's more wonderful than ever, and if it holds good we'll never see Johnny again."

Chapter 8

OUT-BUSH

CONSIDERING ourselves homeless, the Maluka decided that we should "go bush" for a while during Johnny's absence, beginning with a short tour of inspection through some of the southern country of the run; intending, if all were well there, to prepare for a general horse-muster along the north of the Roper. Nothing could be done with the cattle until "after the Wet".

Only Dan and the inevitable black "boy" were to be with us on this preliminary walkabout; but all hands were to turn out for the muster, to the Quiet Stockman's dismay.

"Thought they mostly sat about and sewed," he said in the quarters. Little did the Sanguine Scot guess what he was doing when he "culled" needlework from the "mob" at Pine Creek.

The walkabout was looked upon as a reprieve, and when a traveller, expressing sympathy, suggested that "it might sicken her a bit of camp life", Jack clung to that hope desperately.

"A dress rehearsal for the cattle-musters later on," Dan called the walkabout, looking with approval on my cartridge belt and revolver; and after a few small mobs of cattle had been rounded up and looked over, he suggested "rehearsing that part of the performance where the missus gets lost, and catches cows and milks 'em".

"Now's your chance, missus," he shouted, as a scared, frightened beast broke from the job in hand, and went crashing through the undergrowth. "There's one all by herself to practise on." Dan's system of education, being founded on object lessons, was mightily convincing; and for that trip, anyway, he had a very humble pupil to instruct in the "ways of telling the signs of water at hand".

All day we zig-zagged through scrub and timber, visiting

waterholes and following up cattle-pads; the solitude of the bush seemed only a pleasant seclusion; and the deep forest glades, shady pathways leading to the outside world; but at night, when the camp had been fixed up in the silent depths of a dark Leichhardt-pine forest, the seclusion had become an isolation that made itself felt, and the shady pathways, miles of dark treacherous forest between us and our fellow men.

There is no isolation so weird in its feeling of "cut-offness" as that of a night camp in the heart of the bush. The flickering camp fire draws all that is human and tangible into its charmed circle, and without, all is undefinable darkness and uncertainty. Yet it was in this night camp among the dark pines, with even the stars shut out, that we learnt that out-bush "Houselessness" need not mean "Homelessness"—a discovery that destroyed all hope that "this would sicken her a bit".

As we were only to be out one night, and there was little chance of rain, we had nothing with us but a little tucker, a bluey each, and a couple of mosquito nets. The simplicity of our camp added intensely to the isolation; and as I stood among the dry, rustling leaves, looking up at the dark, broad-leaved canopy above us, with my "swag" at my feet, the Maluka called me a "poor homeless little mite".

A woman with a swag sounds homeless enough to Australian ears, but Dan, with his habit of looking deep into the heart of things, didn't "exactly see where the homelessness came in".

We had finished supper, and the Maluka, stretching himself luxuriously in the firelight, made a nest in the warm leaves for me to settle down in. "You're right, Dan," he said, after a short silence, "when I come to think of it, I don't exactly see myself where the homelessness comes in. A bite and a sup and a faithful dog, and a guidwife by a glowing hearth, and what more is needed to make a home. Eh, Tiddle'ums?"

Tiddle'ums, having for some time given the whole of her heart to the Maluka, nestled closer to him, and Dan gave an appreciative chuckle, and pulled Sool'em's ears. The conversation promised to suit him exactly.

53

"Never got farther than the dog myself," he said. "Did I, Sool'em, old girl?" But Sool'em, becoming effusive, there was a pause until she could be persuaded that "nobody wanted none of her licking tricks". As she subsided Dan went on with his thoughts uninterrupted: "I've seen others at the guidwife business, though, and it didn't seem too bad, but I never struck it in a camp before."

The Maluka suggested that perhaps he had "got farther than the dog" without knowing it, and the idea appealing to Dan, he "reckoned it must have been that". But his whimsical mood had slipped away. And as he sat looking into the fire, with his thoughts far away in the past, the Maluka began to croon contentedly at "Home, Sweet Home", and, curled up in the warm, sweet nest of leaves, I listened to the crooning until everything but the crooning became vague and indistinct, and, beginning also to see into the heart of things, I learned that when a woman finds love and comradeship out-bush, little else is needed to make even the glowing circle of a camp fire her home circle.

Without any warning the Maluka's mood changed. "There is nae luck aboot her house, there is nae luck at a'," he shouted lustily, and Dan, waking from his reverie with a start, rose to the tempting bait.

"No *luck* about *her* house!" he said. "It's the others that have no luck that strike a good, comfortable, well-furnished house first go off, and never get an ounce of educating. They stay chained to their houses as surely as ever a dog was chained to its kennel. But it'll never come to that with the missus. Something's bound to happen to Johnny, just to keep her from ever having a house. Poor Johnny, though," he added, warming up to the subject. "It's hard luck for him. He's a decent little chap. We'll miss him"; and he shook his head sorrowfully, and looked round for applause.

The Maluka said it seemed a pity that Johnny had been allowed to go to his fate; but Dan was in his best form.

"It wouldn't have made any difference," he said tragically. "He'd have got fever if he'd stayed on, or a tree would have fallen on him. He's doomed if the missus keeps him to his contract."

"Oh, well! He'll die in a good cause," I said cheerfully, and Dan's gravity deserted him.

"You're the dead finish!" he chuckled; and without further ceremony, beyond the taking off of his boots, rolled into his mosquito net for the night.

We heard nothing further from him until that strange rustling hour of the night — that hour half-way between midnight and dawn, when all nature stirs in its sleep, and murmurs drowsily in answer to some mysterious call.

Nearly all bushmen who sleep with the warm earth for a bed will tell of this strange wakening moment, of that faint touch of half-consciousness, that whispering stir, strangely enough, only perceptible to the *sleeping* children of the bush — one of the mysteries of nature that no man can fathom, one of the delicate threads with which the Wizard of the Never-Never weaves his spells. "Is all well, my children?" comes the cry from the watchman of the night; and with a gentle stirring the answer floats back, "All is well".

Softly the pine forest rustled with the call and the answer; and as the camp roused to its dim half-consciousness, Dan murmured sleepily, "Sool'em, old girl"; then after a vigorous rustling among the leaves (Sool'em's tail returning thanks for the attention), everything slipped back into unconsciousness until the dawn. As the first grey streak of dawn filtered through the pines, a long-drawn-out cry of "Day-li-ght" — Dan's camp reveille — rolled out of his tent, and Dan rolled out after it, with even less ceremony than he had rolled in.

On our way back to the homestead, Dan suggested that the "missus might like to have a look at the dining room"; we turned into the towering timber that borders the Reach, and for the next two hours rode on through soft, luxurious shade; and all the while the fathomless, spring-fed Reach lay sleeping on our left.

The Reach always slept; for nearly twelve miles it lay, a swaying garland of heliotrope and purple water-lilies, gleaming through a graceful fringe of palms and rushes and scented shrubs, touched here and there with shafts of sunlight, and murmuring and rustling with an attendant host of gorgeous butterflies and flitting birds and insects.

Dan looked on the scene with approving eyes. "Not a bad place to ride through, is it?" he said. But gradually as we rode on a vague depression settled down on us, and when Dan finally decided he "could do with a bit more sunshine", we followed him into the blistering noontide glare with almost a sigh of relief.

It is always so. These wondrous waterways have little part in that mystical holding power of the Never-Never. They are only pleasant places to ride through and—leave behind; for their purring slumberous beauty is vaguely suggestive of the beauty of a sleeping tiger—a sleeping tiger with deadly fangs and talons hidden under a wonder of soft allurement; and when exiles in the towns sit and dream, their dreams are all of stretches of scorched grass and quivering sun-flecked shade.

In the honest sunlight Dan's spirits rose, and as I investigated various byways he asked "where the sense came in of tying up a dog that was doing no harm running loose. It warn't as though she's taken to chivvying cattle," he added as, a mob of inquisitive steers trotting after us, I hurried Roper in among the riders; and then he wondered "how she'll shape at her first muster".

The rest of the morning he filled in with tales of cattle musters—tales of stampedes and of cattle rushing over camps and "mincing chaps into sawdust"—until I was secretly pleased that the coming muster was for horses.

But Jack's reprieve was to last a little longer. When all was ready for the muster, word came in that outside blacks were in all along the river, and the Maluka deciding that the risks were too great for the missus in long-grass country, the plans were altered, and I was left at the homestead in the Dandy's care.

"It's an ill wind that blows nobody any good," the Maluka said, drawing attention to Jack's sudden interest in the proceedings.

Apart from sterling worth of character, the Dandy was all contrast to the Quiet Stockman; quick, alert, and sociable, and brimming over with quiet tact and thoughtfulness, and the Maluka knew I was in good hands. But the Dandy had his work to attend to; and after watching till the bush had swallowed up the last of the pack team, I went to the wood heap for company or consolation. Had the Darwin ladies seen me then, they would have been justified in saying, "I told you so".

There was plenty of company at the wood heap, but the consolation was doubtful in character. Goggle-Eye and three other old blackfellows were gossiping there, and after a peculiar grin of welcome they expressed great fear lest the homestead should be attacked by "outside" blacks during the Maluka's absence. "Might it," they said, and offered to sleep in the garden near me, as no doubt "missus would be frightened fellow" to sleep alone.

"Me big mob frightened fellow longa wild blackfellow," Goggle-Eye said, rather overdoing the part; and the other old rascals giggled nervously, and said "My word!" But sly, watchful glances made me sure they were only probing to find if fear had kept the missus at the homestead. Of course, if it had, a little harmless bullying for tobacco could be safely indulged in when the Dandy was busy at the yards.

Fortunately, Dan's system of education provided for all emergencies; and remembering his counsel to "die rather than own to a blackfellow that you were frightened of anything", I refused their offer of protection, and declared so emphatically that there was nothing in heaven or earth that I was afraid to tackle single-handed, that I almost believed it myself.

There was no doubt *they* believed it, for they murmured in admiration, "My word! Missus big mob cheeky fellow all right". But in their admiration they forgot that they were supposed to be quaking with fear themselves, and took no precautions against the pretended attack; and deciding "there was nothing in the yarn", the Dandy slept in the Quarters and I in the House, leaving the doors and windows open as usual.

When this was reported at dawn by Billy Muck, who had taken no part in the intimidation scheme, a wholesome awe crept into the old men's admiration, for a blackfellow is fairly logical in these matters.

To him, the man who crouches behind barred doors is a coward and may be attacked without much risk, while he who relies on his own strength appears as a Goliath defying the armies of a nation, and is best left alone, lest he develop into a Samson annihilating Philistines. Fortunately for my reputation, only the Dandy knew that we considered open doors easier to get out of than closed ones, and that my revolver was to be fired to call him from the Quarters if anything alarming occurred.

"You'll have to live up to your reputation now," the Dandy said, and, brave in the knowledge that he was within coo-ee, I ordered the old men about most unmercifully, leaving little doubt in their minds that "missus was big mob cheeky fellow".

Billy Muck and Jimmy had been absent from the wood heap. Had they been present, knowing the old fellows well, I venture to think there would have been no intimidation scheme floated.

As the Dandy put it, "altogether the time passed pleasantly", and when the Maluka returned we were all on the best of terms, having reached the phase of friendship when pet names are permissible. The missus had become "Gadgerrie" to the old men and certain privileged lubras. What it means I do not know, excepting that it seemed to imply fellowship. Perhaps it means "old pal" or "mate", or, judging from the tone of voice that accompanied it, "old girl", but more probably, like Maluka, untranslatable. The Maluka was always Maluka to the old men and to some of us who imitated them.

Dan came in the day after the Maluka, and, hearing of our "affairs", took all the credit of it to himself.

"Just shows what a bit of educating'll do," he said. "The Dandy would have had a gay old time of it if I hadn't put you up to their capers"; and I had humbly to acknowledge the truth of all he said.

"I don't say you're not promising well," he added, satisfied with my humility. "If Johnny'll only stay away long enough, we'll have you educated up to doing without a house."

Within a week it seemed as though Johnny was aiding and abetting Dan in his scheme of education; for he sent in word that his "cross-cut saw", or something equally important, had "doubled up on him", and he was going back to Katherine to "see about it straight off".

Chapter 9

"TEA BIN FINISSEM"

BEFORE the mustered horses were drafted out, everyone at the homestead, blacks, whites and Chinese, went up to the stockyard to "have a look at them".

Dan was in one of his superior moods. "Let's see if she knows anything about horses," he said condescendingly, as the Quiet Stockman opened the mob up a little to show the animals to better advantage. "Show us your fancy in this lot, missus." "Certainly," I said, affecting particular knowledge of the subject, and Jack wheeled with a quick, questioning look, suddenly aware that, after all, a woman *might* be only a fellow man; and as I glanced from one beautiful animal to another he watched keenly, half expectant and half incredulous.

It did not take long to choose. In the foreground stood a magnificent brown colt, that caught and held the attention, as it watched every movement with ears shot forward and nostrils quivering; and as I pointed it out Jack's boyish face lit up with surprise and pleasure.

"Talk of luck!" Dan cried, as usual withholding the benefit of the doubt. "You've picked Jack's fancy."

But it was Jack himself who surprised everyone, for, forgetting his monosyllables, he said with an indescribable ring of fellowship in his voice, "She's picked out the best in the whole mob," and turned back to his work among the horses with his usual self-possession.

Dan's eyes opened wide. "Whatever's come to Jack?" he said; but seemed puzzled at the Maluka's answer that he was "only getting educated". The truth is that every man has his vulnerable point, and Jack's was horses.

When the mob had been put through the yards, all the unbroken horses were given into the Quiet Stockman's care, and for the next week or two the stockyard became the only place of real interest; for the homestead, waiting for the Wet to lift, had settled down to store lists, fencing, and stud books.

It was not the horses alone that were of interest at the yards; the calm, fearless, self-reliant man who was handling them was infinitely more so. Nothing daunted or disheartened him; and in those hours spent on the stockyard fence, in the shade of a spreading tree, I learnt to know the Quiet Stockman for the man he was.

Jack's horse-breaking was a battle for supremacy of mind over mind, not mind over matter — a long course of careful training and schooling, in which nothing was broken, but all bent to the control of a master. Working always intelligent obedience, not cowed stupidity, he appeared at times to be almost reasoning with the brute mind, as he helped it to solve the problems of its schooling; penetrating dull stupidity with patient reiteration, or wearing down stubborn opposition with steady, unwavering persistence, and always rewarding ultimate obedience with gentle kindness and freedom.

Step by step, the training proceeded. Submission first, then an establishment of perfect trust and confidence between horse and man, without which nothing worth having could be attained.

After that, in orderly succession the rest followed; toleration of handling, reining, mouthing, leading on foot, and on horseback, and in due time saddling and mounting. One thing at a time and nothing new until the old was so perfected that when all was ready for the mounting — from a spectacular point of view — the mounting was generally disappointing. Just a little rearing and curvetting, then a quiet, trusting acceptance of this new order of things.

Half a dozen horses were in hand at once, and, as with children at school, some quickly got ahead of the others, and every day the interest grew keener and keener in the individual character of the horses. At the end of a week Jack announced that he was "going to catch the brown colt" next day. "It'll be worth seeing," he said; and from the Quiet Stockman that was looked upon as a very pressing invitation.

From the day of the draughting he had ceased altogether to avoid me, and in the days that followed had gradually realised that a horse could be more to a woman than as a means of locomotion; and now no longer drew the line at conversations.

When we went up to the yards in the morning, the brown colt was in a small yard by itself, and Jack was waiting at the gate, ready for its "catching".

With a laugh at the wild rush with which the colt avoided him, he shut himself into the yard with it, and moved quietly about, sometimes towards it and sometimes from it; at times standing still and looking it over, and at other times throwing a rope or sack carelessly down, waiting until his presence had become familiar, and the colt had learned that there was nothing to fear from it.

There was a curious calmness in the man's movements, a fearless repose that utterly ignored the wild rushes, and as a natural result they soon ceased; and within just a minute or two the beautiful creature was standing still, watching in quivering wonder.

Gradually a double rope began to play in the air with ever-increasing circles, awakening anew the colt's fears; and as these in turn subsided, without any apparent effort, a long running noose flickered out from the circling rope, and, falling over the strong young head, lay still on the arching neck.

The leap forward was terrific; but the rope brought the colt up with a jerk; and in the instant's pause that followed the Quiet Stockman braced himself for the mad rearing plunges that were coming. There was literally only an instant's pause, and then with a clatter of hoofs the plungings began, and were met with muscles of iron and jaw set like a vice, as the man, with heels dug into the ground, dragged back on the rope, yielding as much as his judgment allowed — enough to ease the shocks, but not an inch by compulsion.

Twice the rearing, terrified creature circled round him, and then the rope began to shorten to a more workable length. There was no haste, no flurry. Surely and steadily the rope shortened (but the horse went to the man, not the man to the horse; that was to come later). With the shortening of the rope the compelling power of the man's will forced itself into the brute mind; and, bending to that will, the wild leaps and plungings took on a vague suggestion of obedience—a going *with* the rope, not against it; that was all. An erratic going, perhaps, but enough to tell that the horse had acknowledged a master. That was all Jack asked for at first and, satisfied, he relaxed his muscles and, as the rope slackened, the horse turned and faced him; and the marvel was how quickly it was all over.

But something was to follow, that once seen could never be forgotten—the advance of the man to the horse.

With barely perceptible movement, the man's hands stole along the rope at a snail's pace. Never hurrying, never stopping, they slid on, the colt watching them as though mesmerised. When within reach of the dilated nostrils, they paused and waited, and slowly the sensitive head came forward snuffling, more in bewilderment than fear at this new wonder, and as the dark twitching muzzle brushed the hands, the head drew sharply back, only to return again in a moment with greater confidence.

Three or four times the quivering nostrils came back to the hands before they stirred, then one lifted slowly and lay on the muzzle, warm and strong and comforting, while the other creeping up the rope, slipped on to the glossy neck, and the catching was over.

For a little while there was some gentle patting and fondling, to a murmuring accompaniment of words; the horse standing still with twitching ears the while. Then came the test of victory—the test of the man's power and the creature's intelligence. The horse was to go to the man, at the man's bidding alone, without force or coercion. "The better they are the sooner you learn 'em that," was one of Jack's pet theories, while his proudest boast—his only boast, perhaps—was that he's "never been beaten on that yet".

"They have to come sooner or later if you stick at 'em," he had said, when I marvelled at first to see the great creatures come obediently to the click of his tongue or fingers. So far in all his wide experience the latest had been the third day. That, however, was rare; more frequently it was a matter of hours, sometimes barely an hour, while now and then—incredulous as it may seem to the layman—only minutes.

Ten minutes before Jack put the brown colt to the test it had been a wild, terrified, plunging creature, and yet, as he stepped back to try its intelligence and submission, his face was confident and expectant.

Moving slowly backwards, he held out one hand—the hand that had proved all kindness and comfort—and, snapping a finger and thumb, clicked his tongue in a murmur of invitation.

The brown ears shot forward to attention at the sound, and as the head reached out to investigate the snapping fingers repeated the invitation, and without hesitation the magnificent creature went forward obediently until the hand was once more resting on the dark muzzle.

The trusting beauty of the surrender seemed to break some spell that had held us silent since the beginning of the catching. "Oh, Jack! Isn't he a beauty?" I cried, unconsciously putting my admiration into a question.

But Jack no longer objected to questions. He turned towards us with soft, shining eyes. "There's not many like him," he said, pulling at one of the flexible ears. "You could learn him anything." It seemed so, for after trying to solve the problem of the roller and bit with his tongue when it was put into his mouth, he accepted the mystery with quiet, intelligent trust; and as soon as he was freed from it, almost courted further fondling. He would let no one but Jack near him, though. When we entered the yard the ears went back and the whites of the eyes showed. "No one but me for a while," Jack said, with a strange ring of ownership in his voice, telling that it is a good thing to have a horse that is yours, and yours only.

While the Quiet Stockman had been the centre of interest, a good many things had been going wrong at the homestead. Sam began by breaking both china cups, and letting the backbone slip out of everything in his charge.

Fowls laid out and eggs became luxuries. Cream refused to rise on the milk. It seemed impossible to keep meat sweet.

Jimmy lost interest in the gathering of firewood and the carrying of water; and as a result, the water-butts first shrank, then leaked, finally lay down, a medley of planks and iron hoops. A swarm of grasshoppers passed through the homestead, and to use Sam's explicit English: "Vegetables bin finissem all about"; and by the time fresh seeds were springing the Wet returned with renewed vigour, and flooded out the garden. Then stores began to fail, including soap and kerosene, and writing paper and ink threatened to "peter out". After that the lubras, in a private quarrel during the washing of clothes, tore one of the "couple of changes" of blouses sadly; and the mistress of a cattle station was obliged to entertain guests at times in a pink cambric blouse patched with a washed calico flour-bag, no provision having been made for patching. Then just as we were wondering what else could happen, one night, without the slightest warning, the very birds migrated from the lagoon, carrying away with them the promise of future pillows, to say nothing of a mattress; and the Maluka was obliged to go far afield in search of non-migrating birds.

Dan wagged his head and talked wise philosophy, with these disasters for the thread of his discourse; but even he was obliged to own that there was a limit to education when Sam announced that "Tea bin finissem all about".

He had found that the last eighty-pound tea chest contained tinware when he opened it to replenish his tea caddy. Tea had been ordered, and the chest was labelled tea clearly enough, to show that the fault lay in Darwin; but that was poor consolation to us, the sufferers.

The necessities of the bush are few; but they are necessities; and Billy Muck was sent in to the Katherine post-haste, to beg, borrow, or buy tea from Mine Host. But in spite of Mine Host's efforts to keep us going, twice again, before the waggons came, we found ourselves begging tea from travellers.

It was only March, and the waggons had to wait till the Wet lifted; but in our need everyone felt sure that "the Wet would lift early this year".

"Generally does with the change of moon before Easter,"

65

the traveller said, and flying off at a tangent, I asked when Easter was, unwittingly setting the homestead a tough problem.

Nobody could say for certain. But Dan "knew a chap once who could reckon it by the moon"; and the Maluka felt inspired to work it out. "It's simple enough," he said. "The first Friday—or is it Sunday?—*after* the first full moon *after* the twenty-first of March."

"Twenty-fifth, isn't it?" the Dandy asked, complicating matters from the beginning.

The traveller reckoned it'd be new moon about Monday or Tuesday, which seemed near enough at the time; and the full moon was fixed for the Tuesday or Wednesday fortnight from that.

"That ought to settle it," Dan said; and so it might have if anyone had been sure of Monday's date; but we all had different convictions about that, varying from the ninth to the thirteenth.

After much ticking off of days upon fingers, with an old newspaper as "something to work from", the date of the full moon was fixed for the twenty-fourth or twenty-fifth of March, unless the moon came in so late on Tuesday that it brought the full to the morning of the twenty-sixth.

"Seems getting a bit mixed," Dan said, and matters were certainly complicated.

If we were to reckon from the twenty-first Easter was in March, but if from the twenty-fifth, in April—if the moon came in on Monday, but March in either case if the full was on the twenty-sixth.

Dan suggested "giving it best". "It 'ud get anybody dodged," he said, hopelessly at sea; but the Maluka wanted to "see it through". "The new moon should clear most of it up," he said, "but you've given us a teaser this time, little 'un."

The new moon should have cleared everything up if we could have seen it, but the Wet coming on in force again, we saw nothing till Thursday evening when it was too late to calculate with precision.

Dan was for having two Easters, and "getting even with it that way"; but Sam unexpectedly solved the problem for us.

"What was the difficulty?" he asked, and listened to the explanation attentively. "Bunday!" he exclaimed at the finish, showing he had fully grasped the situation. Of course, he knew all about Bunday! Wasn't it so many weeks after the Chinaman's New Year festival? And in a jargon of pidgin-English he swept aside all moon discussions and fixed the date of "Bunday" for the twenty-eighth of March, "which," as Dan wisely remarked "proved that somebody was right"; but whether the Maluka or the Dandy or the moon, he forgot to specify. "The old heathen to beat us all, too," he added, "just when it had got us all dodged." Dan took all the credit of the suggestion to himself. Then he looked philosophically on the toughness of the problem: "Anyway," he said, "the missus must have learnt a bit about beginning at the beginning of things. Just think what she'd have missed if anyone had known when Easter was right off!"

What she'd have missed, indeed. Exactly what the townsman misses, as long as he remains in a land where everything can be known "right off ".

But a new idea had come to Dan. "Of course," he said, "as far as that goes, if Johnny does turn up she ought to learn a thing or two while he's moving the dining room up to the house"; and he decided to welcome Johnny on his return.

He had not long to wait, for in a day or two Johnny rode into the homestead, followed by a black boy carrying a cross-cut saw. This time he hailed us with a cheery:

"*Now* we shan't be long."

Chapter 10

A TINY HOME IN THE WILDERNESS

IT had taken over six weeks to "get hold of Little Johnny"; but as the Dandy had prophesied, once he started, he "made things hum in no time".

"Now we shan't be long," he said, flourishing a tape measure; and the Dandy was kept busy for half a day "wrestling with the calculating".

That finished, the store was turned inside out and a couple of "boys" sent in for "things needed", and after them more "boys" for more things, and then other "boys" for other things, until travellers must have thought the camp blacks had entered into a walking competition. When everything necessary was ordered, "all hands" were put to sharpen saws and tools, and the homestead shrieked and groaned all day with harsh, discordant raspings. Then a camp was pitched in the forest, a mile or so from the homestead; a sawpit dug, a platform erected, and before a week had passed an invitation was issued for the missus to "come and see a tree felled". "Laying the foundation stone," the Maluka called it.

Johnny, of course, welcomed us with a jovial "Now we shan't be long", and shouldering a tomahawk, led the way out of the camp into the timber.

House hunting in town does not compare favourably with the timber-hunting for a house in a luxuriant tropical forest. Sheltered from the sun and heat, we wandered about in the feathery undergrowth, while the Maluka tested the height of the giant timber above us with shots from his bull-dog revolver, bringing down twigs and showers of leaves from the topmost branches, and sending flocks of white cockatoos up into the air with squawks of amazement.

Tree after tree was chosen and marked with the tomahawk, each one appearing taller and straighter and more beautiful than any of its fellows — until, finding ourselves back at the camp, Johnny went for his axe and left us to look at the beauty around us.

"Seems a pity to spoil all this, just to make four walls to shut the missus in from anything worth looking at," Dan murmured as Johnny reappeared. "They won't make anything as good as this up at the house." Johnny, the unpoetical, hesitated, perplexed. Philosophy was not in his line. "'Tisn't too bad," he said, suddenly aware of the beauty of the scene; and then, the tradesman coming to the surface: "I reckon *my* job'll be a bit more on the plumb, though," he chuckled, and, delighted with his little joke, shouldered his axe and walked towards one of the marked trees, while Dan speculated aloud on the chances a man had of "getting off alive" if a tree fell on him.

"Trees don't fall on a man that knows how to handle timber," the unsuspecting Johnny said briskly; and as Dan feared that "fever was her only chance then", he spat on his hands and, sending the axe home into the bole of the tree with a clean, swinging stroke, laid the foundation stone — the foundation stone of a tiny home in the wilderness, that was destined to be the dwelling place of great joy and happiness and sorrow.

The Sanguine Scot had prophesied rightly. There being "time enough for everything in the Never-Never", there was time for "many pleasant rides along the Reach, choosing trees for timber".

But the rides were the least part of the pleasure. For the time being, the silent Reach forest had become the hub of our little universe. All was life and bustle and movement there. Every day fresh trees were felled and chopping contests entered into by Johnny and the Dandy; and as the trees fell in quick succession, black boys and lubras armed with tomahawks swarmed over them, to lop away the branches, before the trunks were dragged by the horses to the mouth of the sawpit. Everyone was happy and light-hearted, and the work went merrily forward, until a great pile of tree trunks lay ready for the sawpit.

Then a new need arose; Johnny wanted several yards of strong string, and a "sup" of ink, to make guiding lines on the timber for his saw; but as only sewing cotton was forthcoming, and the Maluka refused to part with one drop of his precious ink, we were obliged to go down to the beginning of things once more: two or three lubras were set to work to convert the sewing-cotton into tough, strong string, while others prepared a substitute for the ink from burnt water-lily roots.

The sawing of the tree trunks lasted for nearly three weeks, and the Dandy, being the underman in the pit, had anything but a merry time. Down in the pit, away from the air, he worked; pulling and pushing, pushing and pulling, hour after hour, in a blinding stream of sawdust.

When we offered him sympathy and a gossamer veil, he accepted the veil gratefully, but waved the sympathy aside, saying it was "all in the good cause". Nothing was ever a hardship to the Dandy, excepting dirt.

Johnny, being a past-master in his trade, stood on the platform in the upper air, guiding the saw along the marked lines; and as he instructed us all in the fine art of pit-sawing, Dan decided that the building of a house, under some circumstances, could be an education in itself.

"Thought she might manage to learn a thing or two out of it," he said. "The building of it is right enough. It all depends what she uses it for when Johnny's done with it."

As the pliant saw coaxed beams, and slabs, and flooring boards out of the forest trees I grew to like beginning at the beginning of things, and realised there was an underlying truth in Dan's whimsical reiteration that "the missus was in luck when she struck this place"; for beams and slabs and flooring boards wrested from Nature amid merry-making and philosophical discourses are not as other beams and slabs and flooring boards. They are old friends and fellow-adventurers, with many a good tale to tell, recalling comical situations in their reminiscences with a vividness that baffles description.

Perhaps those who live in homes with the beginning of things left behind in forests they have never seen, may think chattering planks a poor compensation for unpapered, rough-boarded walls and unglazed window frames. Let them try it before they judge, remembering always that, before a house can be built of old friends and memories, the friends must be made and the memories lived through.

But other things besides the sawing of timber were in progress.

The Easter moon had come in dry and cool, and at its full the Wet lifted, as our traveller had foretold. Sam did his best with Bunday, serving hot rolls with mysterious markings on them for breakfast, and by midday he had the homestead to himself, the Maluka and I being camped at Bitter Springs and everyone else being elsewhere.

Dan was away beyond the northern boundary, going through the cattle, judging the probable duration of "outside waters" for that year. The Quiet Stockman was away beyond the southern boundary, rounding up wanderers and stragglers among the horses, and the station was face to face with the year's work, making preparations for the year's mustering and branding — for with the lifting of the Wet everything in the Never-Never begins to move.

"After the Wet" rivers go down, the north-west monsoon giving place to the south-east trades; bogs dry up everywhere, opening all roads; travellers pass through the stations from all points of the compass — cattle buyers, drovers, station owners, telegraph people — all bent on business, and all glad to get moving after the long compulsory inaction of the Wet; and lastly, that great yearly cumbrous event takes place; the starting of the "waggons", with their year's stores for Inside.

The first batch of travellers had little news for us. They had heard that the teams were loading up, and couldn't say for certain, and, finding them unsatisfactory, we looked forward to the coming of the "Fizzer", our mailman, who was almost due.

Eight mails a year was our allowance, with an extra now and then through the courtesy of travellers. Eight mails a year against eight hundred for the townsfolk. Was it any wonder that we all found we had business at the homestead when the Fizzer was due there?

When he came this trip he was, as usual, brimming over with news: personal items, public gossip, and the news that the horse teams had got most of their loading on, and that the Macs were getting their bullocks under way. Two horse waggons and a dray for far "Inside", and three bullock waggons for the nearer distances, comprised the "waggons" that year. The teamsters were Englishmen; but the bullock-punchers were three Macs — an Irishman, a Highlander, and the Sanguine Scot.

Six waggons, and about six months' hard travelling, in and out, to provide a year's stores for three cattle stations and two telegraph stations. It is not surprising that the freight per ton was what it was — twenty-two pounds per ton for the Elsey, and upwards of forty pounds for "Inside". It is this freight that makes the grocery bill such a big item on stations out-bush, where several tons of stores are considered by no means a large order.

Close on the heels of the Fizzer came other travellers, with the news that the horse teams had "got going" and the Macs had "pulled out" to the Four Mile. "Your trunks'll be along in no time now, missus," one of them said. "They've got 'em all aboard."

The Dandy did some rapid calculations: "Ten miles a day on good roads," he said; "one hundred and seventy miles. Tens into that, seventeen days. Give 'em a week over for unforeseen emergencies, and call it four weeks." It sounded quite cheerful and near at hand, but a belated thunderstorm or two, and consequent bogs, nearly doubled the four weeks.

Almost every day we heard news of the teams from the now constant stream of travellers; and by the time the timber was all sawn and carted to the house to fulfil the many promises there, they were at the Katherine.

But the year's stores were on the horse teams, and the station, having learnt from bitter experience of the past, now sent in its own waggon for the bulk of the stores, as soon as they were known to be at the Katherine; and so the Dandy set off at once.

"You'll see me within a fortnight, bar accidents," he called back, as the waggon lurched forward towards the slip-rails.

The Dandy out of sight, Johnny went back to his work, which happened to be hammering curves out of sheets of corrugated iron.

"Now we shan't be long," he shouted, hammering vigorously; and when I objected to the awful din, he reminded me, with a grin, that it was "all in the good cause". When "smoothed out", as Johnny phrased it, the iron was to be used for capping the piles that the house was built upon, "to make them little white ants stay at home".

"We'll smooth all your troubles out, if you give us time," he shouted, returning to the hammering after his explanation with even greater energy. But by dinner time someone had waddled into our lives who was to smooth most of the difficulties out of it, to his own and our complete satisfaction.

Just as Sam announced dinner a cloud of dust creeping along the horizon attracted our attention.

"Foot travellers!" Dan decided; but something emerged out of the dust, as it passed through the slip-rails, that looked very like a huge mould of white jelly on horseback.

Directly it sighted us it rolled off the horse, whether intentionally or unintentionally we could not say, and leaving the beast to the care of chance, unfolded two short legs from somewhere and waddled towards us—a fat, jovial Chinese John Falstaff.

"Good day, boss! Good day, missus! Good day, all about," he said in cheerful salute, as he trundled towards us like a ship's barrel in full sail. "Me new cook, me—" and then Sam appeared and towed him into port.

"Well, I'm blest!" Dan exclaimed, staring after him. "What *have* we struck?"

But Johnny knew, as did most Territorians. "You've struck Cheon, that's all," he said. "Talk of luck! He's the jolliest old josser going."

The "jolliest old josser" seemed difficult to repress; for already he had eluded Sam and, reappearing in the kitchen doorway, waddled across the thoroughfare towards us.

"Me new cook!" he repeated, going on from where he had left off. "Me Cheon!" and then in queer pidgin English, he solemnly rolled out a few of his many qualifications.

"Me savey all about," he chanted. "Me savey cook 'im, and gard'in', and milk 'im, and chuckie, and fishin', and shootin' wild duck." On and on he chanted through a varied list of accomplishments, ending up with an application for the position of cook. "Me sit down? Eh, boss" he asked, moon-faced and serious.

"Please yourself!" the Maluka laughed, and with a flash of white teeth and an infectious chuckle, Cheon laughed and nodded back; then, still chuckling, he waddled away to the kitchen and took possession there, while we went to our respective dinners, little guessing that the truest-hearted, most faithful, most loyal old "josser" had waddled into our lives.

Chapter 11

"ME SAVEY ALL ABOUT"

CHEON rose at cock-crow ("fowl-sing-out", he preferred to call it), and began his duties by scornfully refusing Sam's bland offer of instruction in the "ways" of the homestead.

"Me savey all about," he said, with a majestic wave of his hands, after expressing supreme contempt for Sam's ways; so Sam applied for his cheque, shook hands all round, and withdrew smilingly.

Sam's account being satisfactorily "squared", Cheon's name was then formally entered in the station books as cook and gardener, at twenty-five shillings a week. That was the only vacancy he ever filled in the books; but in our life at the homestead he filled almost every vacancy that required filling, and there were many.

There was nothing he could not and did not do for our good; and it was well that he refused to be instructed in anybody's ways, for his own were delightfully disobedient and unexpected and entertaining. Not only had we "struck the jolliest old josser going", but a born ruler and organiser into the bargain. He knew best what was good for us, and told us so, and, meekly bending to his will, our orders became mere suggestions to be entertained and carried out if approved of by Cheon, or dismissed as "silly-fellow" with a Podsnapian wave of his arm if they in no way appealed to him.

Full of wrath for Sam's ways, and bubbling over with trundling energy, he calmly appropriated the whole staff, as well as Jimmy, Billy Muck, and the rejected, and within a week had put backbone into everything that lacked it, from the water butts to old Jimmy.

The first two days were spent in a whirlwind of dust and rubbish, turned out from unguessed-at recesses, and Cheon's jovial humour, suiting his helpers to a nicety, the rubbish was dealt with amid shouts of delight and enjoyment; until Jimmy, losing his head in his lightness of heart, dug Cheon in the ribs and, waving a stick over his head, yelled in mock fierceness: "Me wild-fellow blackfellow. Me myall-fellow."

Then Cheon came out in a new role. Without a moment's hesitation, his arms and legs appeared to fly out all together in Jimmy's direction, completely doubling him up.

"Me myall-fellow, too," Cheon said calmly, master of himself and the situation. Then, chuckling at Jimmy's discomfiture, he went on with his work, while his helpers stared open-eyed with amazement; an infuriated Chinese catherine-wheel being something new in the experience of a blackfellow. It was a wholesome lesson, though, and no one took liberties with Cheon again.

The rubbish disposed of, leaking water butts and the ruins of collapsed water butts were carried to the billabong, swelled in the water, hammered and hooped back into steadfast, reliable water butts, and trundled along to their places in a merry, joyous procession.

With Cheon's hand on the helm, cream rose on the milk from somewhere. The meat no longer turned sour. An expert fisherman was discovered among the helpers — one Bob by name. Cheon's shot-gun appeared to have a magnetic attraction for wild duck. A garden sprang up by magic, grasshoppers being literally chased off the vegetables. The only thing we lacked was butter; and after a week of order and cleanliness and dazzlingly varied menus, we wondered how we had ever existed without him.

It was no use trying to wriggle from under Cheon's foot once he put it down. At the slightest neglect of duty, lubras or boys were marshalled and kept relentlessly to their work until he was satisfied; and woe betide the lubras who had neglected to wash hand, and pail, and cow, before sitting down to their milking. The very fowls that laid out-bush gained nothing by their subtlety. At the faintest sound of a cackle, a dozing lubra was roused by the point of Cheon's toe, as he shouted excitedly above her: "Fowl sing out! That way! Catch 'im egg! Go on!" pointing out the direction with much pantomime; and as the egg basket filled to overflowing he either chuckled with glee or expressed further contempt for Sam's ways.

But his especial wrath was reserved for the fowl roosts over his sleeping quarters. "What's 'er matter! Fowl sit down close up kitchen!" he growled in furious gutturals, whenever his eyes rested on them; and as soon as time permitted he mounted to the roof, and, boiling over with righteous indignation, hurled the offending roosts into space.

New roosts were then nailed to the branches of a spreading coolibah tree, a hundred yards or so to the north of the buildings, the trunk encircled with zinc to prevent snakes or wild cats from climbing into the roosts; a moveable ladder staircase made, to be used by the fowls at bedtime, and removed as soon as they were settled for the night, lest the cats or snakes should make unlawful use of it (Cheon always foresaw every contingency); and finally "boys" and lubras were marshalled to wean the fowls from their old love.

But the weaning took time, and proved most entertaining; and while the fowls were being taught by bitter experience to bend to Cheon's will, the homestead pealed with shoutings and laughter.

Busy as he was, Cheon found time to take the missus also under his ample wing, and protect her from everything — even herself. "Him too muchee little fellow," he said to the Maluka, to explain his attitude towards his mistress; and the Maluka, chuckling, shamefully encouraged him in his ways.

Every suggestion the missus made was received with an amused "No good that way, missus! Me savey all about." Her methods with lubras were openly disapproved, and her gardening ridiculed to all comers: "White woman no good, savey gard'n," he reiterated; but was fated to apologise handsomely in that direction later on.

Still, in other things the white woman was honoured as became her position as never Sam had honoured her. Without any discrimination, Sam had summoned all at meal times with a booming teamster's bell, thus placing the gentry on a level with the Quarters; but, as Cheon pointed out, what could be expected of one of Sam's ways and caste? It was all very well to ring a peremptory bell for the Quarters — its caste expected to receive and obey orders; but gentry should be graciously notified that all was ready, when it suited their pleasure to eat; and from the day of Sam's departure, the House was honoured with a sing-song: "Din-ner! Boss! Missus" at midday, with changes rung at "Bress-fass" or "Suppar"; and no written menu being at its service, Cheon supplied a chanted one, so that before we sat down to the first course we should know all others that were to come.

But the person Cheon most approved of at the homestead was Johnny; for not only had Johnny helped him in many of his wild efforts at carpentry, but was he not working in the good cause?

"What's 'er matter, missus only got one room?" Cheon had said, angry with circumstances, and daily and hourly he urged Johnny to work quicker.

"What's the matter, indeed!" Johnny echoed, mimicking his furious gutturals, and sawing, planing, and hammering with untiring energy, pointed out that he was doing his best to give her more.

Finding the process slow with only one man at work, Cheon suggested the Maluka might lend a hand in his spare time (station books being considered recreation); and when Dan came in with a mob of cattle from the Reach country, he hinted that cattle could wait, and that Dan could employ his time better.

But Dan also was out of patience with circumstances, and growled that "they'd waited quite long enough as it was", for the work of the station was at a deadlock for want of stores. They had been sadly taxed by the needs of travellers, and we were down to our last half-bag of flour and sugar, and a terrifyingly small quantity of tea; soap, jams, fruit, kerosene, and all such had long been things of the past. The only food we had in quantities was meat, vegetables and milk. Where we would have been without Cheon no one can tell.

To crown all, we had just heard that the Dandy was delayed in a bog with a broken shaft, but he eventually arrived in time to save the situation, but not before we were quite out of tea. He had little to complain of in the way of welcome when his great piled-up waggon lumbered into the homestead avenue and drew up in front of the store.

The horse teams were close behind, the Dandy said, but Mac was "having a gay time" in the sandy country, and sent in a message to remind the missus that she was still in the Land of Wait-a-while. The reminder was quite unnecessary.

There was also a message from Mine Host. "I'm sending a few cuttings for the missus," it read. Cuttings he called them; but the back of the waggon looked like a nurseryman's van; for all a-growing and a-blowing and waiting to be planted out, stood a row of flowering, well-grown plants in tins: crimson hibiscus, creepers, oleanders, and all sorts. A man is best known by his actions, and Mine Host best understood by his kindly thoughtfulness.

The store was soon full to overflowing, and so was our one room, for everything ordered for the house had arrived—rolls of calico, heavy and unbleached, mosquito netting, blue matting for the floors, washstand ware, cups and saucers, and dozens of smaller necessities piled in every corner of the room.

"There won't be many idle hands round these parts for a while," a traveller said, looking round the congested room, and he was right, for, having no sewing machine, a gigantic hand-sewing contract was to be faced. The ceilings of both rooms were to be calico, and a dozen or so seams were to be over-sewn for that; the strips of matting were to be joined together and bound into squares, and after that a herculean task undertaken: the making of a huge mosquito-netted dining room, large enough to enclose the table and chairs, so as to ensure our meals in comfort—for the flies, like the poor, were to be with us always.

This net was to be nearly ten feet square and twelve feet high, with a calico roof of its own drawn taut to the ceiling of the room, and walls of mosquito netting, weighted at the foot with a deep fold of calico, and falling from ceiling to floor, with a wide overlapping curtain for a doorway. Imagine an immense four-poster bed-net, ten by ten by twelve, swung taut within a larger room, and a fair idea of the dining net will have been formed. A room within a room, and within the inner room we hoped to find a paradise at mealtime in comparison with the purgatory of the last few months.

But the sewing did not end at that. The lubras' methods of washing had proved most disastrous to my meagre wardrobe; and the resources of the homestead were taxed to the utmost to provide sufficient patching material to keep the missus even decently clothed.

"Wait for the waggons," the Maluka sang cheerily every time he found me hunting in the store (unbleached calico or mosquito netting being unsuitable for patching).

Cheon openly disapproved of this stage of affairs, and was inclined to blame the Maluka. A good husband usually provides his wife with sufficient clothing, he insinuated; but when he heard that further supplies were on the bullock waggon, he apologised, and as he waddled about kept one ear cocked to catch the first sound of the bullock bells. "Bullocky jump four miles," he informed us; from which we inferred that the sound of the bells would travel four miles. Cheon's English generally required paraphrasing.

Almost every day some fresh garment collapsed. Fortunately a holland dress was behaving beautifully. "A staunch little beast," the Maluka called it. That, however, had to be washed every alternate day; and, fearing possible contingencies, I was beginning a dress of unbleached calico when the Maluka, busy among the stores, came on a roll of bright pink galatea ordered for the lubras' dresses, and brought it to the house in triumph.

Harsh, crudely pink, galatea! Yet it was received as joyfully as ever a woman received a Paris gown; for although necessity may be the mother of invention, she more often brings thankful hearts into this world.

A hank of coarse, bristling, white braid was also unearthed from among the stores, and within three days the galatea had become a sturdy white-braided blouse and skirt that promised to rival the "staunch little beast" in staunchheartedness.

By the time it was finished, Johnny and the Dandy had all the flooring boards down in the dining room, and before the last nail was in Cheon and the Maluka had carried in every available stick of furniture, and spread it about the room to the greatest possible advantage. The walls were still unfinished, and doors and window frames gaped; but what did it matter? The missus had a dining room, and as she presided at her supper table in vivid pink and the pride of possession, Cheon looked as though he would have liked to shake hands with everyone at once, but particularly with Johnny.

"Looks A1," the Maluka said, alluding to the stiff, aggressive frock, and took me "bush" with him, wearing the blouse and a holland riding skirt that had also proved itself a true, staunch friend.

Dan, the Quiet Stockman, and the Dandy had already gone "bush" in different directions; for with the coming of the year's stores, horse-breaking, house-building, trunks, and waggons had all stepped into their proper places—a very secondary one—and cattle had come to the front, and would stay there, as far as the men were concerned, until next Wet.

Where runs are huge, and fenceless, and freely watered, the year's mustering and branding is no simple task. Our cattle were scattered through a couple of thousand square miles of scrub and open-timbered country, and therefore each section of the run had to be gone over again and again; each mob, when mustered, travelled to the nearest yard and branded.

Every available day of the Dry was needed for the work; but there is one thing in the Never-Never that refuses to take a secondary place—the mailman; and at the end of a week we all found, once again, that we had business at the homestead; for six weeks had slipped away since our last mail day, and the Fizzer was due once more.

Chapter 12

THE FIZZER

THE Fizzer was due at sundown, and for the Fizzer to be due meant that the Fizzer would arrive; and by six o'clock we had all got cricks in our necks, with trying to go about as usual, and keep an expectant eye on the north track.

The Fizzer is unlike every type of man excepting a bush mailman. Hard, sinewy, dauntless, and enduring, he travels day after day and month after month, practically alone—"on me Pat Malone", he calls it—with or without a black boy, according to circumstances, and five trips out of his yearly eight throwing dice with death along the dry stages, and yet at all times as merry as a grig, and as chirrupy as a young grasshopper.

With a light-hearted, "So long, chaps", he sets out from Katherine on his thousand-mile ride, and with a cheery "What ho, chaps! Here we are again!" rides in again within five weeks with that journey behind him.

A thousand miles on horseback, "on me Pat Malone", into the Australian interior and out again, travelling twice over three long dry stages and several shorter ones, and keeping strictly within the Government time limit, would be a life-experience to the men who set that limit—if it wasn't a death-experience. "Like to see one of 'em doing it 'emselves," says the Fizzer. Yet never a day late, and rarely an hour, he does it eight times a year, with a "So long, chaps", and a "Here we are again".

The Fizzer was due at sundown, and at sundown a puff of dust rose on the track, and as a cry of "Mail oh!" went up all round the homestead, the Fizzer rode out of the dust.

"Hullo! What ho, boys," he shouted in welcome, and the next moment we were in the midst of his clattering team of pack-horses.

82

For five minutes everything was in confusion; horse bells and hobbles jingling and clanging, harness rattling, as horses shook themselves free, and packbags, swags, and saddles came to the ground with loud, creaking flops. Everyone was lending a hand, and the Fizzer, moving in and out among the horses, shouted a medley of news and welcome.

"News? Stacks of it," he shouted. The Fizzer always shouted. "The gay time we had at the Katherine! Here, steady with that pack-bag. It's breakables! Sore back here, fetch along the balsam. What ho, Cheon!" as Cheon appeared and greeted him as an old friend. "Heard you were here. You're the boy for my money. You *bally* ass! Keep 'em back from the water there." This last was for the black boy. It took discrimination to fit the Fizzer's remarks on to the right person. Then, as a pack-bag dropped at the Maluka's feet, he added: "That's the station lot, boss. Full bags, missus! Two on 'em. You'll be doing the disappearing trick in half a mo'."

In "half a mo' " the seals were broken, and the mail matter shaken out on the ground. A cascade of papers, magazines, and books, with a fat, firm little packet of letters among them; forty letters in all—thirty of them falling to my lot—thirty fat, bursting envelopes, and in another "half mo' " we had all slipped away in different directions—each with our precious mail matter—doing the "disappearing trick" even to the Fizzer's satisfaction.

The Fizzer smiled amiably after the retreating figures, and then went to be entertained by Cheon. He expected nothing else. He provided feasts all along his route, and was prepared to stand aside while the bush-folk feasted. Perhaps in the silence that fell over the bush homes, after his mail bags were opened, his own heart slipped away to dear ones, who were waiting somewhere for news of our Fizzer.

Eight mails *only* in a year is not all disadvantage. Townsfolk who have eight hundred tiny doses of mail matter doled out to them, like men on sick diet, can form little pleasure of that feast of "full bags and two on 'em", for like thirsty camels we drank it all in—every drop of it—in long, deep, satisfying draughts. It may have been a disadvantage, perhaps, to have been so thirsty; but then only the thirsty soul knows the sweetness of slaking that thirst.

After a full hour's silence the last written sheet was laid down, and I found the Maluka watching and smiling.

"Enjoyed your trip south, little 'un?" he said, and I came back to the bush with a start, to find the supper dead cold. But then supper came every night and the Fizzer only once in forty-two.

At the first sound of voices, Cheon bustled in, "New-fellow tea, I think," he said, and bustled out again with the teapot (Cheon had had many years' experience of bush mail-days), and in a few minutes the unpalatable supper was taken away and cold roast beef and tomatoes stood in its place.

After supper, as we went for our evening stroll, we stayed for a little while where the men were lounging, and after a general interchange of news the Fizzer's turn came.

News! He had said he had stacks of it, and he now bubbled over with it. The horse teams were "just behind", and the Macs almost at the front gate. The Sanguine Scot? Of course, he was all right; always was, but reckoned bullock-punching wasn't all it was cracked up to be; thought his troubles were over when he got out of the sandy country, but hadn't reckoned on the black soil flats. "Wouldn't be surprised if he took to punching something else besides bullocks before he's through with it," the Fizzer shouted, roaring with delight at the recollection of the Sanguine Scot in a tight place. On and on he went with his news, and for two hours afterwards, as we sat chewing the cud of our mail-matter, we could hear him laughing and shouting and "chuckling".

At daybreak he was at it again, shouting among his horses, as he culled his team of "done-ups", and soon after breakfast was at the head of the south track with all aboard.

"So long, chaps!" he called. "See you again half-past eleven, four weeks"; and by "half-past eleven four weeks" he would have carried his precious freight of letters to the yearning, waiting men and women hidden away in the heart of Australia, and be out again, laden with Inside letters for the outside world.

At all seasons of the year he calls the first two hundred miles of this trip a "kid's game". "Water somewhere nearly every day, and a decent camp most nights." And although he

84

speaks of the next hundred and fifty as being a "bit off during the Dry", he faces its seventy-five mile dry stage, sitting loosely in the saddle, with the same cheery "So long, chaps".

Five miles to "get a pace up"—a drink, and then that seventy miles of dry, with any "temperature they can spare from other parts", and not one drop of water in all its length for the horses. Straight on top of that, with the same horses and the same temperature, a run of twenty miles, mails dropped at Newcastle Waters, and another run of fifty into Powell's Creek, dry or otherwise, according to circumstances.

"Takes a bit of fizzing to get into the Powell before the fourth sundown," the Fizzer says—for, forgetting that there can be no change of horses, and leaving no time for a "spell" after the "seventy-five mile dry"—the time limit for that one hundred and fifty miles, in a country where four miles an hour is good travelling on good roads, has been fixed at three and a half days. "Four, they call it," says the Fizzer, "forgetting I can't leave the water till midday. Takes a bit of fizzing all right"; and yet at Powell's Creek no one has yet discovered whether the Fizzer comes at sundown, or the sun goes down when the Fizzer comes.

"A bit off," he calls that stage, with a schoolboy shrug of his shoulders; but at Renner's Springs, twenty miles further on, the shoulders set square, and the man comes to the surface. The dice-throwing begins there, and the stakes are high—a man's life against a man's judgment.

Some people speak of the Fizzer's luck, and say he'll pull through, if anyone can. It is luck, perhaps—but not in the sense they mean—to have the keen judgment to know to an ounce what a horse has left in him, judgment to know when to stop and when to go on—for that is left to the Fizzer's discretion; and with that judgment the dauntless courage to go on with, and win through, every task attempted.

The Fizzer changes horses at Renner's Springs for the "Downs trip"; and as his keen eyes run over the mob, his voice raps out their verdict like an auctioneer's hammer. "He's fit. So is he. Cut that one out. That colt's A1. The chestnut's done. So is the brown. I'll risk that mare. That black's too fat." No hesitation; horse after horse rejected or approved, until the team is complete; and then driving them before him he faces the Open Downs — the Open Downs, where the last mailman perished; and only the men who know the Downs in the Dry know what he faces.

For five trips out of the eight, one hundred and thirty miles of sun-baked, crab-holed, practically trackless plains, no sign of human habitation anywhere, cracks that would swallow a man — "hardly enough wood to boil a quart pot", the Fizzer says, and a sun-temperature hovering about 160° (there is no shade-temperature on the Downs); shadeless, trackless, sun-baked, crab-holed plains, and the Fizzer's team a moving speck in the centre of an immensity that, never diminishing and never changing, moves onward with the team; an immensity of quivering heat and glare, with that one tiny living speck in its centre, and in all that hundred and thirty miles one drink for the horses at the end of the first eighty. That is the Open Downs.

"Fizz!" shouts the Fizzer. "That's where the real fizzing gets done, and nobody that hasn't tried it knows what it's like."

He travels its first twenty miles late in the afternoon, then, unpacking his team, "let's 'em go for a roll and a pick, while he boils a quart pot" (the Fizzer carries a canteen for himself); "spells" a bare two hours, packs up again and travels all night, keeping to the vague track with a bushman's instinct, "doing" another twenty miles before daylight; unpacks for another spell, pities the poor brutes "nosing round too parched to feed", may "doze a bit with one ear cocked", and then packing up again, "punches 'em along all day", with or without a spell. Time is precious now. There is a limit to the number of hours a horse can go without water, and the thirst of the team fixes the time limit on the Downs. "Punches 'em along all day, and into water close up sundown", at the deserted Eva Downs station.

"Give 'em a drink at the well there," the Fizzer says as unconcernedly as though he turned on a tap. But the well is old and out of repair, ninety feet deep, with a rickety old wooden windlass; fencing wire for a rope; a bucket that the Fizzer has "seen fit to plug with rag on account of it leaking a bit", and a trough, stuffed with mud at one end by the resourceful Fizzer. Truly the Government is careful for the safety of its servants. Added to all this, there are eight or ten horses so eager for a drink that the poor brutes have to be tied up and watered one at a time; and so parched with thirst that it takes three hours' drawing before they are satisfied—three hours out of twenty-seven spent in the saddle, and half that time "punching" jaded beasts along; and yet they speak of the "Fizzer's luck".

"Real fine old water, too," the Fizzer shouts in delight, as he tells his tale. "Kept in the cellar for our special use. Don't indulge in it much myself. Might spoil my palate for newer stuff, so I carry enough for the whole trip from Renner's."

If the Downs have left deep lines on the Fizzer's face, they have left none in his heart. Yet at that well the dice-throwing goes on just the same.

Maybe the Fizzer feels "a bit knocked out with the sun", and the water for his perishing horses ninety feet below the surface; or "things go wrong" with the old windlass, and everything depends on the Fizzer's ingenuity. The odds are very uneven when this happens—a man's ingenuity against a man's life, and death playing with loaded dice. And every letter the Fizzer carries past that well costs the public just twopence.

A drink at the well, an all-night's spell, another drink, and then away at midday, to face the tightest pinch of all—the pinch where death won with the other mailman. Fifty miles of rough, hard, blistering, scorching "going", with worn and jaded horses.

The old programme all over again. Twenty miles more, another spell for the horses (the Fizzer never seems to need a spell for himself), and then the last lap of thirty, the run into Anthony's Lagoon, "punching the poor beggars along somehow". "Keep 'em going all night", the Fizzer says, "and if you should happen to be at Anthony's on the day I'm due there you can set your watch for eleven in the morning when you see me coming along". I have heard somewhere of the Pride of Harness.

Sixteen days is the time limit for those five hundred miles, and yet the Fizzer is expected because the Fizzer is due; and to a man who loves his harness no praise could be sweeter than that. Perhaps one of the brightest thoughts for the Fizzer as he "punches" along those desolate Downs is the knowledge that a little before eleven o'clock in the morning Anthony's will come out and, standing with shaded eyes, will look through the quivering heat, away into the Downs, for that tiny moving speck. When the Fizzer is late there, death will have won at the dice-throwing.

I suppose he got a salary. No one ever troubled to ask. He was expected, and he came, and in our selfishness we did not concern ourselves beyond that.

It is men like the Fizzer who, "keeping the roads open", lay the foundation stones of great cities; and yet when cities creep into the Never-Never along the Fizzer's mail route, in all probability they will be called after Members of Parliament and the Prime Ministers of that day, grandsons, perhaps, of the men who forgot to keep the old well in repair, while our Fizzer and the mailman who perished will be forgotten; for townsfolk are apt to forget the beginning of things.

Three days' spell at Anthony's, to wait for the Queensland mailman from the "other side" (another Fizzer, no doubt, for the bush mail-service soon culls out the unfitted), an exchange of mail bags, and then the Downs must be faced again with the same team of horses. Even the Fizzer owns that "tackling the Downs for the return trip's a bit sickening; haven't had time to forget what it feels like, you know," he explains.

Inside to Anthony's, three days' spell, over the Downs again, stopping for another drink at that well, along the stage "that's a bit off", and back to the "kid's game", dropping mail bags in twos and threes as he goes in, and collecting others as he comes out, to say nothing of the weary packing and unpacking of his team. That is what the Fizzer had to do by half-past eleven four weeks.

But every man's life runs parallel with other lives, and while the Fizzer was "punching along" his dry stages events were moving rapidly with us; while perhaps, away in the hearts of towns, men and women were "winning through the dry stages" of their lives there.

Chapter 13

PATIENCE REWARDED AT LAST

SOON after the Fizzer left us the horse-teams came in, and went on, top-heavy with stores for Inside; but the "Macs" were now thinking of the dry stages ahead, and were travelling at the exasperating rate of about four miles a day, as they "nursed the bullocks" through the good grass country.

Dan had lost interest in waggons, and was anxious to get among the cattle again; but with the trunks so near, the house growing rapidly, and days of sewing waiting, I refused point-blank to leave the homestead just then.

Dan tried to taunt me into action, and reviewed the "kennel" with critical eyes. "Never saw a dog making its own chain before," he said to the Maluka as I sat among billows of calico and mosquito netting. But the homemaking instinct is strong in a woman, and the musterers went out west without the missus. The Dandy being back at the Bitter Springs superintending the carting of new posts for the stockyard there, the missus was left in the care of Johnny and Cheon.

"Now we shan't be long," said Johnny, and Cheon believing him, expressed great admiration for Johnny, and superintended the scrubbing of the walls, while I sat and sewed, yard after yard of over-sewing, as never woman sewed before.

The walls were erected on what is known as the drop-slab panel system—upright panels formed of three-foot slabs cut from the outside slice of tree trunks, and dropped horizontally, one above the other, between grooved posts—a simple arrangement, quickly run up and artistic in appearance—outside, a horizontally fluted surface, formed by the natural curves of the timber, and inside, flat, smooth walls. As in every third panel there was a door or a window, and as the horizontal slabs stopped within two feet of the ceiling, the building was exceedingly airy, and open on all sides.

Cheon, convinced that the system was all Johnny's, was delighted with his ingenuity. But as he insisted upon the walls being scrubbed as soon as they were up, and before the doors and windows were in, Johnny had one or two good duckings, and narrowly escaped many more; for lubras' methods of scrubbing are as full of surprises as all their methods.

First soap is rubbed on the dry boards, then vigorously scrubbed into a lather with wet brushes, and after that the lather is sluiced off with artificial waterspouts whizzed up the walls from full buckets. It was while the sluicing was in progress that Johnny had to be careful; for many buckets missed their mark, and the waterspouts shot out through the doorways and window frames.

Wearing a mackintosh, I did what I could to prevent surprises, but without much success. Johnny fortunately took it all as a matter of course. "It's all in the good cause," he chuckled, shaking himself like a water-spaniel after a particularly bad misadventure; and described the "performance" with great zest to the Maluka when he returned. The sight of the clean walls filled the Maluka also with zeal for the cause; and in the weeks that followed walls sprouted with corner shelves and brackets—three wooden kerosene cases became a handy series of pigeon-holes for magazines and papers. One panel in the dining room was completely filled with book shelves, one above the other, for our coming books. Great sheets of bark, stripped by the blacks from the ti-tree forest, were packed a foot deep above the rafters to break the heat reflected from the iron roof, while beneath it the calico ceiling was tacked up. And all the time Johnny hammered and whistled and planed, finishing the bathroom and "getting on" with the office.

The Quiet Stockman, coming in, was pressed into the service, and grew quite enthusiastic, suggesting substitutes for necessities, until I suggested cutting off the tails of every horse on the run, to get enough horsehair for a mattress.

"Believe the boss'ud do it himself if she asked him," he said in the Quarters; and in his consternation suggested bangtailing the cattle during the musters.

"Just the thing," Dan decided; and we soon saw, with his

assistance, a vision of our future mattress walking about the run on the ends of cows' tails.

"Look's like it's going to be a dead-heat," Johnny said, still hammering, when the Dandy brought in word that the "Macs" were within twelve miles of the homestead. And when I announced next day that the dining net was finished and ready for hanging, he also became wildly enthusiastic.

"Told you from the beginning we shouldn't be long," he said, flourishing a hammer and brimming over with suggestions for the hanging of the net. "Rope'll never hold it," he declared; "fencing wire's the thing"; so fencing wire was used, and after a hard morning's work pulling and straining the wire and securing it to uprights, the net was in its place, the calico roof smooth and flat against the ceiling, and its curtains hanging to the floor, with strong, straight saplings run through the folded hem to weigh it down. Cheon was brimming over with admiration for it.

"My word, boss! Missus plenty savey," he said. (Cheon invariably discussed the missus in her presence.) "Chinaman woman no more savey likee that," and, bustling away, dinner was soon served inside the net.

Myriads of flies, balked in their desire, settled down on the outside, and while we enjoyed our dinner in peace and comfort, Cheon hovered about like a huge bloated buzz fly himself, chuckling around the outside among the swarms of balked flies, or coming inside to see if "any fly sit down inside".

"My word, boss! Hear him sing-out sing-out. Missus plenty savey," he reiterated, and then calling a Chinese friend from the kitchen, stood over him, until he also declared that "missus *blenty* savey", with good emphasis on the *blenty*.

The net was up by midday, and at ten o'clock at night the slow, dull clang of a bullock-bell crept out of the forest. Cheon was the first to hear it. "Bullocky come on," he called, waddling to the house and waking us from our first sleep; and as the deep-throated bell boomed out again the Maluka said drowsily: "The homestead's only won by a head. Mac's at the Warlochs."

At "fowl-sing-out" we were up, and found Bertie's Nellie

91

behind the black boys' humpy shyly peeping round a corner. With childlike impetuosity she had scampered along the four miles from the Warlochs, only to be overcome with unaccountable shyness.

" 'Allo, missus!" was all she could find to say, and the remainder of the interview she filled in with wriggling and giggles.

Immediately after breakfast Mac splashed through the creek at a hand-gallop, and, dashing up to the house, flung himself from his horse, the same impetuous, warm-hearted "Brither Scot".

"Patience rewarded at last," he called in welcome; and when invited to "come ben the hoose to the dining room", was, as usual, full of congratulations. "My! We are some!" he said, examining every detail. But as he also said that "the Dandy could get the trunks right off if we liked to send him across with the dray", we naturally "liked", and Johnny and the Dandy, harnessing up, went with him, and before long the verandah and rooms were piled with trunks.

Fortunately Dan was "bush" again among the cattle, or his heart would have broken at this new array of links for the chain.

Once the trunks were all in, Mac, the Dandy, and Johnny retired to the Quarters after a few more congratulations, Johnny continuing his flourishes all the way across. Cheon, however, with his charming disregard for conventionality, being interested, settled himself on one of the trunks to watch the opening of the others.

To have ordered him away would have clouded his beaming happiness; so he remained, and told us exactly what he thought of our possessions, adding much to the pleasure of the opening of the trunks. If any woman would experience real pleasure, let her pack all her belongings into trunks—all but a couple of changes of everything—and go away out-bush, leaving them to follow "after the Wet" per bullock waggon, and when the reunion takes place the pleasure will be forthcoming. If she can find a Cheon to be present at the reunion, so much the better.

Some of our belongings Cheon thoroughly approved of; others were passed over as unworthy of notice, and others were held up to chuckling ridicule. A silver teapot was pounced upon with a cry of delight (tinware being considered far beneath the dignity of a missus, and seeing Sam had broken the china pot soon after its arrival, tinware had graced our board for some time).

And a brass lamp was looked upon as a monument of solid wealth. "Him gold," he decided, insisting it was in the face of all denials. "Him gold. Me savey gold all right. Me live longa California long time," he said, bringing forward a most convincing argument, and, dismissing the subject with one of his Podsnapian waves, he decided that a silver-coloured composition flower-bowl in the form of a swan was solid silver: "Him sing out all a same silver," he said, making it ring with a flick of his finger and thumb when I differed from him, and knowing Cheon by now, we left it at that for the time being.

After wandering through several trunks and gloating over blouses, and skirts, and house linen, and old friends, the books were opened up, and before the Maluka became lost to the world, Cheon favoured them with a passing glance. "Big mob book," he said indifferently, and turned his attention to the last trunk of all.

Near the top was a silver filigree candlestick moulded into the form of a convolvulus flower and leaf—a dainty little thing, but it appeared ridiculous to Cheon's commonsense mind.

"Him silly fellow," he scoffed, and appealed to the Maluka for his opinion: "him silly fellow? Eh, boss?" he asked.

The Maluka was half buried in books. "Um," he murmured absently, and that clinched the matter for all time. "Boss bin talk silly fellow!" Cheon said, with an approving nod toward the Maluka, and advised packing the candlestick away again. "Plenty room sit down longa box," he said truthfully, putting it into an enormous empty trunk and closing the lid, leaving the candlestick a piece of lonely splendour hidden under a bushel.

But the full glory of our possessions was now to burst upon Cheon. The trunk we were at was half filled with all sorts of cunning devices for kitchen use, intended for the mistress's pantry of that commodious station home of past ignorant imagination. A mistress's pantry forsooth, in a land where houses are superfluous, and luxuries barred, and at a homestead where the mistress had long ceased to be anything but the little missus — something to rule or educate or take care of, according to the nature of her subordinates.

In a flash I knew all I had once been, and quailing before the awful proof before me, presented Cheon with the whole collection of tin and enamel ware, and packed him off to the kitchen before the Maluka had time to lose interest in the books.

Everything was exactly what Cheon most needed, and he accepted everything with gleeful chuckles — everything except a kerosene Primus burner for boiling a kettle. That he refused to touch. "Him go bang," he explained, as usual explicit and picturesque in his English.

After gathering his treasures together he waddled away to the kitchen, and at afternoon tea we had sponge cakes, light and airy beyond all dreams of airy lightness, no one having yet combined the efforts of Cheon, a flour dredge, and an egg-beater, in his dreams.

All afternoon we worked, and by the evening the dining room was transformed; blue cloths and lace runners on the deal side table and improvised pigeon-holes; nick-nacks here and there on tables and shelves and brackets; pictures on the walls; "kent" faces in photograph frames among the nick-nacks; a folding carpet-seated armchair in a position of honour; cretonne curtains in the doorway between the rooms, and inside the shimmering white net a study in colour effect — blue and white matting on the floor, a crimson cloth on the table, and on the cloth Cheon's "silver" swan sailing in a sea of purple, blue, and heliotrope water-lilies. But best of all were the books — row upon row of old familiar friends; nearly two hundred of them filling the shelved panel as they looked down upon us.

Mac was dazzled with the books. "Hadn't seen so many together since he was a nipper"; and after we had introduced him to our favourites, we played with our new toys like a parcel of children, until supper time.

The waggons spelled for two days at the Warlochs, and we saw much of the "Macs". Then they decided to "push on"; for not only were others farther "In" waiting for their waggons, but daily the dry stages were getting longer and drier, and the shorter his dry stages are, the better a bullock-puncher likes them.

With well-nursed bullocks, and a full complement of them—the "Macs" had twenty-two per waggon for their dry stages—a "thirty-five mile dry" can be "rushed", the waggoners getting under way by three o'clock one afternoon, travelling all night with a spell or two for the bullocks by the way, and "punching" them into water within twenty-four hours.

"Getting over a fifty-mile dry" is, however, a more complicated business, and suggests a treadmill. The waggons are "pulled out" ten miles in the late afternoon, the bullocks unyoked and brought back to the water, spelled most of the next day, given a last drink and travelled back to the waiting waggons by sundown; yoked up and travelled on all that night and part of the next day; once more unyoked at the end of the forty miles of the stage; taken *forward* to the next water, and spelled and nursed up again at this water for a day or two; travelled back again to the waggons, and again yoked up, and finally brought forward in the night with the loads to the water.

Fifty miles dry with loaded waggons being the limit for mortal bullocks, the Government breaks the "seventy-five" with a "drink" sent out in tanks on one of the telegraph station waggons. The stage thus broken into a "thirty-five mile dry", with another of forty on top of that, becomes complicated to giddiness in its backings, and fillings, and goings, and comings, and returnings.

As each waggon carries only five tons, all things considered, from thirty to forty pounds a ton is not a high price to pay for the cartage of stores to Inside.

But although the "getting in" with the stores means much to the bush-folk, "getting out" again is the ultimate goal of the waggoners.

There is time enough for the trip, but only good time, before the roads will be closed by the dry stages growing to impossible lengths for the bullocks to recross; and if the waggoners lose sight of their goal, and loiter by the way, they will find themselves "shut in" Inside, with no prospect of getting out until the next Wet opens the road for them.

The Irish Mac held records for getting over stages; but even he had been "shut in" once, and had sat kicking his heels all through a long Dry, wondering if the showers would come in time to let him out for the next year's loading, or if the Wet would break suddenly, and further shut him in with floods and bogs.

"Might a bullock-puncher have the privilege of shaking hands with a lady?" the Irish Mac asked, extending an honest, horny hand; and the privilege, if it were one, was granted. Finally all was ready, and the waggons, one behind the other, each with its long swaying line of bullocks before it, slid away from the Warloch Ponds and crept into the forest, looking like three huge snails with shells on their backs, Bertie's Nellie watching, wreathed in smiles.

Johnny, generally repairing the homestead now, admired the garden and declared everything would be "A1 in no time".

"Wouldn't know the old place," he said, a day or two later, surveying his own work with pride. Then he left us, and for the first time I was sorry the house was finished.

Just as we were preparing to go out-bush for reports, Dan came in with a mob of cattle for branding and the news that a yard on the northern boundary was gone from the face of the earth.

"Clean gone since last Dry," he reported; "burnt or washed away, or both."

Rather than let his cattle go, he had travelled in nearly thirty miles with the mob in hand, but "reckoned" it wasn't "good enough".

The Maluka also considered it not "good enough", and decided to run up a rough branding wing at once on the holding yard at the Springs; and while Dan saw to the branding of the mob the Maluka looked out his plans.

"Did you get much hair for the mattress?" I asked, all in good faith, when Dan came down from the yards to the house to discuss the plans, and Dan stood still, honestly vexed with himself.

"Well! I'm blest!" he said, "if I didn't forget all about it," and then tried to console me by saying I wouldn't need a mattress till the mustering was over. "Can't carry it round with you, you know," he said, "and it won't be needed anywhere else." Then he surveyed the house with his philosophical eye.

"Wouldn't know the old place," Johnny had said, and Dan "reckoned" it was "all right as houses go"; adding with a chuckle, "Well, she's wrastled with luck for more'n four months to get it, but the question is what's she going to use it for now she's got it?" For over four months we had wrestled with luck for a house, only to find we had very little use for it for the time being, that is, until the next Wet. It couldn't be carried out-bush from camp to camp, and finding us at a loss for an answer, Dan suggested one himself.

"Of course!" he said, as he eyed the furnishings with interest, "it 'ud come in handy to pack the chain away in, while the dog was out enjoying itself!" and we left it at that. It *came* in handy to pack the chain away in while the dog was enjoying itself, for within twenty-four hours we were camped at the Bitter Springs, and two weeks passed before the homestead saw us again.

Chapter 14

"REAL GLAD TO SEE YOU"

THE two weeks gone, the next midday we rode into the homestead thoroughfare, where Cheon and Tiddle'ums welcomed us with enthusiasm, but Cheon's enthusiasm turned to indignation when he found we were only in for a day or two.

"What's er matter?" he ejaculated. "Missus no more stockrider"; but a letter waiting for us at the homestead made "bush" more than ever imperative; a letter from the foreman of the telegraphic repairing line party, asking for a mob of killers, and fixing a date for its delivery to one "Happy Dick".

"Spoke just in the nick of time," Dan said; but as we discussed plans Cheon hinted darkly that the Maluka was not a fit and proper person to be entrusted with the care of a woman, and suggested that he should undertake to treat the missus as she should be treated, while the Maluka attended to the cattle.

But Fate interfering to keep the missus in at the homestead with an influenza sore throat, Dan went out alone to find the Quiet Stockman and the "killers" for Happy Dick, and before a week was out the Maluka and Cheon had won each other's undying regard because of their treatment of the missus.

Then the musterers coming in with Happy Dick's bullocks and a great mob of mixed cattle for the yards, and Happy Dick due to arrive by midday, Cheon's hands were full with other matters.

There was a roly-poly pudding to make for Dan, baked custard for the Dandy, jam tarts for Happy Dick, cake and biscuits for all comers, in addition to a dinner and supper waiting to be cooked for fifteen black boys, several lubras, and half-a-dozen hungry white folk. Cheon had his own peculiar form of welcome for his many favourites, regaling each one of them with delicacies of their particular liking, each and every time they came in.

Happy Dick, also, had his own peculiar form of welcome. "Good day! Real glad to see you!" was *his* usual greeting. Sure of his own welcome wherever he went, he never waited to hear it, but hastened to welcome all men into his fellowship. "Real glad to see you," he would say, with a ready smile of comradeship; and it always seemed as though he had added: "I hope you'll make yourself at home while with me." In some mysterious way, Happy Dick was at all times the host, giving liberally of the best he had to his fellow men.

He was one of the pillars of the Line Party. "Born in it, I think," he would say. "Don't quite remember," adding with his ever-varying smile, "Remember when it was born, anyway."

When the "Overland Telegraph" was built across the Australian continent from sea to sea, a clear broad avenue, two chains wide, was cut for it through bush and scrub and dense forests, along the backbone of Australia, and in this avenue the Line Party was "born" and bred—a party of axemen and mechanics under the orders of a foreman, whose duty it is to keep the "Territory section" of the line in repair, and this avenue free from the scrub and timber that spring up unceasingly in its length.

In unbroken continuity this great avenue runs for hundreds upon hundreds of miles, carpeted with feathery grasses and shooting scrubs, and walled in on either side with dense, towering forest or lighter and more scattered timber. On and on it stretches in utter loneliness, zig-zagging from horizon to horizons beyond, and guarding those two sensitive wires at its centre, as they run along their single line of slender galvanised posts, from the great bush that never ceases in its efforts to close in on them and engulf them. A great broad highway, waiting in its loneliness for the generations to come, with somewhere in its length the Line Party camp, and here and there, within its thousand miles, a chance traveller or two; here and there a horseman with pack-horse ambling and grazing along behind him; here and there a trudging speck with a swag across its shoulders, and between them one, two, or three hundred miles of solitude;

here and there a horseman riding, and here and there a footman trudging on, each unconscious of the others.

From day to day they travel on, often losing the count of the days, with those lines always above them, and those beckoning posts ever running on before them; and as they travel, now and then they touch a post for company—shaking hands with Outside, daily realising the company and comfort those posts and wires can be. Here at least is something in touch with the world, something vibrating with the lives and actions of men, and an ever-present friend in dire necessity. With those wires above him, any day a traveller can cry for help in the Territory, if he call while he yet has strength to climb one of those friendly posts and cut that quivering wire—for help that will come speedily, for the cutting of the telegraph wire is as the ringing of an alarm bell throughout the Territory. In all haste the break is located, and food, water, and every human help that suggests itself sent out from the nearest telegraph station. There is no official delay—there rarely is in the Territory—for by some marvellous good fortune, there everything belongs to the Department in which it finds itself.

Just as Happy Dick is one of the pillars of the Line Party, so the Line Party is one of the pillars of the line itself. Up and down this great avenue, year in, year out, it creeps along, cutting scrub and repairing as it goes, and moving cumbrous main camps from time to time, with its waggon loads of stores, tents, furnishings, flocks of milking goats, its fowls, its gramophone, and Chinese cook. Month after month it creeps on, until reaching the end of the section, it turns round to creep out again.

Year in, year out, it had crept in and out, and for twenty years Happy Dick had seen to its peace and comfort. Nothing ever ruffled him. "All in the game" was his nearest approach to a complaint, as he pegged away at his work, in between whiles going to the nearest station for killers, carting water in tanks out to "dry stage camps", and doing any other work that found itself undone. Dick's position was as elastic as his smile.

He considered himself an authority on three things only:

the Line Party, dog fights, and cribbage. All else, including his dog Peter and his cheque book, he left to the discretion of his fellow-men.

Peter — a speckled, drab-coloured, prick-eared creature, a few sizes larger than a fox terrier — could be kept in order with a little discretion, and by keeping hands off Happy Dick; but all the discretion in the Territory, and a unanimous keeping-off of hands, failed to keep order in the cheque book.

The personal payment of salaries to men scattered through hundreds of miles of bush country being impracticable, the department pays all salaries due to its servants into their bank accounts at Darwin, and therefore when Happy Dick found himself the backbone of the Line Party, he also found himself the possessor of a cheque book. At first he was inclined to look upon it as a poor substitute for hard cash; but after the foreman had explained its mysteries, and taught him to sign his name in magic tracery, he became more reconciled to it, and drew cheques blithely, until one for five pounds was returned to a creditor; no funds — and in due course returned to Happy Dick.

"No good?" he said to the creditor, looking critically at the piece of paper in his hands. "Must have been writ wrong. Well, you've only yourself to blame, seeing you wrote it," then added magnanimously, mistaking the creditor's scorn: "Never mind, write yourself out another. I don't mind signing 'em."

The foreman and the creditor spent several hours trying to explain banking principles, but Dick "couldn't see it". "There's stacks of 'em left!" he persisted, showing his book of fluttering bank cheques. Finally, in despair, the foreman took the cheque book into custody, and Dick found himself poor once more.

But it was only for a little while. In an evil hour he discovered that a cheque from another man's book answered all purposes if it bore that magic tracery, and Happy Dick was never solvent again. Gaily he signed cheques, and the foreman did all he could to keep pace with him on the cheque-book block; but as no one, excepting the accountant in the Darwin bank, knew the state of his account from day to day, it was like taking a ticket in a lottery to accept a cheque from Happy Dick.

"Real glad to see you," Happy Dick said in hearty greeting to us all as he dismounted, and we waited to be entertained. Happy Dick had his favourite places and people, and the Elsey community stood high in his favour. "Can't beat the Elsey for a good dog fight and a good game of cribbage," he said, every time he came in or left us; and that from Happy Dick was high praise. At times he added: "Nor for a square meal neither", thereby inciting Cheon to further triumphs for his approval.

As usual, Happy Dick "played" the Quarters cribbage and related a good dog fight—"Peter's latest"— and, as usual before he left us, his pockets were bulging with tobacco—the highest stakes used in the Quarters—and Peter and one Brown, the Maluka's own special fox terrier, had furnished him with materials for a still newer dog-fight recital. As usual, he rode off with his killers, assuring us that he would "be along again soon", and as usual, he had hunted through the store, and taken anything he "really needed", paying, of course, by cheque; but when he came to sign that cheque, after the Maluka had written it, he entered the dining room for the first time since its completion.

With calm scrutiny he took in every detail, including the serviettes as they lay folded in their rings on the waiting dinner table, and before he left the homestead he expressed his approval in the Quarters:

"Got everything up to the knocker, haven't they?" he said. "Often heard toffs decorated their tables with rags in hobble rings, but never believed it before."

Happy Dick gone, Cheon turned his attention to the health of the missus; but Dan, persuading the Maluka that "all she needed was a breath of fresh air", we went bush for a tour of inspection.

Chapter 15

"EVERY DAY MUST SEEM THE SAME"

THE travellers had also carried out an extra mail for us, and, opening it, we found the usual questions of the South folk.

"Whatever do you do with your time?" they all asked. "The monotony would kill me," some declared. "Every day must seem the same," said others; everyone agreeing that life out-bush was stagnation, and all marvelling that we did not die of ennui.

"Whatever do you do with your time?" The day the travellers left was devoted to housekeeping duties — "spring cleaning", the Maluka called it, while Dan drew vivid word-pictures of dogs cleaning their own chains. The day after that was filled in with preparations for a walkabout, and the next again found us camped at Bitter Springs. Monotony! when of the thirty days that followed these three every day was alike only in being different from any other, excepting in their almost unvarying menu: beef and damper and tea for a first course, and tea and damper and jam for a second. They also resembled each other, and all other days out-bush, in the necessity of dressing in a camp mosquito net. "Stagnation!" they called it, when no day was long enough for its work, and almost every night found us camped a day's journey from our breakfast camp.

It was August, well on in the Dry, and on a cattle station in the Never-Never "things hum" in August. All the surface waters are drying up by then, and the outside cattle — those scattered away beyond the borders — are obliged to come in to the permanent waters, and must be gathered in and branded before the showers scatter them again.

We were all together at the Springs: Dan, the Dandy, the Quiet Stockman, ourselves, every horse-"boy" that could be mustered, a numerous staff of camp "boys" for the Dandy's work, and an almost complete complement of dogs.

Everyone of the company had his special work to attend to; but everyone's work was concerned with cattle, and cattle only. The musterers were to work every area of country again and again, and the Dandy's work began in the building of the much-needed yard to the north-west.

We breakfasted at the Springs all together, had dinner miles apart, and all met again at the Stirling for supper. Dan and ourselves dined also at the Stirling on damper and "push" and vile-smelling blue-black tea. The damper had been carried in company with some beef and tea, in Dan's saddle-pouch; the tea was made with the thick, muddy, almost putrid water of the fast-drying waterhole, and the "push" was provided by force of circumstances, the pack teams being miles away with the plates, knives, and forks.

Around the Stirling are acres of red-coloured queer-shaped, uncanny white-ant hills, and camped among these we sat, each served with a slice of damper that carried a smaller piece of beef upon it, providing the "push" by cutting off small pieces of the beef with a penknife, and "pushing" them along the damper to the edge of the slice, to be bitten off from there in hearty mouthfuls.

No butter, of course. In Darwin, eight months before, we had tasted our last butter on shipboard, for tinned butter, out-bush, in the tropics, is as palatable as castor oil. The tea had been made in the Maluka's quart-pot, our cups having been carried dangling from our saddles, in the approved manner of the bush-folk.

We breakfasted at the Springs, surrounded by the soft forest beauty; ate our dinner in the midst of grotesque ant-hill scenery, and spent the afternoon looking for a lost waterhole.

The Dandy was to build his yard at this hole when it was found, but the difficulty was to find it. The Sanguine Scot had "dropped on it once", by chance, but lost his bearing later on. All we knew was that it was there, to be found somewhere in that corner of the run — a deep, permanent hole, "back in the scrub somewhere", according to the directions of the Sanguine Scot.

Of course, the black boys could have found it; but it is the habit of black boys to be quite ignorant of the whereabouts of all lost or unknown waters, for when a blackfellow is "wanted" he is looked for at water, and in his wisdom he keeps any "water" he can a secret from the white folk, an unknown "water" making a safe hiding-place when it suits a blackfellow to obliterate himself for a while.

Eventually we found our hole, after long wanderings and futile excursions up gullies and by-ways, and, riding into the Stirling camp at sundown, found the Dandy there, busy at the fire, with a dozen or so of large silver fish spread out on green leaves beside him.

"Good enough!" Dan cried at the first sight of them, and the Dandy explained that the boys had caught "shoals of 'em" at his dinner camp at the Fish Hole, assuring us that the water there was "stiff with 'em". But the Dandy had been busy elsewhere. "Good enough!" Dan had said at the sight of the fish, and, pointing to a billy full of clear sweet water that was just thinking of boiling, the Maluka echoed the sentiment if not the words.

"Dug a soakage along the creek a bit and got it," the Dandy explained; and as we blessed him for his thoughtfulness, he lifted up a clean cloth and displayed a pile of crisp Johnny cakes. "Real slap up ones," he assured us, breaking open one of the crisp, spongy rolls. It was always a treat to be in camp with the Dandy; everything about the man was so crisp and clean and wholesome.

As we settled down to supper, the Fizzer came shouting through the ant hills, and, soon after, the Quiet Stockman rode into camp. Our Fizzer was always the Fizzer. "Hullo! What ho! Now for it!" he shouted in welcome, as he came shouting on to the camp fire; and then he surveyed our supper: "Struck it lucky, as usual," he declared, helping himself to a couple of fish from the fire and breaking open one of the crisp Johnny cakes. "Can't beat grilled fish and hot rolls by much, to say nothin' of tea." The Fizzer was one of those happy, natural people who always find the supply exactly suited to the demand.

But if our Fizzer was just our Fizzer, the Quiet Stockman was changing every day. He was still the Quiet Stockman, and always would be, speaking only when he had something to say, but he was learning that he had much to say that was worth saying, or, rather, much that others found worth listening to; and that knowledge was squaring his shoulders and bringing a new ring into his voice.

Around the camp fires we touch on any subject that suggests itself, but at the Stirling that night, four of us being Scottish, we found Scotland and Scotsmen an inexhaustible topic, and before we turned in were all of Jack's opinion that "you can't beat the Scots". Even the Dandy and the Fizzer were converted; and Jack having realised that there are such things as Scotswomen — Scots-hearted women — a new bond was established between us.

No one had much sleep that night, and before dawn there was no doubt left in our mind about the outside cattle coming in. It seemed as though every beast on the run must have come in to the Stirling that night for a drink. Every waterhole out-bush is as the axis of a great circle, cattle pads narrowing into it like the spokes of a wheel, from every point of the compass. Along these pads around the Stirling mob after mob of cattle came in in single file, treading carelessly, until each old bull leader, scenting the camp, gave its low, deep, drawn-out warning call that told of danger at hand. After that rang out, only an occasional snapping twig betrayed the presence of the cattle as they crept cautiously in for the drink that must be procured at all hazards. But after the drink the only point to be considered was safety, and in a crashing stampede they rushed out into the timber. Till long after midnight they were at it, and as Brown and I were convinced that every mob was coming straight over our net, we spent an uneasy night. To make matters worse, just as the camp was settling down to a deep sleep after the cattle had finally subsided, Dan's camp reveille rang out.

It was barely three o'clock, and the Fizzer raised an indignant protest of: "Moonrise, you bally ass".

"Not it," Dan persisted, unfortunately bent on argument; "not at this quarter of the moon, and besides it was moonlight all evening", and that being a strong peg to hang his argument on, investigating heads appeared from various nets. "Seem to think I don't know dawn when I see it," Dan added, full of scorn for the camp's want of observation; but before we had time to wither before his scorn, Jack turned the tables for us with his usual quiet finality: "That's the west you're looking at," he said. "The moon's just set"; and the curtain of Dan's net dropped instantly.

"Told you he was a bally ass," the Fizzer shouted in his delight, and promising Dan something later on, he lay down to rest.

Dan, however, was hopelessly roused. "Never did that before," gurgled out of his net, just as we were dropping off once more; but a withering request from the Dandy to "gather experience somewhere else", silenced him till dawn, when he had the wisdom to rise without further reveille.

After breakfast we all separated again; the Dandy to his yard-building at the Yellow Hole, and the rest of us, with the cattle boys, in various directions, to see where the cattle were, each party with its team of horses, and carrying in its pack a bluey, an oilskin, a mosquito net, a plate, knife and fork apiece, as well as a "change of duds" and a bit of tucker for all; the bite of tucker to be replenished with a killer when necessary, the change of duds to be washed by the boys also when necessary, and the plate to serve for all courses, the fastidious turning it over for the damper and jam course.

The Maluka spent one day with Dan beyond the "front gate"—Brown and missus wagging along behind as a matter of course—another day passed boundary riding, inspecting waterholes, and doubling back to the Dandy's camp to see his plans; then, picking up the Quiet Stockman, we struck out across country, riding four abreast through the open forest lands, and were camped at sundown in the thick of the cattle, miles from the Dandy's camp, and thirty miles due north from the homestead. "Whatever do you do with your time?" asked the South folk.

Dan was in high spirits: cattle were coming in everywhere, and another beautiful permanent "water" had been discovered in unsuspected ambush. To know all the waters of a run is important, for they take the part of fences, keeping the cattle in certain localities; and as cattle must stay within a day's journey or so of water, an unknown water is apt to upset a man's calculations.

As the honour of finding the hole was all Dan's, it was named D.S. in his honour, and we had waited beside it while he cut his initials deep into the trunk of a tree, deploring the rustiness of his education as he carved. The upright stroke of the D was simplicity itself, but after that complications arose.

"It's always got me dodged which way to turn the darned thing," Dan said, scratching faint lines both ways, and standing off to decide the question. We advised turning to the right, and the D was satisfactorily completed; but S proved the "dead finish" and had to be wrestled with separately.

"Can't see why they don't name a chap with something that's easily wrote," Dan said, as we rode forward with our united team of horses and boys swinging along behind us, and M and T and O were quoted as examples. "Reading's always had me dodged," he explained. "Left school before I had time to get it down and wrestle with it."

"There's nothing like reading and writing," the Quiet Stockman broke in, with an earnestness that was almost startling; and as he sat that evening in the firelight poring over the "Cardinal's Snuffbox", I watched him with a new interest.

Jack's reading was very puzzling. He always had the same book—that "Cardinal's Snuffbox"—and pored over it with a strange persistence that could not have been inspired by the book. There was no expression on his face of lively interest or pleasure, just an intent, dogged persistence; the strong, firm chin set as though he was colt-breaking. Gradually, as I watched him that night, the truth dawned on me: the man was trying to teach himself to read. The "Cardinal's Snuffbox"! and the only clue to the mystery a fair knowledge of the alphabet learned away in a childish past. In truth, it takes a deal to "beat the Scots", or, what is even better, to make them feel that they are beaten.

As I watched, full of admiration for the proud, strong character of the man, he looked up suddenly, and in a flash knew that I knew. Flushing hotly, he rose, and "thought he would turn in"; and Dan, who had been discussing education most of the evening, decided to "bottle off a bit of sleep too, for next day's use", and opened up his swag.

"There's one thing about not being too good at the reading trick," he said, surveying its contents; "a chap doesn't need to carry books round with him to put in the spare time."

"Exactly," the Maluka laughed. He was lying on his back, with an open book face downwards on his chest, looking up at the stars. He always had a book with him, but, booklover as he was, it rarely got further than his chest when we were in the camp. Life out-bush is more absorbing than books.

"Of course, reading's handy enough for them as don't lay much stock on education," Dan owned, stringing his net between his mosquito-pegs; then, struck with a new idea, he "wondered why the missus never carries books around. Anyone 'ud think she wasn't much at the reading trick herself," he said. "Never see you at it, missus, when I'm round."

"Lay too much stock on education," I answered, and, chuckling, Dan retired into his net, little guessing that when he was "round", his own self, his quaint outlook on life, and the underlying truth of his inexhaustible, whimsical philosophy were infinitely more interesting than the best book ever written.

But the Quiet Stockman seemed perplexed at the answer. "I thought reading 'ud learn you most things," he said, hesitating beside his own net; and before we could speak, the corner of Dan's net was lifted and his head reappeared. "I've learned a deal of things in my time," he chuckled, "but *reading* never taught me none of 'em." Then his head once more disappeared, and we tried to explain matters to the Quiet Stockman. The time was not yet ready for the offer of a helping hand.

At four in the morning we were roused by a new camp reveille of Starlight. "Nothing like getting off early when mustering's the game," Dan announced. By sun-up the musterers were away, and by sundown we were coming in to Bitter Springs, driving a splendid mob of cattle before us.

As the yard of the Springs came into view, we were making plans for the morrow, and admiring the fine mattress swinging before us on the tails of the cattle; but there were cattle buyers at the Springs who upset all our plans, and left no time for the bang-tailing of the mob in hand.

The buyers were Chinese drovers, authorised by their Chinese masters to buy a mob of bullocks. "Want big mob," they said. "Cash. Got money here," producing a signed cheque ready for filling in.

A Chinese buyer always pays "cash" for a mob—by cheque—generally taking care to withdraw all cash from the bank before the cheque can be presented, and, as a result, a dishonoured cheque is returned to the station, reaching the seller some six or eight weeks after the sale. Six or eight weeks more then pass in demanding explanations, and six or eight more obtaining them, and after that just as many more as Chinese slimness can arrange for before a settlement is finally made. "Cash," the drover repeated insinuatingly at the Maluka's unfathomable "Yes?" Then, certain that he was inspired, added "Spot Cash!"

But already the Maluka had decided on a plan of campaign, and, echoing the drover's "Spot Cash", began negotiations for a sale; and within ten minutes the drovers retired to their camp, bound to take the mob when delivered, and inwardly marvelling at the Maluka's simple trust.

Dan was appalled at it; but, always deferential where the Maluka's business insight was concerned, only "hoped he knew that them chaps needed a bit of watching".

"Their cash does," the Maluka corrected, to Dan's huge delight; and, leaving the musterers to go on with their branding work, culling each mob of its prime bullocks as they mustered, he set about finding someone to "watch the cash", and four days later rode into the Katherine Settlement, with Brown and the missus, as usual, at his heels.

For four days the Maluka argued with Chinese slimness before he felt satisfied that his cash was in safe keeping, while the Wag and others did as they wished with their spare time. Then, four days later, again Cheon and Tiddle'ums were hailing us in welcome at the homestead.

But their joy was short-lived, for as soon as the homestead affairs had been seen to, and a fresh swag packed, we started out-bush again to look for Dan and his bullocks, and, coming on their tracks at our first night camp, by following them up next morning we rode into the Dandy's camp at the Yellow Hole well after midday, to find ourselves surrounded by the stir and bustle of a cattle camp.

"Whatever do you do with your time?" asked the townsfolk, sure that life out-bush is stagnation, but forgetting that life is life wherever it may be lived.

The drovers disposed of within three days, another day passed travelling the remaining mob of mixed cattle to the Bitter Springs' yard for their branding, with all sorts of cattle incidents by the way; and the following midday again, as we arrived within sight of the homestead, Dan was congratulating the Maluka on the "missus being educated up to doing without a house". Then he suddenly interrupted himself: "Well, I'm blest!" he said. "If we didn't forget all about the bang-tailing that mob for her mattress."

We undoubtedly had, but two or three nights, or thereabouts, with the warm, bare ground for a bed, had made me indifferent to mattresses, and hearing that, Dan became most hopeful of "getting her properly educated yet".

Cheon greeted us with his usual enthusiasm, and handed the Maluka a letter containing a request for a small mob of bullocks within three weeks.

"Nothing like keeping the ball rolling," Dan said, also waxing enthusiastic, while the South folk remained convinced that life out-bush is stagnation.

Chapter 16

THE "WORKING LIABILITY COMPANY"

DAN and the Quiet Stockman went out to the north-west immediately, to "clean up there" before getting the bullocks together; but the Maluka settling down to arrears of bookkeeping, with the Dandy at his right hand, Cheon once more took the missus under his wing, feeding her up and scorning her gardening efforts.

"The idea of a white woman thinking she could grow watermelons," he scoffed, when I planted seeds, having decided on a carpet of luxuriant green to fill up the garden beds until the shrubs grew. The Maluka advised "waiting", and the seeds coming up within a few days, Cheon, after expressing surprise, prophesied an early death or a fruitless life.

Billy Muck, however, took a practical interest in the watermelons, and to incite him to water them in our absence, he was made a shareholder in the venture. As a natural result, the Staff, the Rejected and the Shadows immediately applied for shares — pointing out that they, too, carried water to the plants — and the watermelon beds became the property of a Working Liability Company, with the missus as Chairman of Directors.

The shadows were as numerous as ever, the rejected on the increase, but the staff was, fortunately reduced to three for the time being; or, rather, reduced to two, and increased again to three. Judy had been called "bush" on business, and the Macs, having got out in good time, Bertie's Nellie had been obliged to resign and go with the waggons, under protest, of course, leaving one Rosy and Jimmy's Nellie, augmented by one of the most persistent of all the shadows — a tiny child lubra, Bett-Bett. As the melons grew apace, throwing out secondary leaves in defiance of Cheon's prophecies, Billy Muck grew more and more enthusiastic, and, usurping the position of Chairman of Directors, he inspired the shareholders with so much zeal that the prophecies were almost fulfilled through a surfeit of watering. But Cheon's attitude towards the watermelons did not change, although he had begun to look with favour upon mail-matter and station books, finding in them a power that could keep the Maluka at the homestead.

For two full weeks after our return from the drovers' camp our life was exactly as Cheon would have it—peaceful and regular, with an occasional single day out-bush; and when the Maluka in his leisure began to fulfil his long-standing promise of a fence around my garden, Cheon expressed himself well pleased with his reform.

But even the demands of station books and accumulated mail-matter can be satisfied in time, and Dan reporting that he was "getting going with the bullocks", Cheon found his approval had been premature; for, to his dismay, the Maluka abandoned the fence and began preparations for a trip "bush". "Surely the missus was not going?" he said; and next day we left him at the homestead, a lonely figure, seated on an overturned bucket, disconsolate, and fearing the worst.

It was late in September when Dan reported in, and four weeks slipped away with the concerns of cattle and cattle buyers and cattle duffers, and as we moved hither and thither the watermelons leafed and blossomed and fruited, to Billy's delight and Cheon's undisguised amazement, and the Line Party creeping in, crept first into the borders and then into camp at the Warlochs, and Happy Dick's visits, dog fights, and cribbage became part of the station routine. Now and then a traveller from Inside passed out, but as the roads Inside were rapidly closing in, none came from the Outside going in. Because of that there were no extra mails, and towards the end of October we were wondering how we were "going to get through the days until the Fizzer was due again", when Dan and Jack came in unexpectedly for a consultation.

"Run clean out of flour," Dan announced, with a wink and a mysterious look towards the black world, as he dismounted at the head of the homestead thoroughfare; then, after inquiring for the "education of the missus", he added with further winks and mystery, that it only needed a "surprise party" to round off her education properly, but it was after supper before he found a fitting opportunity to explain his winks and mystery. Then, joining us, as we lounged in the open starry space between the billabong and the house, he wagged his head wisely, declaring "she had got on so well with her education that it 'ud be a pity not to finish her off properly". Then, dropping his bantering tone, he reported a scatter-on among the river cattle.

"I wasn't going to say anything about it before the 'boys'," he said, "but it's time someone gave a surprise party down the river"; and a "scatter-on" meaning "blacks in", the Maluka readily agreed to a surprise patrol of the river country, that being forbidden ground for blacks' camps.

"It's no good going unless it's going to be a surprise party," Dan reiterated; and when the Quiet Stockman was called across from the Quarters, he was told that "there wasn't going to be no talking before the boys".

Further consultations being necessary, Dan feared arousing suspicion, and to ensure his surprise party, and to guard against any word of the coming patrol being sent out-bush by the station "boys", he indulged in a little dust-throwing; and there was much talking in public about going "out to the north-west for the boss to have another look round there", and much laying of deep plans in private.

Finally, it was decided that the Quiet Stockman and his "boys" were to patrol the country north from the river while we were to keep to the south banks and follow the river down to the boundaries in all its windings, each party appointed to camp at the Red Lily lagoons second night out, each, of course, on its own side of the river. It being necessary for Jack to cross the river beyond the Springs, he left the homestead half a day before us — public gossip reporting that he was "going beyond the Waterhouse horse mustering", and Dan, finding dust-throwing highly diverting, shouted after him that he "might as well bring some fresh relays to the Yellow Hole in a day or two", and then giving his attention to the packing of swags and pack-bags, "reckoned things were just about fixed for a surprise party".

Chapter 17

A "SURPRISE PARTY"

AT our appointed time we left the homestead, taking the north-west track for over a mile to continue the dust-throwing; and for the whole length of that mile Dan reiterated the "advantages of surprise parties", and his opinion that "things were just about properly fixed for one"; and when we left the track abruptly and set off across country at right angles to it, Sambo's quick, questioning, suspicious glance made it very evident that he, for one, had gleaned no inkling of the patrol, which naturally filled Dan with delight.

"River to-night, Sambo," he said airily; but after that one swift glance Sambo rode after us as stolid as ever — Sambo was always difficult to fathom — while Dan spent the afternoon congratulating himself on the success of his dust-throwing, proving with many illustrations that "it's the hardest thing to spring a surprise on blacks. Something seems to tell 'em you're coming," he explained. "Some chaps put it down to second-sight or thought-reading."

When we turned in Dan was still chuckling over his cute handling of the trip. "Bluffed 'em this time all right," he assured us, little guessing that the blacks at the "Red Lilies", thirty miles away, and other little groups of blacks travelling down the river towards the lagoons were conjecturing on the object of the Maluka's visit — "something having told them we were coming".

The "something", however, was neither second-sight nor thought-reading, but a very simple, tangible "something". Sambo had gone for a stroll from our camp about sundown, and one of Jack's boys had gone for a stroll from Jack's camp, and soon afterwards two tell-tale telegraphic columns of smoke, worked on some blackfellow dot-dash system, had risen above the timber, and their messages had also been duly noted down at Red Lilies and elsewhere, and acted upon. The Maluka was on the river, and when the Maluka was about it was considered wisdom to be off forbidden ground; not that the blacks feared the Maluka, but no one cares about vexing the goose that lays the golden eggs.

On stations in the Never-Never the blacks are supposed to camp either in the homesteads, where no man need go hungry, or right outside the boundaries on waters beyond the cattle, travelling in or out as desired, on condition that they keep to the main travellers' tracks—blacks among the cattle have a scattering effect on the herd, apart from the fact that "black in" generally means cattle killing.

Of course, no man ever hopes to keep the blacks absolutely obedient to this rule; but the judicious giving of an old bullock at not too rare intervals, and always at corroboree times, the more judicious winking at cattle killing on the boundaries, where cattle scaring is not all disadvantage, and the even more judicious giving of a hint when a hint is necessary, will do much to keep them fairly well in hand. Anyway, it will discourage them from openly harrying and defiantly killing, which in humanity is surely all any man should ask.

The Maluka being more than willing to give his fair percentage, a judicious hint from him was generally taken quietly and for the time discreetly obeyed, and it was a foregone conclusion that our "surprise party" would only involve the captured with general discomfiture; but the Red Lilies being a stronghold of the tribe, and a favourite hiding-place for "outsiders", emergencies were apt to occur "down the river", and we rode out of camp with rifles unslung and revolvers at hand.

Dan's sleep had in no wise lessened his faith in the efficiency of dust-throwing, and as we set out he "reckoned" the missus would "learn a thing or two about surprise parties this trip". We all did, but the blackfellows gave the instruction.

All morning we rode in single file, following the river through miles of deep gorges, crossing here and there stretches of grassy country that ran in valleys between gorge and gorge, passing through deep ti-tree forests at times, and now and then clambering over towering limestone ridges that blocked the way, with, all the while, the majestic Roper flowing deep and wide and silent on our left, between its water-lily fringed margins.

For over two hours we rode, prying into and probing all sorts of odd nooks and crannies before we found any sign of blacks, and then, Roper giving the alarm, everyone sat to attention. Roper had many ways of amusing himself when travelling through bush, but one of his greatest delights was nosing out hidden blackfellows. At the first scent of one his ears would prick forward, and if left to himself, he would carry his rider into an unsuspected blacks' camp, or stand peering into the bushes at a discomfited blackfellow, who was busy trying to think of some excuse to explain his presence and why he had hidden.

As Roper's ears shot forward and he turned aside towards a clump of thick-set bushes, Dan chuckled in expectation; but all Roper found was a newly deserted gundi camp, and fresh tracks travelling eastwards—tracks left during the night—after our arrival at the river, of course.

Dan surveyed the tracks, and his chuckles died out, and, growing sceptical of the success of the surprise party, he followed them for a while in silence, Sambo riding behind, outwardly stolid, but, no doubt, inwardly chuckling.

Other eastward-going tracks a mile or so further on made Dan even more sceptical, and further tracks again set him harking back to his theory of "something always telling 'em somehow", and, losing interest in the hunt, he became showman of the Roper river scenery.

But gorges and ridges were not all Dan had to show us. Twice in our thirty-five miles of the Roper—about ten miles apart—wide-spreading rocky arches completely span the river a foot or so beneath its surface, forming natural crossing-places; for at them the full volume of water takes what Dan called a "duck-under", leaving only smoothly flowing shallow streams, a couple of hundred yards wide, running over the rocky bridgeways. The first "duck-under" occurs in a ti-tree valley, and, marvelling at the wonder of the rippling streamlet—so many yards wide and so few in length, with that deep, silent river for its source and estuary—we loitered in the pleasant forest glen, until Dan,

117

coming on further proofs of a blackfellow's "second-sight" along the margins of the duck-under, he turned away in disgust, and as we followed him through the great forest he treated us to a lengthy discourse on thought-reading.

The Salt Creek, coming into the Roper with its deep, wide estuary, interrupted both Dan's lecture and our course, and following along the creek to find the crossing, we left the river, and before we saw it again a mob of "brumbies" had lured us into a "drouth" that even Dan declared was the "dead finish".

Brumby horses being one of the problems of the run, and the destruction of brumby stallions imperative, as the hunt was apparently off, the brumby mob proved too enticing to be passed by, and for an hour and more it kept us busy, the Maluka and Dan being equally "set on getting a stallion or two".

As galloping after brumbies when there is no trap to run them into is about as wise as galloping after a flight of swallows, we followed at a distance when they galloped, and stalked them against the wind when they drew up to reconnoitre: beautiful, clean-limbed, graceful creatures, with long flowing manes and tails floating about them, galloping freely and swiftly as they drove their mares before them, or stepping with light, dancing tread as they drew up and faced about, with the mares now huddled together behind them. Three times they drew up and faced about, and each time a stallion fell before the rifles, then, becoming more wary, they led us further and further back, evading the rifles at every halt, until finally they galloped out of sight, and beyond all chance of pursuit. Then, Dan, discovering he had acquired the "drouth", advised "giving it best" and making for the Spring Hole in Duck Creek.

"Could do with a drop of spring water," he said; but Dan's luck was out this trip, and the Spring Hole proved a slimy bog "alive with dead cattle", as he himself phrased it. Three dead beasts lay bogged on its margin, and held as in a vice, up to their necks in slime and awfulness, stood two poor living brutes. They turned piteous, terrified eyes on us as we rode up, and then Dan and the Maluka, firing in mercy, the poor heads drooped and fell; and the bog with a sickening sigh sucked them under.

As we watched, horribly fascinated, Dan indulged in soliloquy—a habit with him when ordinary conversation seemed out of place. " 'Awful dry Wet we're having,' sez he," he murmured, " 'the place is alive with dead cattle. Fact,' sez he, 'cattle's dying this year that never died before.' " Then remarking that "this sort of thing" wasn't "exactly a thirst quencher", he followed up the creek bank into a forest of cabbage-tree palms — tall, feathery-crested palms everywhere, taller even than the forest trees; but never a sign of water.

It was then two o'clock, and our last drink had been at breakfast—soon after sun-up; and for another hour we pegged wearily on, with that seven hours' "drouth", done horses, the beating sun of a Territory October overhead, Brown stretched across the Maluka's knees on the verge of apoplexy, and Sool'em panting wearily on.

By three o'clock we struck water in the Punch Bowl—a deep volcanic hole, bottomless, the blacks say, but apparently fed beneath by the river; but long before then Dan's chuckle had died out, and soliloquies had ceased to amuse him.

At the first sight of the water we revived, and as Brown and Sool'em lay down and revelled on its margin, Dan "took a pull as an introduction", and then, after unpacking the team and getting the fire going for the billy, he opened out the tucker-bags, having decided on a "fizz" as a "good quencher".

"Nothing like a fizz when you've got a drouth on," he said (mixing soda and cream of tartar into a cup of water, and drinking deeply). As he drank, the "fizz" scattered its foam all over his face and beard, and after putting down the empty cup with a satisfied sigh, he joined us as we sat on the pebbly incline, waiting for the billy to boil, and with the tucker-bags dumped down around and about us. "Real refreshing that!" he said, drawing a red handkerchief from his belt and mopping his spattered face and beard, adding, as he passed the damp handkerchief over his ears and neck, with chuckling exaggeration: "Tell you what! A fizz 'ud be a great thing if you were short of water. You could get a drink and have a good wash-up with the one cupful."

With the "fizz", Dan's interest in education revived, and after dinner he took up the role of showman of the Roper scenery once more, and had us scrambling over boulders and cliffs along the dry bed of the creek that runs back from the Punch Bowl, until, having clambered over its left bank into a shady glen, we found ourselves beneath the gem of the Roper — a wide-spreading banyan tree, with its propped-up branches turning and twisting in long winding leafy passages and balconies, over a feathery grove of young palm trees that had crept into its generous shade.

Here and there the passages and balconies graded one to another's level, all being held together by innumerable stays and props, sent down from branch to branch, and from branches to the grassy turf beneath; and one sweeping limb, coming almost to the ground in a gentle incline before twisting away and up again, made ascent so simple that the menfolk sent the missus for a "stroll in mid-air", sure that no white woman's feet had yet trodden those winding ways. And as she strolled about the tree — not climbed — hindered only by her holland riding-skirt, Brown followed, anxiously but cautiously. Then, the spirit of vandalism taking hold of the Maluka, he cut the name of the missus deep into the yielding bark.

There are some wonderful trees on the Elsey, but not one of them will compare with the majesty and grandeur of that old banyan. Away from the world it stands, beyond those rocky ways and boulders, with its soft shade, sweeping curves, and feathery undergrowth, making a beautiful world of its own. For years upon years it has stood there — maybe for centuries — sending down from its branches those props for its old age, bountiful with its shade, and indifferent whether its pathways be trodden by white feet or black.

After the heat and "drouth" we could have loitered in that pleasant shade; but we were due at the Red Lilies "second night out"; and it being one of the unwritten laws of a "surprise party" to keep appointments — "the other chaps worrying a bit if you don't turn up" — soon after four o'clock we were out in the blazing heat again, following the river now along its higher flood-bank, through grassy plains and open forest land.

By five o'clock Dan was prophesying that "it 'ud take us all we knew to do the trick in daylight", but at six o'clock, when we were still eight miles from the Red Lilies, the Maluka settled the question by calling for a camp there and then. "The missus had had enough," the Maluka decided, and Dan became anxious. "It's that drouth that's done it," he lamented; and although agreeing with the Maluka that Jack would survive a few hours' anxiety, regretted he had "no way of letting him know". (We were not aware of the efficiency of smoke signalling.)

We turned back a short distance for better watering for horses, settling down for the night at the second "duck-under" — McMinn's bar — within sound of the rushing of many waters; for here the river comes back to the surface with a mighty roar and swirling currents. "Knock-up camp," Dan christened it in his pleasant way, and Sambo became unexpectedly curious. "Missus knock up?" he asked, and the Maluka nodding, Sambo's question was forgotten until the next midday.

By then we had passed the Red Lily lagoons, and ridden across the saltbush plain, and through a deep belt of tall, newly sprung green grass that hugged the river there just then, and having been greeted by smug, smiling old black-fellows, were saluting Jack across two or three hundred feet of water as we stood among our horses.

"Slewed!" Jack called in answer, through hollowed hands. "Didn't worry. Heard — the missus — had — knocked — up," and Dan leaned against his horse, limp with amazement.

"Heard the missus had knocked up," he gasped. "Well, I'm blowed! Talk of surprise parties!" and the old blackfellows looked on, enjoying the effect.

"Blackfellow plenty savey," they said loftily, and Dan was almost persuaded to a belief in debbil-debbils, until our return to the homestead, when Jimmy's Nellie divulged the Court secret; then Dan ejaculated another "Well, I'm blowed!" with the theory of second-sight and thought-reading falling about his ears.

After a consultation across the river in long-drawn out syllables, Jack decided on a horse muster for the return trip—genuine this time—and went on his way, after appointing to meet us at Knock-up camp next evening. But our horses refusing to leave the deep green feed, we settled down just where we were, beside the river, and formed a curious camping-ground for ourselves, a small space hacked out and trampled down, out of the dense rank grass that towered above and around us.

But this was to be a record trip for discomfort. Dan, on opening out the tucker-bags, announced ruefully that our supply of meat had "turned on us"; and as our jam tin had "blown", we feared we were reduced to damper only, until the Maluka unearthed a bottle of anchovy paste, falsely labelled "Chicken and Ham". "Lot's wife," Dan called it, after tackling some as a relish.

Birds were everywhere about the lagoons—ducks, shags, great geese, and pigmy geese, hovering and settling about them in screaming clouds; and after dinner, deciding we "might as well have a bit of game for supper", we walked across the open saltbush plain to the Big Red Lily. But revolvers are hardly the thing for duck shooting, and the soft-nosed bullets of the Maluka's rifle reducing an unfortunate duck to a tangled mass of blood and feathers, we were obliged to accept, willy-nilly, the prospect of damper and "Lot's wife" for supper. But our hopes died hard, and we sneaked about the gorgeous lagoons, revolvers in hand, for a good hour, "learning a thing or two about the lagoons" from Dan as we sneaked.

Getting nothing better than one miserable shag by our revolvers, we faced damper and "Lot's wife" about sundown, returning to camp through a dense Leichhardt-pine forest, where we found myriads of bat-like creatures, inches long, perhaps a foot, hanging head downwards from almost every branch of every tree. "Flying foxes," Dan called them, and Sambo helped himself to a few, finding "Lot's wife" unsatisfying; but the white folk "drew the line at varmints".

"Had bandicoot once for me Christmas dinner," Dan informed us, making extra tea "on account of 'Lot's wife'" taking a bit of washing down". Then, supper over, the problem of watering the horses had to be solved. The margins of the lagoons were too boggy for safety, and as the horses, fearing alligators apparently, refused the river, we had a great business persuading them to drink out of the camp mixing dish.

The sun was down before we began; and long before we were through with the tussle, peculiar shrilling cries caught our attention, and, turning to face down stream, we saw a dense cloud approaching—skimming along and above the river: a shrilling, moving cloud, keeping all the while to the river, but reaching right across it, and away beyond the tree tops. Swiftly it came to us and sped on, never ceasing its peculiar cry; and as it swept on, and we found it was made up of innumerable flying creatures, we remembered Dan's "flying foxes". In unbroken continuity the cloud swept out of the pine forest, along the river, and past us, resembling an elongated kaleidoscope, all dark colours in appearance; for, as they swept by, the shimmering creatures constantly changed places—gliding downwards as they flew, before dipping for a drink, to rise again with swift, glancing movement, shrilling that peculiar cry all the while. Like clouds of drifting fog they swept by, and in such myriads that, even after the Maluka began to time them, full fifteen minutes passed before they began to straggle out, and twenty before the last few stragglers were gone. Then, as we turned up-stream to look after them, we found that there the dense cloud was rising and fanning out over the tree tops. The evening drink accomplished, it was time to think of food.

Dan welcomed the spectacle as an "impromptu bit of education. Learnt something meself, even," he said with lordly superiority. "Been out-bush forty years, and never struck *that* before."

But it had taken so long to persuade the horses that a drink could proceed out of a mixing dish that it was time to turn in by then, and Dan proceeded to clear a space for a sleeping ground with a tomahawk. "Seems no end of education once you start," he chuckled, hacking at a stubborn tussock. "Reckon no other woman ever learned to make a bed with a

123

tomahawk." Then Sambo created a diversion by asking for the loan of a revolver before taking a message to the blacks' camp.

"Big mob bad fellow blackfellow sit down longa island," he explained; and Dan, whimsical under all circumstances, "noticed the surprise party wasn't exactly going off without a hitch". "Couldn't have fixed up better for them if they've got a surprise party of their own up their sleeves," he added ruefully, looking round at the dense wall of grass about us; and as he and the Maluka swung the two nets not six feet apart, we were all of one mind that "getting murdered was an experience we could do nicely without".

A cheerful nightcap; but such was our faith in Sool'em and Brown as danger signals that the camp was asleep in a few minutes. Perhaps also because such alarms were by no means the exception: the bush-folk would get little sleep if they lay awake whenever they camped near doubtful company. But the Red Lilies were beyond our boundaries, and shrill cries approaching the camp at dawn brought us all to our elbows, to find only the flying foxes returning to the pine forest, fanning inwards this time.

After giving the horses another drink, and breakfasting on damper and "Lot's wife", we moved on again, past the glory of the lagoons, to further brumby encounters, carrying a water-bag on a pack-horse by way of precaution against further "drouths". But such was the influence of "Lot's wife" that long before midday the bag was empty, and Dan was recommending bloater paste as a "grand thing for breakfast during the Wet, seeing it keeps you dry all day long".

Further damper and "Lot's wife" for dinner, and an afternoon of thirst, set us all dreading supper, and about sundown three very thirsty, forlorn white folk were standing by the duck-under "Knock-up camp", waiting for the Quiet Stockman. But an opportune "catch" of duck gave us heart for further brumby encounters, another night's camp out-bush. And the following morning as we rode towards the homestead, Dan "reckoned" that from an educational point of view the trip had been a pronounced success.

Chapter 18

BILLY MUCK, RAINMAKER

JUST before midday—five days after we had left the homestead—we rode through the southern slip rails to find the Dandy at work "cleaning out a soakage" on the brink of the billabong, with Cheon enthusiastically encouraging him. The billabong, we heard, had threatened to "peter out" in our absence, and riding across the now dusty wind-swept enclosure we realised that November was with us, and that the Dry was preparing for its final fling—"just showing what it could do when it tried".

With the South-east Trades to back it up, it was fighting desperately against the steadily-advancing North-west Monsoon, drying up, as it fought, every drop of moisture left from last Wet. There was not a blade of green grass within sight of the homestead, and everywhere dust whirled, and eddied, and danced, hurled all ways at once in the fight, or gathered itself into towering centrifugal columns, to speed hither and thither, obedient to the will of the elements.

Half the heavens seemed part of the Dry, and half part of the Wet; dusty blue to the south-east, and dark banks of clouds to the north-west, with a fierce beating sun at the zenith. Already the air was oppressive with electric disturbances, and Dan, fearing he would not get finished unless things kept humming, went out-bush next morning, and the homestead became once more the hub of our universe—the south-east being branded from that centre. Every few days a mob was brought in and branded, and disbanded; hours were spent on the stockyard fence; pack-teams were packed, unpacked, and repacked; and every day grew hotter and hotter, and every night more and more electric; and as the days went by we waited for the Fizzer, hungry for mail-matter with a six weeks' hunger.

When the Fizzer came in he came with his usual lusty

shouting, but varied his greeting into a triumphant: "Broken the record this time, missus. Two bags as big as a house and a few et-cet-eras!" And presently he staggered towards us, bent with the weight of a mighty mail. But a Fizzer without news would not have been our Fizzer, and as he staggered along we learned that Mac was coming out to clear the run of brumbies. "Be along in no time now," the Fizzer shouted. "Fallen clean out with bullock-punching. Wouldn't put his worst enemy to it. Going to tackle something that'll take a bit of jumping round." Then the mailbags and etceteras came down in successive thuds, and no one was better pleased with its detail than our Fizzer: fifty letters, sixty-nine papers, dozens of books and magazines, and parcels of garden cuttings.

"Last you for the rest of the year by the look of it," the Fizzer declared later, finding us at the house walled in with a litter of mail-matter. Then he explained his interruption. "I'm going straight on at once," he said, "for me horses are none too good as it is, and the lads say there's a bit of good grass at the nine-mile"; and, going out, we watched him set off.

"So long!" he shouted, as cheerily as ever, as he gathered his team together. "Half-past eleven four weeks."

But already the Fizzer's shoulders were setting square, for the last trip of the "Dry" was before him—the trip that perished the last mailman—and his horses were none too good.

"Good luck!" we called after him. "Early showers!" and there was a note in our voices brought there by the thought of that gaunt figure at the well—rattling its dice box as it waited for one more round with our Fizzer: a note that brought a bright look into the Fizzer's face, as with an answering shout of farewell he rode on into the forest. And watching the sturdy figure, and knowing the luck of our Fizzer—that luck that had given him his fearless judgment and steadfast, courageous spirit—we felt his cheery "Half-past eleven four weeks" must be prophetic, in spite of those long dry stages, with their beating heat and parching dust eddies—stages eked out now at each end with other stages of "bad going".

"Half-past eleven four weeks," the Fizzer had said, and as we returned to our mail-matter, knowing what it meant to our Fizzer, we looked anxiously to the north-west, and "hoped the showers" would come before the "return trip of the Downs".

In addition to the fifty letters for the house, the Fizzer had left two others at the homestead to be called for—one being addressed to Victoria Downs (over two hundred miles to our west), and the other to—

> F. BROWN, Esq.,
> In Charge of Stud Bulls going West
> via Northern Territory.

The uninitiated may think that the first was sent out by mistake, and that the second was too vaguely addressed; but both letters went into the rack to await delivery, for the faith in the wisdom of our Postal Department was great: it makes no mistakes, and to it—in a land where everybody knows everybody else, and all his business, and where it has taken him—an address could never be too vague. The bush-folk love to say that when it opened out its swag in the Territory it found red tape had been forgotten, but having a surplus supply of common sense on hand, it decided to use that in its place.

And so it would seem. "Down South" envelopes are laboriously addressed with the names of stations and vias here and vias there; and throughout the Territory men move hither and thither to compulsion or freewill, giving never a thought to an address; while the Department, knowing the ways of its people, delivers its letters in spite of, not because of, these addresses. It reads only the name of the man that heads the address of his letters, and sends the letters to where the man happens to be. Provided it has been clearly stated which Jones is meant, the Department will see to the rest, although it is wise to add Northern Territory for the guidance of post offices "Down South". "Jones travelling with cattle for Wave Hill," reads the Department; and that gossiping friendly wire reporting Jones as "just leaving the Powell", the letter lies in the Fizzer's loose-bag until he runs into Jones's mob; or a mail coming in for Jones, Victoria

River, when this Jones is on the point of sailing for a trip south, *his* mail is delivered on shipboard; and as the Department goes on with its work, letters for east go west, and for west go south—in mailbags, loose-bags, travellers' pockets, or per black boy—each one direct to the bush-folk as a migrating bird to its destination.

But, painstaking as our Department is with our mail matter, it excels itself in its handling of telegrams. Southern red tape has decreed—no doubt wisely as far as it goes—that telegrams shall travel by official persons only; but out-bush official persons are few, and apt to be on duty elsewhere when important telegrams arrive; and it is then that our Department draws largely on that surplus supply of common sense.

Always deferential to the South, it obediently pigeon-holes the telegram to await some official person; then, knowing that a delay of weeks will probably convert it into so much waste paper, it writes a "duplicate", and goes outside to send it "bush" by the first traveller it can find. If no traveller is at hand, the "Line" is "called up" and asked if anyone is going in the desired direction from elsewhere; if so, the "duplicate" is repeated "down the line", but if not, a traveller is created in the person of a black boy by means of a bribing stick of tobacco. No extra charge, of course. Nothing is an extra in the Territory. "Nothing to do with the Department," says the chief, "merely the personal courtesy of our officers." May it be many a long day before the forgotten shipment of red tape finds its way to the Territory to strangle the courtesy of our officers!

Nothing finds itself outside this courtesy. The Fizzer brings in great piles of mail-matter, unweighed and unstamped, with many of the envelopes bursting, or, at times, in place of an envelope, a request for one; and "our officers", get to work with their "courtesy", soon put all in order, not disdaining even the licking of stamps or the patching or renewing of envelopes. Letters and packets are weighed, stamped and repaired—often readdressed where addresses for South are blurred; stamps are supplied for outgoing mail-matter and telegrams, postage-dues and duties paid on all incoming letters and parcels—in fact, nothing is left for us to do but to pay expenses incurred when the account is rendered at the end of each six months. No doubt our Department would also read and write our letters for us if we wished it, as it does, at times, for the untutored.

Wherever it can, it helps the bush-folk, and they, in turn, doing what they can to help it in its self-imposed task, are ever ready to "find room somewhere" in packbags or swags for mail-matter in need of transport assistance; and within a day or two of the Fizzer's visit a traveller passed through going east who happened to know that the "chap from Victoria Downs was just about due at Hodgson going back west", and one letter went forward in his pocket en route to its owner. But before the other could be claimed Cheon had opened the last eighty-pound chest of tea, and the homestead fearing the supply might not be equal to the demands of the Wet the Dandy was despatched in all haste for an extra loading of stores. And all through his absence, as before it, and before the Fizzer's visit, Dan and the elements "kept things humming".

Daily the soakage yielded less and less water, and daily Billy Muck and Cheon scrimmaged over its yield, for Billy's melons were promising to pay a liberal dividend, and Cheon's garden was crying aloud for water. Every day was filled with flies, and dust, and prickly heat, and the South-east Trades skirmished and fought with the North-west Monsoon, until the willy-willys, towering higher and higher, sped across the plain incessantly, and whirled, and spun, and danced like storm witches, in and out and about the homestead enclosure, leaving its acres all dust, and only dust, with the house, lightly festooned in creepers now, and set in its deep-green luxuriant garden of melons, as a pleasant oasis in a desert of glare and dust.

Then, things coming to a climax in a succession of dry thunderstorms, two cows died in the yards from exhaustion, and Dan was obliged to "chuck it".

"Not too bad, though," he said, reviewing the year's work.

Until the billabong "petering out" altogether, and the soakage threatening to follow suit, he gave his attention to the elements.

"Never knew the showers so late," he growled, and the

homestead was inclined to agree that it was the "dead finish"; but remembering then our Fizzer was battling through the last stage of the Dry, we were silent, and Dan remembering also, devoted himself to the "missus", she being also a person of leisure now.

For hours we "pitched" near the restful green of the melon beds, and as we "pitched" the Maluka ran fencing wires through two sides of the garden fence. And, as the fence grew, Dan lent a hand here and there; Cheon haunted the vegetable patch like a disconsolate ghost; while Billy Muck, the rainmaker, hovered bat-like over his melons, lending a hand also with the fence when called upon. As Cheon mourned, his garden also mourned, but when the melons began to mourn, at the Maluka's suggestion Billy visited the Reach with two buckets and his usual following of dogs, and after a two-mile walk gave the melons a drink.

Next day Billy Muck pressed old Jimmy into the service, and the Reach being visited twice, the melons received eight buckets of water. Then Cheon tried every wile he knew to secure four buckets for his garden. "Only four," he pleaded, lavish in his bribes. But Billy and Jimmy had "knocked up longa carry water", and Cheon watched them settle down to smoke, on the verge of tears. Then, a traveller coming in with the news that heavy rain had fallen in Darwin—news gleaned from the gossiping wire—Cheon was filled with jealous fury at the good fortune of Darwin, and taunted Billy with rain-making taunts. "If he were a rainmaker," he taunted, "he would make a little when he wanted it, instead of walking miles with buckets." The taunts rankling Billy's royal soul, he retired to the camp to see about it.

"Hope he does the trick," the traveller said, busy unpacking his team. "Could do with a good bath fairly soon." But Dan cautioned him to "have a care", settling down in the shade to watch proceedings. "These early showers are a bit tricky," he explained. "Can't tell how long they'll last. Heard of a chap once who reckoned it was good enough for a bath, but by the time he'd got himself nicely soaped the shower was travelling on ten miles a minute, and there wasn't another drop of rain for a fortnight, which wasn't too pleasant for the prickly heat."

The traveller filled in Dan's evening, and gave the Quarters a fresh start, and then just before the sundown we felt the first breath of victory from the monsoon — just a few cool, gusty puffs of wind, that was all, and we ran out to enjoy them, only to scurry back into shelter, for our first shower was with us. In pelting fury it rushed upon us out of the north-west, and rushing upon us, swept over us and away from us into the south-east, leaping from horizon to horizon in the triumph of victory.

As a matter of course, it left a sweltering awfulness behind it, but it was a promise of better things; and even as Dan was inquiring with a chuckle "whether that chap in the Quarters had got a bath out of it", a second pelting fury rushed over us, filling Cheon's heart with joy and Billy with importance. Unfortunately it did not fill the water-butts with water, but already the garden was holding up its head, and Billy was claiming that he had scored a win.

"Well?" he said, waylaying Cheon in the garden. "Well, me rainmaker? Eh?" and Cheon's superstitious heart bowed down before such evidence.

A ten-minutes' deluge half an hour later licked up every grain of dust, filled the water-butts to overflowing, brought insect pests to life as by magic, left a shallow pool in the heart of the billabong, and added considerably to Billy's importance. Had not Brown of the Bulls come in during that ten-minutes' deluge, Cheon would probably have fallen to offering sacrifices to Billy. As it was, he could only load him with plum cake before turning his attention to the welcoming of Brown of the Bulls.

During the evening another five-minutes' deluge gladdened our hearts, and soon after breakfast-time Happy Dick was across. "To see how you've fared," he said; and then, to the diversion of Brown of the Bulls, Cheon and Happy Dick rejoiced together over the brimming water-butts and mourned because the billabong had not done better, regretting the while that the showers were so "patchy".

Then, while Happy Dick was assuring us that "both Warlochs were bankers", the Sanguine Scot rode in through the slip-rails at the north track, waving his hat in greeting, and with Bertie and Bertie's Nellie tailing along behind him.

"Back again!" Mac called, light-hearted as a schoolboy just escaped from drudgery, while Bertie's Nellie, as a matter of course, was overcome with ecstatic giggles.

Chapter 19

"FOUR DOZEN EGG SIT DOWN"

AS a matter of course, Bertie's Nellie quietly gathered the reins of management into her own hands, and, as a matter of course, Jimmy's Nellie indulged in ear-splitting continuous protest.

As a matter of course, we left the servant problem to work out its own solution; and, also as a matter of course, the Sanguine Scot was full of plans for the future, but particularly bubbling over with the news that he had secured Tam-o'-Shanter for a partner in the brumby venture.

"He'll be along in a few days," he explained, confident that he was "in luck this time all right", and remembering Tam among the horses at the Katherine, we congratulated him.

As a matter of course, our conversation was all of brumbies, and Mac was also convinced that "when you reckoned everything up there was a good thing in it".

"Of course, it'll take a bit of jumping round," he agreed. But the Wet was to be devoted to the building of a strong holding-yard, a "trap", and a "wing", so as to be able to get going directly the Wet lifted; and, knowing the run well and the extent of the brumby mobs on it, Mac then and there set to work to calculate the "sized mob" that could be "got together after the Wet", listening with interest to the account of our brumby encounters out east.

But long before we had done with the brumbies, Dan had become Showman of the Showers.

"See anything?" he asked, soon after sun-up, waving his hands towards the northern slip-rails, as we stood at the head of the thoroughfare speeding our parting guests; and then he drew attention to the faintest greenish tinge throughout the homestead enclosure—such a clean-washed-looking enclosure now.

"That's going to be grass soon," he said, and, the sun

coming out with renewed vigour after another shower, by midday he had gathered a handful of tiny blades half an inch in length with a chuckling "What did I tell you?"

By the next midday, grass, inches tall, was rippling all around the homestead in the now prevalent north-west breeze, and Dan was preparing for a trip out-bush to see where the showers had fallen, and Mac and Tam coming in as he went out, Mac greeted us with a jocular: "The flats get greener every year about the Elsey."

"Indeed!" we said, and Mac, overcome with confusion, spluttered an apology: "Oh, I say! Look here! I didn't mean to hit off at the missus, you know!" and then catching the twinkle in Tam's eyes, stopped short, and with a characteristic shrug, "reckoned he was making a fair mess of things".

Mac would never be other than our impetuous brither Scot, distinct from all other men, for the bush never robs her children of their individuality. In some mysterious way she clean-cuts the personality of each of them, and keeps it sharply clean-cut; and just as Mac stood apart from all men, so Tam also stood apart, the quiet, self-reliant man we had seen among the horses, and as Mac built castles, and made calculations, Tam put his shoulder to the drudgery, and before Mac quite knew what had happened, he was hauling logs and laying foundations for a brumby trap in the south-east country, while Bertie's Nellie found herself obliged to divide her attention between the homestead and the brumby camp.

As Mac hauled and drudged, the melons paid their first dividend; half-past eleven four weeks drew near, and out of the south came the Fizzer, loping once more in his saddle, with the year's dry stages behind him, and the set lines gone from his shoulders, shouting as he came, "Hullo! What ho!! Here's a crowd of us!"

But the Fizzer, being always the Fizzer, sun-up next morning found him packing up and declaring that "half a day at the Elsey gave a man a fresh start".

And Dan also was packing up—a "duplicate" brought in by the Fizzer having necessitated his presence in Darwin, and as he packed up he assured us he would be back in time

for the Christmas celebrations, even if he had to swim for it;
but before he left he paid a farewell visit to the Christmas
dinner. "In case of accidents," he explained. "Mightn't see it
again. Looks like a case of one apiece," he added, surveying
with interest the plumpness of six young pullets Cheon was
cherishing under a coop.

"Must have pullet longa Clisymus," Cheon had said, and
all readily agreeing, "Of course!" he had added, "Must have
really good Clisymus"; and another hearty "Of course"
convincing him we were at one with him in the matter of
Christmas, he entered into details.

"Must have pig poodinn, and almond, and Clisymus cake,
and mince pie," he chuckled, and then, after confiding that
he had heard of the prospective glories of a Christmas dinner
at the Pine Creek "Pub", the heathen among us urged us to
do honour to the Christian festival.

"Must have top-fellow Clisymus longa Elsey," he said, and
even more heartily we agreed, "Of course", giving Cheon
carte blanche to order everything as he wished us to have it.
"We were there to command," we assured him; and
accepting our services, Cheon opened the ball by sending
Dandy in to the Katherine on a flying visit to do a little
shopping, and, pending the Dandy's return, we sat down
and made plans.

The House and the Quarters should join forces that day,
Cheon suggested, and dine under the eastern verandah. "No
good two-fellow dinner longa Clisymus," he said. And the
blacks, too, must be regaled in their humpy. "Must have
vealer longa blackfellow Clisymus," Cheon ordered, and
Jack's services being bespoken for Christmas Eve, to "round
up a vealer", it was decided to add a haunch of "vealer" to our
menu as a trump card—vealers being rarities at Pine Creek.
Our only regret was that we lived too far from civilisation to
secure a ham; but we had a vealer and a faith in Cheon, and
waited expectantly for the Dandy, sure the Elsey would
"come out top-fellow".

And as we waited for the Dandy, the Line Party moved on
to our northern boundary, taking with it possible Christmas
guests; the Fizzer came in and went on, to face a "merry
Christmas with damper and beef served in style on a pack-

bag", also regretting empty mail-bags—the Southern mail having been delayed en route. Tam and the Sanguine Scot accepted invitations to the Christmas dinner; and the Wet broke in one terrific thunderclap, as the heavens, opening, emptied a deluge over us.

In that mighty thunderclap the Wet rushed upon us with a roar of falling waters, and with them Billy Muck appeared at the house verandah dripping like a beaver to claim further credit.

"Well?" he said again, "Me rainmaker, eh?" and the Maluka shouted above the roar and din:

"You're the boy for my money, Billy! Keep her going!" and Billy kept her going to such purpose that by sun-up the billabong was a banker. Cheon was moving over the face of the earth with the buoyancy of a child's balloon, and Billy had five inches of rain to his credit. Also the fringe of birds was back at the billabong, having returned with as little warning as it had left, and once more its ceaseless chatter became the undertone of the homestead.

At sun-up Cheon had us in his garden, sure now that Pine Creek could not possibly outdo us in vegetables, and the Dandy coming in with every commission fulfilled we felt ham was a mere detail.

But Cheon's cup of happiness was to brim over that day, for after answering every question hurled at him, the Dandy sang cheerfully: "He put in his thumb and pulled out a plum," and dragged forth a ham from its hiding-place, with a laughing "What a good boy am I."

With a swoop Cheon was on it, and the Dandy, trying to regain it, said, "Here, hold hard! I've to present it to the missus with a bow and the compliments of Mine Host." But Cheon would not part with it, and so the missus had the bow and the compliments and Cheon the ham.

Lovingly he patted it and asked us if there ever was such a ham? Or ever such a wonderful man as Mine Host? Or ever such a fortunate woman as the missus? Had any other woman such a ham or such a friend in need? And bubbling over with affection for the whole world, he sent Jackaroo off for mistletoe, and presently the ham, all brave in Christmas finery, was hanging like a gay wedding bell in the kitchen doorway. Then the kitchen had to be decorated, also in mistletoe, to make a fitting setting for the ham, and after that the fiat went forth. No one need expect either eggs or cream before "Clisymus"—excepting, of course, a sick traveller came in—another Mac—he must be kept in condition to do justice to our "Clisymus" fare.

What a week it was—all festivities, and meagre fare, and whirring egg-beaters, and thunderstorms, and downpours, and watermelon dividends, and daily visits to the vegetable patch; where Happy Dick was assured, during a flying visit, that we were sure of seven varieties of vegetables for "Clisymus".

But alas for human certainty! Even then swarms of grasshoppers were speeding towards us, and by sundown were with us.

In vain Cheon and the staff, the rejected, Bett-Bett, every shadow, and the missus danced war-dances in the vegetable patch, and chivvied and chased, and flew all ways at once; the grasshoppers had found green stuff exactly to their liking, and coming in clouds, settled, and feasted, and flew upwards, and settled back, and feasted, and swept on, leaving poor Cheon's heart as barren of hope as the garden was of vegetables. Nothing remained but pumpkins, sweet potatoes, and Cheon's tardy watermelons, and the sight of the glaring blotches of pumpkins filled Cheon with fury.

"Pumpee-kin for Clisymus!" he raved, kicking furiously at the hideous wens. Not if he knew it! and going to some stores left in our care by the Line Party, he openly stole several tins of preserved vegetables. "Must have vegetable longa Clisymus," he said, feeling his theft amply justified by circumstances, but salved his conscience by sending a gift of eggs to the Line Party as a donation towards *its* "Clisymus".

Then, finding everyone sympathetic, he broached a delicate subject. By some freak of chance, he said, the missus was the only person who had succeeded in growing good melons this year, and taking her to the melon beds, which the grasshoppers had also passed by, he looked longingly at three great fruits that lay like mossy green boulders among the rich foliage. "Just chance," he reiterated, and surely the missus would see that chance also favoured our "Clisymus".

"A Clisymus without dessert would be no Clisymus at all," he continued, pressing each fruit in turn between loving hands until it squeaked in response. "Him close up ripe, missus. Him sing out!" he said, translating the squeak.

But the missus appeared strangely inattentive, and in desperation Cheon humbled himself and apologised handsomely for former scoffings. Not chance, he said, but genius! Never was there white woman like the missus! "Him savey all about," he assured the Maluka. "Him plenty savey gardin." Further, she was a woman in a thousand! A woman all China would bow down to! Worth ninety-one hundred pounds in any Chinese matrimonial market. "A valuable asset," the Maluka murmured.

It was impossible to stand against such flattery. Billy Muck was hastily consulted, and out of his generous heart voted two of the mossy boulders to the white folk, keeping only one for "blackfellow all about".

Nothing was amiss now but Dan's non-appearance and the egg-beater whirring merrily on, by Christmas Eve the Dandy and Jack, coming in with wild duck for breakfast and the vealer, found the kitchen full of triumphs and Cheon wrestling with an immense pudding. "Four dozen egg sit down," he chuckled, beating at the mixture. "One bottle port wine, almond, raisin, all about, more better'n Pine Creek all right"; and the homestead taking a turn at the beating "for luck", assured him that it "knocked spots off Pine Creek".

"Must have money longa poodin'!" Cheon added, and our wealth lying also in a cheque book, it was not until after a careful hunt that two threepenny bits were produced, when one, with a hole in it, went in "for luck", and the other followed as an omen for wealth.

The threepenny bits safely in it, it took the united efforts of the homestead to get the pudding into a cloth and thence into a boiler, while Cheon explained that it would have been larger if only we had had a larger boiler to hold it. As it was, it had to be boiled out in the open, away from the buildings, where Cheon had constructed an ingenious trench to protect the fire from rain and wind.

Four dozen eggs in a pudding necessitates an all-night boiling, and because of this we offered to share "watches" with Cheon, but were routed in a body. "We were better in bed," he said. What would happen to his dinner if anyone's appetite failed for want of rest? There were too few of us as it was, and, besides, he would have to stay up all night in any case, for the mince pies were yet to be made, in addition to brownie and another plum pudding for the "boys", to say nothing of the hop beer which, if made too soon, would turn with the thunder, and if made too late would not "jump up" in time. He did not add that he would have trusted no mortal with the care of the fires that night.

He did add, however, that it would be as well to dispatch the vealer overnight, and that an early move (about fowl-sing-out) would not be amiss; and, always obedient to Cheon's will, we all turned in, in good time, and becoming drowsy, dreamed of "watching" great mobs of vealers, with each vealer endowed with a plum pudding for a head.

Chapter 20

"MELLY CLISYMUS"

AT earliest dawn we were awakened by wild, despairing shrieks, and were instinctively groping for our revolvers when we remembered the fatted fowls and Cheon's lonely vigil. Turning out, we dressed hastily, realising that Christmas had come, and the pullets had sung their last "sing-out".

When we appeared the stars were still dimly shining, but Cheon's face was as luminous as a full moon as, greeting each and all of us with a "Melly Clisymus", he suggested a task for each and all. Some could see about taking the vealer down from the gallows; six lubras were "rounded up" for the plucking of the pullets, while the rest of us were sent out, through wet grass and thicket, into the cold, grey dawn, to gather in "big, big mob bough and mistletoe" for the beautifying of all things.

How we worked! With Cheon at the helm, everyone was of necessity enthusiastic. The vealer was quartered in double quick time, and the first fitful rays of sunlight found their way to the Creek crossing to light up an advancing army of boughs and mistletoe clumps that moved forward on nimble black legs.

In a gleaming, hustling processing the forest of green boughs advanced, all crimson-flecked with mistletoe and sunlight, and prostrated itself around us in mighty heaps at the head of the homestead thoroughfare. Then the nimble black legs became miraculously endowed with nimble black bodies and arms; soon the gleaming boughs were piled high upon the iron roof of the eastern verandah to keep our impromptu dining-hall cool and fresh. High above the roof rose the greenery, and over the edge of the verandah, throughout its length, hung a deep fringe of green, reaching

140

right down to the ground at the posts. Everywhere among the boughs trailed long strands of bright red mistletoe, while within the leafy bower itself, hanging four feet deep from the centre of the high roof, one dense elongated mass of mistletoe swayed gently in the breeze, its heaped-up scarlet blossoms clustering about it like a swarm of glorious bees.

Cheon interrupted the decorations with a call to "Bressfass! Duck cully and lice", he sang boldly, and then following in a doubtful, hesitating quaver: "I — think — sausage. Must have sausage for Clisymus bress-fass," he said emphatically, as he ushered us to seats, and we agreed with our usual "Of course!" But we found fried balls of minced collops, which Cheon hastened to explain *would* have been sausages if only he had had skins to pack them into.

"Him close up sausage!" he assured us, but that anxious quaver was back in his voice, and to banish all clouds from his loyal old heart, we ate heartily of the collops, declaring they were sausages in all but skins. Skins, we persuaded him, were merely appendages to sausages; barriers, in fact, between men and delectable feasts; and satisfied that we were satisfied, he became all beams once more, and called our attention to the curried duck.

The duck discussed, he hinted that dinner was the be-all and end-all of "Clisymus", and, taking the hint, we sent the preparations merrily forward.

Every chair and stool on the run was mustered; two tables were placed end to end beneath that clustering mistletoe and covered with clean white tablecloths — remembering the story of the rags and hobble rings, we refrained from serviettes — the hop beer was set in canvas water-bags to keep it cool; and Cheon pointing out that the approach from the kitchens was not all that could be desired, an enormous tent-fly was stretched away from the roof of the verandah, extending it half-way to the kitchen, and further greenery was used, decorating it within and without, to make it a fitting passage-way for the transport of Cheon's triumphs. Then Cheon's kitchen decorations were renewed and added to; and after that further suggestions suggested and attended to. Everything that could be done was done, and by eight o'clock all was ready for Cheon's triumphs, all but our appetites and times of day.

By nine o'clock Mac and Tam had arrived, and after everything had been sufficiently admired, we trooped in a body to the kitchen, obedient to a call from Cheon.

Triumph after triumph was displayed, and after listening gravely and graciously to our assurances that already everything was "more better'n Pine Creek last year", Cheon allowed us a glimpse of the pudding through a cloud of steam, the company standing reverently around the fire trench in a circle, as it bent over the bubbling boiler; then scuttling away before us like an old hen with a following of chickens, he led the way to the water-bags, and asked our opinion on the hop beer: "You think him jump-up longa dinner time, eh, boss?" he said anxiously, as the Maluka, holding a bottle between us and the light, examined it critically. "We make him three o'clock longa night-time."

It looked remarkably still and tranquil, but we hoped for the best, and half an hour later were back at the waterbags, called thither to decide whether certain little globules were sediment or air bubbles. Being sanguine, we decided in favour of bubbles, and in another half-hour were called back again to the bags to see that the bubbles were bubbles indeed, having dropped in at the kitchens on our way to give an opinion on veal stuffing and bread sauce; and within another half-hour were peering into the oven to inspect further triumphs of cooking.

Altogether the morning passed quickly and merrily, any time Cheon left us being spent in making our personal appearance worthy of the feast.

Scissors and hand glasses were borrowed, and hair cut and chins shaved, until we feared our Christmas guests would look like convicts. Then the Dandy produced blacking brushes; boots that had never seen blacking before shone like ebony. After that a mighty washing of hands took place, to remove the blacking stain; and then the Quarters settled down to a general "titivation", Tam "cleaning his nails for Christmas" amid great applause.

By eleven o'clock the Dandy was immaculate, the guests

satisfied that they "weren't too dusty", while the Maluka, in
spotless white relieved with silk cummerbund and tie, bade
fair to outdo the Dandy. Even the Quiet Stockman had
succeeded in making a soft white shirt "look as though it had
been ironed once". And then every lubra being radiant with
soap, new dresses, and ribbons, the missus determined not
to be outdone in the matter of Christmas finery, burrowed
into trunks and boxes, and appeared in cream washing silk,
lace fichu, ribbons, rings, and frivolities—finery, by the
way, packed down south for that "commodious station
home".

Cheon was enraptured with the appearance of his
company, and worked, and slaved, and chuckled in the
kitchen as only Cheon could, until at last the critical moment
had arrived. Dinner was ready; but an unforeseen difficulty
had presented itself. How was it to be announced, Cheon
queried, having called the missus to the kitchen for a hasty
consultation, for was it wise to puff up the Quarters with a
chanted summons?

A compromise being decided on as the only possible
course, after the booming teamster's bell had summoned the
Quarters, Cheon, all in white himself, bustled across to the
verandah to call the gentry by word of mouth:—"Dinner!
Boss! Missus!" he sang—careful to specify his gentry, for not
even reflected glory was to be shed over the Quarters. Then,
moving in and out among the greenery as he put finishing
touches to the table here and there, he glided into the
wonders of his Christmas menu: "Soo-up! Chuckie! Ha-am!
Roo-ost Vealer!" he chanted. "Cauliflower! Pee-es! Bee-ens!
Toe-ma-toes! (with a regretful "tinned" in parenthesis)
Shweet Pootay-toes! Bread Sau-ce!" On and on through
mince pies, sweets, cakes and fruits, went the monotonous
chant, the Maluka and the missus standing gravely at
attention, until a triumphant paean of "Plum-m-m Poodinn!" soared upwards as Cheon waddled off through the
decorated verandah extension for his soup tureen.

But a sudden, unaccountable shyness had come over the
Quarters, and as Cheon trundled away, a hurried argument
reached our ears of "Go on! You go first!" "No, you. Here!
none of that"; and then, after a short subdued scuffle, the

Dandy, looking slightly dishevelled, came through the doorway with just the suspicion of assistance from without, and the ice being thus broken, the rest of the company came forward in a body and slipped into whichever seat came handiest.

As all of us, with the exception of the Dandy, were Scottish, four of us being Macs, the Maluka chose our Christmas grace from Bobby Burns; and quietly and reverently our Scots hearts listened to those homely words:

> Some ha'e meat, and canna eat,
> And some wad eat that want it;
> But we ha'e meat, and we can eat,
> And sae the Lord be thankit.

Then came Cheon's turn, and gradually and cleverly his triumphs were displayed.

To begin with, we were served to clear soup—"just to tickle your palates," the Maluka announced, as Cheon in a hoarse whisper instructed him to serve "little-fellow-helps", anxious that none of the keenness should be taken from our appetites. All served, the tureen was whisked away to ensure against further inroads, and then Cheon trundled round the table, removing the soup plates, inquiring of each guest in turn if he found the soup to his liking, and informing all that lubras were on guard in the kitchen, lest the station cats should so far forget themselves as to take an unlawful interest in our dinner.

The soup finished with, Cheon disappeared into the kitchen regions, to reappear almost immediately at the head of a procession of lubras, each of whom carried a *piece de resistance* to the feast: Jimmy's Nellie leading with the six pullets on one great dish, while Bett-Bett brought up the rear with the bread sauce. On through a vista of boughs and mistletoe came the triumphs—how glad we were the way had been made more worthy of their progress—the lubras, of course, were with them, but we had eyes only for the triumphs: those pullets all a-row with plump brown breasts bursting with impatience to reveal the snowy flesh within; marching behind them that great sizzling "haunch" of veal, taxing Rosy's strength to the utmost; then Mine Host's

crisply crumbed ham trudging along, and filling Bertie's
Nellie with delight, with its tightly bunched little wreath of
mistletoe usurping the place of the orthodox paper frill;
behind again vegetable dishes two abreast, borne by the
lesser lights of the staff (lids off, of course; none of our glory
was to be hidden under covers); tailing along with the
rejected and gravy boats came laden soup plates to eke out
the supply of vegetable dishes; and, last of all, that creamy
delight of bread sauce, borne sedately and demurely by Bett-
Bett.

As the triumphs ranged themselves into a semi-circle at
the head of the table, our first impulse was to cheer, but
obeying a second impulse we did something infinitely better,
for, as Cheon relieved his grinning waitresses, we assured
him, collectively and individually and repeatedly, that never
had anyone seen anything in Pine Creek so glorious as even
the dimmest shadow of this feast; and as we reiterated our
assurances, I doubt if any man in all the British Empire was
prouder or more justified in his pride than our Cheon. Cook
and gardener, forsooth Cheon was Cheon, and only Cheon;
and there is no word in the English language to define Cheon
or the position he filled, simply because there was never
another like Cheon.

"Chuckie!" he sang, placing the pullets before the Maluka,
and dispatching Jimmy's Nellie for hot plates; "Roast vealer
for Mac," and as Mac smiled and acknowledged the honour,
Rosy was dismissed. "Boilee Ham" was allotted to the
Dandy; and as Bertie's Nellie scampered away, Cheon
announced other triumphs in turn and in order of merit,
each of the company receiving a dish also in order of merit:
Tam-o'-Shanter contenting himself with a gravy boat, while,
from the beginning, the Quiet Stockman had been honoured
with the hop beer.

Long before the last waitress was relieved, the carvers
were at work, and the company was bubbling over with
merriment. "Have some veal, chaps?" the Sanguine Scot
said, opening the ball by sticking a carving fork into the great
joint, and waving the knife in a general way round the
company; then as the gravy sizzled out in a steaming gurgle,
he added invitingly: "Come on, chaps! This is *veal*, prime

145

stuff! None of your staggering-bob tack"; and the Maluka and the Dandy bidding against him, to Cheon's delight, everyone "came on" for some of everything; for veal and ham and chicken and several vegetables and sauces blend wonderfully together when a Cheon's hand has been at the helm.

The higher the plates were piled the more infectious Cheon's chuckle became, until nothing short of a national calamity could have checked our flow of spirits. Mishaps only added to our enjoyment, and when a bottle of hop beer went off unexpectedly as the Quiet Stockman was preparing to open it, and he, with the best intentions in the world, planted his thumb over the mouth of the bottle, and directed two frothing streams over himself and the company in general, the delight of everyone was unbounded—a delight intensified a hundredfold by Cheon, who, with his last doubt removed, danced and gurgled in the background, chuckling in an ecstasy of joy: "My word, missus! That one beer *plenty* jump up!" As there were no carpets to spoil, and everyone's clothes had been washed again and again, no one's temper was spoiled, and a clean towel quickly repairing all damages, our only regret was that a bottle of beer had been lost.

But the plum pudding was yet to come, and only Cheon was worthy to carry it to the feast; and as he came through the leafy way, bearing the huge mottled ball, as big as a bullock's head—all ablaze with spirits and dancing light and crowned with mistletoe—it would have been difficult to say which looked most pleased with itself, Cheon or the pudding; for each seemed wreathed in triumphant smiles.

We held our breaths in astonishment, each feeling like the entire Cratchit family rolled into one, and by the time we had recovered speech, Cheon was soberly carrying one-third of the pudding to the missus. The Maluka had put it aside on a plate to simplify the serving of the pudding, and Cheon, sure that the Maluka could mean such a goodly slice for no one else but the missus, had carried it off.

There were to be no "little-fellow-helps" this time. Cheon saw to that, returning the goodly slice to the Maluka under protest, and urging all to return again and again for more. How he chuckled as we hunted for the "luck" and the "wealth", like a parcel of children, passing round bushman jokes as we hunted.

"Too much country to work," said one of the Macs, when after a second helping they were both still "missing". "Covered their tracks all right," said another. The Quiet Stockman "reckoned they were bushed all right". "Going in a circle," the sick Mac suggested, and then a shout went up as the Dandy found the "luck" in his last mouthful.

"Perhaps someone's given the 'wealth' to his dog," Tam suggested, to our consternation, for that was more than possible, as the dogs from time to time had received tit-bits from their masters as a matter of course.

But the man who deserved it most was to find it. As we sat sipping tea, after doing our best with the cakes and water-melons, we heard strange gurgles in the kitchen, and then Cheon appeared choking and coughing, but triumphantly announcing that *he* had found the wealth in his first mouthful. "My word! Me close up gobble him," he chuckled, exhibiting the pudding-coated threepence, and not one of us grudged him his good omens. May they have been fulfilled a thousand-fold!

Undoubtedly our Christmas dinner was a huge success—from a blackfellow's point of view it was the most sensible thing we whites had ever organized; for half the vealer, another huge pudding, several yards of sweet currant "brownie", a new pipe apiece, and a few pounds of tobacco found their way to the "hump"; and although headaches may have been in the near future, there was never a heartache among them.

All afternoon we sat and chatted as only the bush-folk can (the bush-folk are only silent when in uncongenial society), "putting in" a fair amount of time writing our names on one page of an autograph album; and as strong brown hands tried their utmost to honour Christmas Day with "something decent in the way of writing", each man declared that he had never written so badly before, while the company murmured: "Oh, *yours* is all right. Look at mine!" And as we chatted on we agreed that, in spite of, or perhaps *because* of, its many acknowledged disadvantages, the simple, primitive bush-life is the sweetest and best of all—sure that although there may have been more imposing or less conventional feasts elsewhere that Christmas Day, yet nowhere in all this old round world of ours could there have been a happier, merrier, healthier-hearted gathering. No one was bored. No one wished himself elsewhere. All were sure of their welcome. All were light-hearted and at ease; although no one so far forgot himself as to pour his hop beer into the saucer in a lady's presence, for, low be it spoken, although the missus had a glass tumbler, there were only two on the run, and the men-folk drank the Christmas healths from cups, and enamel at that; for a willy-willy had taken Cheon unaware when he was laden with a tray containing every glass and china cup fate had left us, and, as by a miracle, those two glasses had been saved from the wreckage.

But enamel cups were no hardships to the bush-folk, and besides, nothing inconvenienced us that day—except perhaps doing justice to further triumphs at afternoon tea; and all we had to wish for was the company of Dan and the Fizzer.

To add to the general comfort, a gentle north-west breeze blew all through the day, besides being what Bett-Bett called a "shady day", cloudy and cool; and to add to the general rejoicing before we had quite done with "Clisymus", an extra mail came in per black boy—a mail sent out to us by the "courtesy of our officers" at the Katherine, "seeing some of the packages felt like Christmas".

It came to us on the verandah. Two very full mailbags borne by two very empty black boys; and in an incredibly short space of time there were two very full black boys and two very empty mailbags; for the mail was our delayed mail, and exactly what we wanted; and the boys had found all they wanted at Cheon's hospitable hands.

But even Christmas Days must come to an end; and as the sun slipped down to the west, Mac and Tam "reckoned it was time to be getting a move on"; and as they mounted amid further Christmas wishes, with saddle-pouches bursting with offerings from Cheon for "Clisymus supper", a strange feeling of sadness crept in among us, and we wondered where "we would all be next Christmas". Then our Christmas guests rode out into the forest, taking with them

the sick Mac, and as they faded from our sight we knew that
the memory of that Christmas Day would never fade out of
our lives; for we bush-folk have long memories and love to
rest now and then beside the milestones of the past.

Chapter 21

THE SCOURGE OF THE WET

A DAY or two after Christmas, Dan came in full of regrets because he had "missed the celebrations", and gratified Cheon's heart with a minute and detailed account of the "Clisymus" at Pine Creek. Then the homestead settled down to the stagnation of the Wet, and as the days and weeks slipped by, travellers came in and went on, and Mac and Tam paid us many visits, as with the weeks we slipped through a succession of anniversaries.

"A year today, Mac, since you sent those telegrams!" we said, near the beginning of those weeks; and, all mock gravity, Mac answered: "Yes! And blocked that Goer! Often wondered what happened to her!"

"A year today, gentlemen," I added a few days later, "since you flung that woman across the Fergusson"; and as Mac enjoyed the reminiscence, the Maluka said: "And forgot to fling the false veneer of civilisation after her."

A few days later again we were greeting Tam at the homestead. "Just a year ago, Tam," we said, "you were . . ." but Tam's horse was young and untutored, and, getting out of hand, carried Tam away beyond the building. "A Tam-o'-Shanter fleeing," the Maluka once more murmured.

Then Dan filled in the days, until one evening just at sundown, when we said:

"A year this sundown, Dan, since we first sampled one of your dampers," and, chuckling, Dan reviewed the details of that camp, and slipping thence into reviewing education. "Somebody's learned a thing or two since then," he chuckled. "Don't notice people catching cows and milking 'em round these parts quite so often."

In the morning came the Quiet Stockman's turn. "There's a little brown filly in the mob I'm just beginning on, cut out for the missus," he said, coming to the house on his way to the stockyard, and we went with him to see the bonnie creature.

"She's the sort that'll learn anything," Jack said, his voice full of admiration. "If the missus'll handle her a bit, I'll learn her everything a horse can learn."

"Gypsy" he had named her, and in a little while the pretty creature was "roped" and standing beneath Jack's caressing hand. "Now, missus," he said—and then followed my first lesson in "handling" until the soft brown muzzle was resting contentedly in my hand. "She'll soon follow you," Jack said eagerly, "you ought to come up every day"; and looking up at the glowing boyish face, I said quietly:

"Just a year today, Jack, since you met us by the roadside," and the strong young giant looked down with an amused light in his eyes. "Just a year," he said, with that quiet smile of his; and that quiet smile, and that amused "Just a year" were more eloquent than volumes of words, and set Dan "reckoning" that "somebody else's been learning a thing or two besides book learning".

But the Dandy was waiting for some tools from the office, and as we went with him he, too, spoke of the anniversaries. "Just a year since you first put foot on this verandah," he said; and that reminiscence brought into the Maluka's eyes that deep look of bush comradeship, as he added: "And became just One of Us."

Before long Mac was reminding us that "a year ago she was wrestling with the servant question", and Cheon coming by we indulged in a negative anniversary. "A year ago, Cheon," we said, "there was no Cheon in our lives," and Cheon pitied our former forlorn conditions as only Cheon could, at the same time asking us what could be expected of one of Sam's ways.

Then other anniversaries crowded on us thick and fast, and with them there crept into the Territory that scourge of the wet season—malaria dysentery, and travellers coming in stricken down with it rested a little while before going on again.

But two of these sick travellers went down to the very gates of death, where one, a little Chinaman, slipped through, blessing the "good boss", who treated all men alike, and

151

leaving an echo of a blessing in old Cheon's loyal heart. But the other sick traveller turned back from those open gates, although bowed with the weight of seventy years, and faced life anew, blessing in his turn "the whitest man" those seventy years had known.

Bravely the worn, bowed shoulders took up the burden of life again, and, as they squared to their load, we slipped back to our anniversaries — once more Jack went bush for the schooling of his colts, once more Mac and Dan went into the Katherine to "see about the ordering of stores", Tam going with them; and as they rode out of the homestead, once more we slipped, with the Dandy, into the Land of Wait-a-while — waiting once more for the Wet to lift, for the waggons to come, and for the Territory to rouse itself for another year's work.

Full of bright hopes, we rested in that Land of Wait-a-while, speaking of the years to come, when the bush-folk will have conquered the Never-Never and lain it at the feet of great cities; and, waiting, and resting, we made merry and planned plans, all unconscious of the great Shadow that was even then hovering over us.

THE
LITTLE BLACK PRINCESS

Chapter 1

BETT-BETT

BETT-BETT must have been a princess, for she was a king's niece; and, if that does not make a princess of anyone, it ought to do so.

She didn't sit—like fairy-book princesses—waving golden sceptres over devoted subjects, for she was just a little bush blackfellow-girl, about eight years old. She had, however, a very wonderful palace—the great, lonely, Australian bush.

She had, also, one devoted subject—a little, speckled dog called Sue; one big trouble—"looking out tucker"; and one big fear—debbil-debbils.

It wasn't all fun being a black princess, for nobody knew what terrible things might happen any minute—as you will see.

Once, when Bett-Bett and Sue were camped with some of the tribe on the Roper River, they were suddenly attacked by the Willeroo blacks, who were their very fiercest enemies. Everybody "ran bush" at once to hide, with the Willeroos full chase after them. In the fright and hurry-scurry, Bett-Bett fell into the river, and at once decided to stay there, for, in spite of the crocodiles, it was the safest place she could think of. She swam under the water to the steep banks, and caught hold of the roots of an old tree. Standing on this, she stuck her nose and mouth out of the water, in the shelter of a water-lily leaf; and, there she stood for a long time without moving a muscle, her little naked black body looking exactly like one of the shadows.

When all was quiet and it was getting dark, she crept out, thinking she would be safe for the night. Sue at once came out from her hiding-place, and, licking Bett-Bett's hand, seemed to say, "My word, that *was* a narrow escape, wasn't it?"

155

Bett-Bett spoke softly to her, and the two of them then hunted about to see if any tucker had been left behind.

Sue very soon found a piece of raw beef; and Bett-Bett made a fire in the scrub, so that nobody could see the smoke. Then, while the supper was cooking, they crouched close to the warmth, for they felt very cold.

By and by, the steak caught fire, and Bett-Bett picked it up between two sticks, and tried to blow it out. Finding she could not manage this, she laid it on the ground, and threw a handful of earth on it; and, at once, the flames died away. She and Sue then grinned at each other as if to say, "Aren't we clever? we know how to manage things, don't we?" and were just settling down to enjoy their supper, when somebody grabbed Bett-Bett from behind, and shouted out, "Hallo! what name you?"

Did you ever see a terribly frightened little black princess? I did, for I saw one then. The Maluka and I were out-bush, camping near the river. We had arrived just about sunset, and, seeing black tracks, had decided to follow them, and found Bett-Bett. Big Mac, one of the stockmen, was with us, and it was he who had caught hold of her; but, if it had been an army of debbil-debbils, she could not have been more frightened.

"Nang ah! piccaninny," I said, meaning "come here, little one". I spoke as kindly as I could, and Bett-Bett saw at once that I was a friend.

She spoke to Sue and came, saying, "Me plenty savey Engliss, Missus!"

This surprised us all, for she looked such a wild little girl. I asked her where she had learnt her "plenty savey Engliss"; and she answered, "Longa you boys", meaning she had picked it up from our homestead boys.

After a little coaxing, she told us the story of the Willeroos, and said "Dank you please, Missus", very earnestly when I asked if she would like to sleep in our camp.

As we went up the bank, I was amused to see that she was munching her beef. It takes more than a good fright to make a blackfellow let go his only chance of supper. After a big meal of damper and honey — "sugar-bag" she called it, — she went to a puddle, and smeared herself all over with mud;

and, when I asked why she did this, she said, "Spose skeeto come on, him bite mud, him no more bite meself"; and I thought her a very wise little person.

As soon as it became dark, she and Sue curled themselves up into a little heap near the fire, and fell asleep for the night.

In the morning, I gave her a blue and white singlet that I had taken from one of the boys' swags. She dressed herself in it at once, and looked just like a gaily coloured beetle, with thin black arms and legs; but she thought herself very stylish, and danced about everywhere with Sue at her heels. Sue was the ugliest dog of any I had seen. She looked very much like a flattened out plum pudding on legs, with ears like a young calf, and a cat's tail.

As we sat at breakfast, I asked Bett-Bett if any mosquitoes had bitten her in the night. "No more," she said, and then added with a grin, "Big mob bin sing out, sing out". She seemed pleased to think how angry they must have been when they found a mouthful of mud, instead of the juicy flesh they expected.

When we were ready to start for the homestead, I asked Bett-Bett if she and Sue would like to come and live with me there. "Dank you please, Missus!" she answered, grinning with delight.

So Bett-Bett found a Missus, and I—well, I found a real nuisance.

Chapter 2

"SHIMMY SHIRTS"

FOR at least a week after we reached the homestead, Bett-Bett was kept busy protecting Sue from the station dogs. We hadn't been home an hour before we heard a fearful yell, and, running to see what could have happened, found that all the dogs on the place had set on the poor little beast, and were trying to worry her to death.

With a shriek, Bett-Bett flew to the rescue. As she ran, she picked up a thick stick, and with it fought and hammered and screamed her way into the biting, yelping mob of dogs; then, picking up the dusty little speckled ball, she fought and hammered and screamed her way out again to a place of safety. There, she sat and crooned over Sue, who licked her face, and tried to say, "How good you are, Bett-Bett!"

I don't know how many fights we had altogether, for the dogs kept at it till they were tired of the fun, which was not before Sue was nearly in tatters.

While Bett-Bett was fighting these battles, I was busy sewing, making clothes for her. To begin with, I made her a bright blue dress, which pleased her very much, and the singlet was kept for a nightdress, for she would not part with it altogether. Then, I made some little white petticoats which she called "shimmy shirts". When these were finished, I began to make a red dress; but oh, dear, the fuss she made! and the fright she got into! In funny pidgin English, and with much waving of her arms, she said that, if you had on a red dress when there was a thunderstorm, the debbil-debbil who made the thunder would "come on" and kill you "deadfellow". When I heard this, of course I made a pink dress, as I didn't want the Thunder debbil-debbil to run off with her. Besides, he might have been angry with me for making red dresses for little native girls.

This debbil-debbil is a funny sort of person, for, although

he gets furious if he sees a lubra dressed in red, it pleases him wonderfully to see an old blackfellow with as much red on as he can find. Do you know, if this Thunder debbil-debbil is roaring dreadfully, and happens to catch sight of an old man with plenty of red handkerchiefs, and scarves of red feathers tied round him, it puts him into such a good temper that he can't help smiling; and then nobody gets hurt. But sometimes even a blackfellow with yards of red stuff wound round him can do nothing to quiet this raging debbil-debbil; then, everybody knows that the lubras have been wearing red dresses. Such wicked, selfish people deserve to be punished; and it's quite a comfort to think that, very soon, Mr Thunder debbil-debbil will get hold of them and "kill them deadfellow". Of course, if anybody gets killed by mistake, it will be their fault, for they should have given all their red things to their husbands.

Billy Muck, one of the wise old men of the tribe, told Bett-Bett this fearful story. Bett-Bett was engaged to be married to Billy Muck, and it was his duty to teach her these things. I fancy Billy made it up, I don't know; but the wise old men, who are supposed to know everything, have a cunning little way of telling awful tales about debbil-debbils, so as to get the best things for themselves.

For ages upon ages, the old men have told the young men and lubras that they must not eat fat turkeys, or the tail of the kangaroo, or, indeed, any of the best things that they find when hunting. If they do, a terrible thing will happen, for a big Hunting debbil-debbil will come on with a rush, and, in a moment, make them very old and weak. "Look at us!" cry the old rascals. "We eat these things, and behold, we are weak old men, with no strength to fight an enemy!" This looks so true that nobody—excepting the old men—cares about eating turkeys and kangaroo tails, and such things.

Bett-Bett believed all these tales, for she was a little black girl, every bit of her. Like all blacks, she had such a generous heart that she could not bear to have anything good without sharing it with everybody. This was rather a nuisance, for, as soon as her clothes were finished, she wanted to give most of them to the other lubras.

"Him no more got goodfellow dress, Missus," she said,

159

almost crying, when I told her she must keep her clothes for herself. I didn't know what to do; it seemed wrong to teach her to be greedy and selfish, so I had to say that I would make the lubras a new dress each.

This made everybody shriek with delight; and, for another week, we had a merry time choosing colours, sewing dresses, and conducting dog fights. Fortunately, the lubras said that shimmy shirts were "silly fellow", or I suppose I would have had to make enough of these to go round as well.

Among the things I had given Bett-Bett was a warm bluey, or rug; and, wrapped in this, she and Sue slept on the bathroom floor every night. She preferred the floor to a bed, and was very funny about my spring mattress. "Him too muchee jump-up jump-up," she said scornfully.

At bedtime, dressed in her gay singlet, she made her bed. First, she spread her bluey out on the floor, and jumped and pranced wildly about till she had managed to fold it in four. Then, she lifted a corner carefully, and she and Sue crept in like a pair of young opossums. While they were settling themselves, the rug bulged and wobbled and wriggled so much that it looked as though it were playing at earthquakes. At last when all was quiet, two pairs of very bright eyes peeped out at the top of the bluey, looking for the supper biscuit that I always had ready. As soon as I offered it, out came a thin black arm; and, then, Bett-Bett, Sue, and biscuit disappeared for the night.

It was no use trying to keep these two apart. They simply could not understand why they should not sleep together; so I told Bett-Bett that Sue must have plenty of baths, and that, if I ever found one single tick on her, the little dog would have to be given a whipping.

The thought of such a fearful punishment for them both made Bett-Bett shiver with fear. She called Sue, and told her all about it, and made her understand that she would have to lie still and be hunted in, so that every horrid little insect could be found and killed. So every day, and many times a day, they had a tick hunt; and Bett-Bett managed to make a great game of it.

She talked to herself all the time, and pretended that the ticks were wicked people, and that she was a terrible debbil-

debbil, who caught them and killed them "deadfellow". How she did grin as she crunched them between two stones!

One morning, Bett-Bett was very quiet on the veranda, with Sue asleep beside her. I wondered what she was doing, and went out to see. She was busy unravelling threads from some pieces of rag, and I asked her what they were for. "Me makem string," she answered, and, taking up a few threads, stuck one of her thin little legs straight out in front of her. Pulling up her dress, she laid the threads on her thigh, and, with the palm of her hand, rolled them quickly backwards and forwards. In a few seconds, she grinned, and held up a little piece of string in her fingers.

I was very interested, and sat watching her till she had made quite a yard; then, to help to amuse her, gave her a big bundle of coloured scraps of rag.

After a day or two, she showed me a pretty little bag that she had made by weaving and knotting this string together.

"You are a good little girl, Bett-Bett" I said. "Now, come and help me tidy your box."

When her clean clothes were neatly in place I found that the shimmy shirts were all missing, and asked where they were.

"Me knock up longa shimmy shirts," Bett-Bett said with a grin, meaning that she was tired of wearing them.

"But where are they?" I said.

"Longa string," she answered cheerfully. "Me bin make em."

Then, I knew that the piles of rag she had unravelled to make into string were her new shimmy shirts.

I was really angry with her now, and set her to sew at a new one. She obeyed with such a cheerful grin that I began to feel quite mean for punishing her, for how could she understand that it was wrong to tear up her own things?

I was just going to tell her to run and play, when I heard a merry little chuckle from under the veranda. Looking to see what the fun was, I found that Bett-Bett was having a tick hunt. She had just found an extra big one between Sue's toes, which she dragged from its hiding place, and threaded on to her needle and cotton. As she held her thread up for me to admire, I saw that she had about a dozen of the horrid creatures, hanging down like a string of beads. I felt quite sick.

"Bett-Bett," I said, "you have done enough sewing; take some soap, and go and give yourself and Sue a good bath."

Off they went to the creek like a pair of gay young wallabies, hopping and skipping over everything.

In a few minutes they were both nearly white with soap lather, dancing a wild sort of corroboree on an old tree trunk. The dance ended suddenly with a leap into "middle water", as Bett-Bett called the deep holes.

They loved a bath, these two—"bogey", the blacks call it—but neither of them would have soap on their faces.

"Him"—meaning the soap—"bite eye belonga me," Bett-Bett explained.

Chapter 3

"SHUT-HIM-EYE QUICKFELLOW"

THE king we were talking about—Bett-Bett's uncle, you know—was called by the tribe Ebimel Wooloomool. The white people had nicknamed him "Goggle Eye"; and he was very proud of his "whitefellow name", as he called it. You see, he didn't know what it meant.

He didn't have a golden sceptre. Australian kings never do; but he had what was quite as deadly—a "magic deathbone". If you had been up to mischief, breaking the laws, or doing anything wrong, it was wise to keep out of the way; for every blackfellow knew that, if he "sang" this bone and pointed it at you, you would very quickly die.

The white man says you die of fright; but, as it is the bone-pointing that gives the fright, it's the bone-pointing that kills, isn't it?

The first time I met Goggle Eye, he was weeding my garden, and I didn't know he was king; I thought he was just an ordinary blackfellow. You see he didn't have a crown, and as he was only wearing a tassel and a belt made from his mother-in-law's hair, it was no wonder I made the mistake. It takes a good deal of practice to tell a king at a glance—when he's naked and pulling up weeds.

I didn't like having even unclothed kings about the homestead, so I said:—"Goggle Eye, don't you think you had better have some more clothes on?"

He grinned and looked very pleased, so I gave him a pair of blue cotton trousers. He put them on at once, just where he was, and asked my advice as to which leg he had better put in first. I advised him as best I could, and finally he was safely into them, right side out, and all else as it should be, to his complete satisfaction.

We gardened for a while, the old blackfellow and I; but, as the sun became hotter, I noticed that he kept pulling his trousers up over his knees. At last he sat down and took one leg right out.

"What's the matter, Goggle Eye?" I asked. "Don't you like your trousers?"

"Him bite me longa knee," he answered, meaning that they pinched him under the knee; then picking up his hoe again, he worked till dinnertime with one leg in and one out, and the belt of the trousers neatly tucked up through his mother-in-law's hair belt. After dinner he took both legs out and worked with the trousers dangling in front of him.

"Too muchee hot-fellow," he explained.

A few days afterwards, I met his lubra with a tucker-bag made of one of the legs!

I was always ready to listen to any old blackfellow telling about the strange laws and customs of the tribe. Very soon, Goggle Eye found this out; and, as sitting in the shade, yarning, suited the old rascal much better than gardening, we had many a long gossip.

I never laughed at their strange beliefs. I found them wonderfully interesting, for I soon saw that, under every silly little bit of nonsense, was a great deal of good sense. At first it appears great nonsense to tell the young men that fat turkeys and kangaroo tails will make them old and weak; but it does not seem silly when we know that it is only a black-fellow's way of providing for old age.

When Goggle Eye found that I never made fun of the laws that he thought so good and wise, he would tell me almost anything that I wanted to know. I was a particular friend of his, but he was not at all pleased with me for bringing Bett-Bett to the homestead; in fact, he was quite cross about it. He said he was her "little bit father", and seemed to think that explained everything. By "little bit father", he meant he was her father's brother, or cousin, or some near relation of his. I really could not see what difference it made, if he was her uncle. I just thought him a very disagreeable old man, and soon forgot all about it.

About a week after, Bett-Bett and I were gardening, and I sent her to the storeroom for a hammer, so that I could fix up some creepers. While she was gone, Goggle Eye came along, and I kept him to help me.

As Bett-Bett came back round the corner of the house, she saw him, and shut her eyes at once; and, of course, the next minute bumped her head on one of the veranda posts.

"Open your eyes, you foolish child," I called, for, with them still tightly shut, she was feeling her way into the house.

"Can't longa Goggle Eye," she answered, and, dropping the hammer on the ground, slipped through the doorway.

"Bring me the hammer, Goggle Eye," I said, turning to him, only to find that his eyes were shut too.

"You silly old thing," I said, "playing baby-tricks," for I thought they were having a game of something like white children's "saw you last"; "bring me that hammer at once, I can't stand on this ladder all day." But he would not move or open his eyes till I told him that Bett-Bett had gone away. When we had finished the creeper, I sent him to the creek for a bucket of water, and called Bett-Bett to come and pull up weeds. She came, but, as she worked, kept one eye on the creek, and, the minute that Goggle Eye's head appeared over the banks, walked towards the house.

"Bett-Bett," I said sternly, "stay here," for I was tired of their silly games.

"Can't, Missus," she answered, stopping, but shutting her eyes, "Goggle Eye little bit father belonga me."

"I can't help that," I said, losing all patience. "Stay here, I want you both."

She stayed; but old Goggle Eye stopped short. He called a lubra, who came and shrieked out something; and Bett-Bett, crying, "Must, Missus, straightfellow", ran round the house to the far side.

"Whatever is the matter with you all?" I said, for I saw now they were not playing a game. "Come here, Goggle Eye, and tell me what this all means. And, Bett-Bett, you stay where you are."

His majesty came, and, sitting down under the veranda, began to tell of one of the strangest customs that the blacks have.

The wise men of the tribe, he explained, have always taught that you must never, never look at any little girl, or lubra, if you are her "little-bit father", or "little-bit brother", or any near relation to her. You must not even speak to her, or listen to her voice, unless she is so far off that you cannot see her face. "That far," said Goggle Eye, pointing to a tree about one hundred yards away.

I was very interested, and asked him what would happen if he broke this law. He answered earnestly: "Spose me look, debbil-debbil take away eye; spose me listen, debbil-debbil take away ear; spose me talk, debbil-debbil take away tongue."

"Dear me," I said, "that would be unpleasant," and, then I asked him why the debbil-debbils didn't come and catch him when he was talking to Maudie. She, I knew, was his sister, and he often spoke to her.

He looked at me very scornfully.

"Him bin come on first time, me bin come on *bee*hind," he said, meaning that she had been born first. She had started first for the world, and he had come on *bee*hind her, and so she was his eldest sister. Evidently, the debbil-debbils allow you to talk to your eldest sister.

When I asked what would happen if he turned a corner suddenly, and, without meaning to, saw his "little-bit-somebody-he-shouldn't'", he answered wisely. "Spose me shut him eye quickfellow, that all right."

"Ebimel Wooloomool," I said, giving him his full name, which always pleased him, "you blackfellows plenty savey."

He smiled a kingly smile at this; and, when I asked him if he would like some flour to make a damper for his supper, said, "Dank you please, Missus," and followed me to the store with a dirty old billy-can in his hand. I gave him some flour, and he carried it down to his camp fire at the creek. In five minutes, he was back with it. "Missus," he said, looking the very picture of misery, "me bin spill him water longa flour; damper no good now;" and he held out his billy-can, and showed me a fearful, sloppy-looking, wet mess.

"Dear me!" I said, "you've put too much water into it."

"You eye," he whined, "me bin spilt him, Missus."

"Never mind," I said, "I'll stiffen it up for you;" and he positively beamed, as I added some more flour. To my surprise, he was back again in a few minutes, saying, "Missus! Me bin spill him nuzzer time."

Then, I saw what he was scheming for: he wanted a big damper.

"You old rogue," I said, "what do you mean, playing tricks on your Missus like this? You know you are doing it on purpose."

He looked so astonished at being found out that I could not help laughing at him, and ended by stiffening his damper for him again.

He grinned into his tin with a very knowing air as he walked away, for he knew quite well that I was amused at his cuteness. When he reached the creek, he turned back to laugh at me; and I called, "Good-bye, Goggle Eye; next time you spoil your damper, you can mend it by yourself."

Chapter 4

"ME KING ALL RIGHT"

HOW to punish Bett-Bett puzzled me more than anything. I often excused her naughty tricks because I thought she knew no better; but, in certain things, I was determined she should obey. The hardest work of all was to stop her from chewing tobacco. When I told her she must not, she smiled sweetly, and, the very first chance she got, begged pieces of "chewbac" from the lubras.

Whipping her was no good, for I couldn't hurt her a little bit. I only seemed to tickle her.

"You too muchee little fellow, Missus," she explained cheerfully.

Any other punishment she got nothing but fun out of.

I gave her sewing to do, and she threaded ticks on to her needle and cotton.

I gave her bread and water for dinner, and she and Sue caught water rats; and Bett-Bett made a fire and cooked them. In fact, they had a splendid picnic.

I took Sue away from her, and chained her up; but the little dog howled so dismally that I was more punished than Bett-Bett.

I shut her in the bathroom by herself. She always called it the "bogey-house"; and she pretended that she was hiding from her enemies, and told Sue awful tales of Willeroo blacks through the cracks under the door.

I could think of nothing else, and was at my wits' end; but the ever-cheerful Bett-Bett continued to chew tobacco.

In despair, I had almost decided to send her back to the bush, when she suggested a fearful punishment herself, of course without meaning to do so.

I was busy painting some shelves one morning, and allowed Bett-Bett to help. She enjoyed it very much, and spattered herself and the ground for yards around with daubs of white. By and by, the heat and the smell of the paint made us both sick. Bett-Bett was very bad, and thought she was going to die. "Me close up deadfellow, Missus," she moaned. Poor little mite! She had never been sick before, and thought that her inside was coming right out. When she was well again, she asked me what had made her so ill; and I said it was the paint.

Next day, she was singing like a young skylark, and chewing away at a piece of tobacco between times.

I was very angry indeed with her, and, deciding to send her "bush", called sternly, "Come here at once, Bett-Bett."

To my surprise she screamed and cried out, "No more, Missus. Me goodfellow; spose you no more make me white-fellow longa paint."

I saw at once what she was afraid of. I had the paint-pot and brush in my hands, and she thought I was going to paint her, to make her sick for punishment. I put them down, and told her to come to me.

"Bett-Bett," I said, "will you be a good girl if I don't paint you this time?"

"You eye, Missus; straightfellow," she sobbed.

"And you will not chew tobacco?" I added.

"No more, Missus; straightfellow," she said, promising "straightfellow", or "honour bright".

"Very well," I said, putting down the brush; "I will not paint you to-day." After that, I had very little trouble with her, for the sight of the paint-pot made her as good as gold.

Bett-Bett loved polishing the silver, particularly the biscuit barrel, which she called "little-fellow billy-can belonga biscuit". One morning, we were busy with it on the veranda, when a shout from the lubras of "Goggle Eye come on" made Bett-Bett scurry round the house like a young rabbit. It was always like this and I began to wish the blacks would be less particular about falling in love with their relations.

As he came along, I saw he had a headache, for he had his wife's waist belt round his head. It is wonderful how quickly a wife's belt or hair-ribbon will charm away a headache. It only fails when she has been up to mischief of any sort. Of course, when a lubra's belt does not cure her husband, he knows she has been naughty, and punishes her as she deserves. The lubras say that the belts do not always speak the truth, but the men say they do. Whichever way it is, they are mean horrid tell-tales.

I told Goggle Eye I was sorry for him; and, as he really looked ill, I gave him a dose of Epsom salts to help the belt cure, and to save Mrs Goggle Eye, the queen, from a beating. He took it, and, then, sitting down under the veranda, nursed his head in his hands—a poor forlorn old king! As he sat with his back to me, I saw a peculiar mark on his shoulder that I had not noticed before, and wondered what it meant.

All blackfellows have thick, ugly scars, up and down and across their bodies and limbs; but Goggle Eye had more than most men.

He told me once that he had made a great many of them himself with a stone knife. After his first corroboree, he had cut himself a good deal to show the tribe that he was a man now, and not afraid of pain. Of course, when any near relatives had died, he had cut himself all over his arms and thighs, to let the spirit know that he was truly sorry. Whenever a blackfellow dies, all his friends cut themselves terribly, because, if the spirit thinks they are not sorry enough, he will very likely send debbil-debbils along to punish them for their hardness of heart.

After a good long "cry cry", the wise men say that the spirit is satisfied—I don't know how they tell—and then everybody rubs hot ashes into the wounds. This heals them very quickly, but it makes the scars into big, ugly weals that will never fade away.

Goggle Eye would talk about this as often as I liked to listen; but, whenever I asked him the meaning of the marks on his back or shoulders, he always answered, "Nuzzing," and either changed the subject or walked away.

Now, when a blackfellow says "nuzzing" like that, it simply means that he is not going to tell, for, when he really does not understand the meaning of a law or custom, he answers, "All day likee that," which means that his fathers did it, and so must he, even if he has forgotten why.

After a while, I saw Goggle Eye feeling among his thick

curly hair for his pipe, and I guessed his headache was better. When he had found it, he filled it ready for a smoke; and I remarked that Mrs Goggle Eye must be a very good lubra. He smiled approval, and said, "My word!" and I thought that, if Mrs Goggle Eye had known everything, she would have given "three cheers for good old Epsom"!

As he sat puffing at his pipe, I wondered if these extra marks had anything to do with his being king, but knew, if I asked questions, he would go away. Instead, I showed him a picture of King Edward VII, and told him that he wore a crown to show that he was king.

He liked this very much, and said so, and then smoked on in silence. At last, pointing to his right arm, he said, "Me king all right".

"My word!" I said, "I think you big mob king."

This pleased the vain old chap immensely.

"Me plenty savey corroboree," he chuckled, rubbing his hands up and down his back; "me savey all about corroboree."

"My word!" I said, to show my great admiration. "Tell me, Goggle Eye," I added.

He hesitated for a while, and then told me that, when a blackfellow has been through a corroboree, his teachers put a mark on him, to show that he understands all about it—a certificate for the examination, I suppose! Of course, a great number of marks means a great deal of knowledge; so it was no wonder that Goggle Eye was proud of his. As he felt his certificates, he chuckled.

"Big mob sit down longa me."

Corroborees are really the books of a tribe, for they have no others. They are not just dancing picnics, as some people think, but lessons, and very hard lessons too, sometimes.

The old men are the teachers, and the head man is the headmaster. They teach the young men all they should know—how to point "death bones", the best way to "sing" people dead, the way to scare debbil-debbils away with bull-roarers and sacred stones, all the laws about marriage, the proper things to eat, how to make rain, and I can't tell what else.

The man who proves in a great many ways that he understands all he should, will one day be king and headmaster. A
black king is not king because his father was so.

As I listened to Goggle Eye's explanation of all this, I
thought how necessary it was to have a wise king, since he
has the care of the special "death-bones", and
"pointing-sticks", and all the sacred charms. No one knows
what terrible things might happen to the tribe if any one
touched these magic charms who did not know how to use
them. Why, he might set a death-bone working, and not be
able to stop it till everybody was dead, or make a mistake and
invite debbil-debbils to come and chivvy everybody about,
when he was meaning to tell them to stay away. It really is
too fearful to think what might happen with a foolish king!

When Goggle Eye stopped talking, I asked him what the
peculiar marks on his shoulder meant.

"What name this one talk, Goggle Eye?" I said, touching it
with my finger.

He was just trying to decide whether it would be all right
to tell a white woman what a black lubra must not hear,
when a wretched little willy-waggletail flew into the veranda
after spiders.

No blackfellow will talk secrets with one of these little birds
about. They say they are the tell-tales of the bush, and are
always spying about, listening for bits of gossip to make
mischief. They call them "jenning-gherries", or mischief
makers, and say they love mischief of all kinds.

"Jenning-gherri come on," said Goggle Eye, pointing to
the little, flitting, flirting bird; and I knew I should hear no
more that day.

"Very well," I said, and, giving him a stick of "chewbac",
sent him back to his camp, and called Bett-Bett.

She came, carrying old "Solomon Isaacs", our white
cockatoo, on her wrist, and asked me why he had no legs.

"But he has," I said; "he has two"; and I touched them to
show her.

"No, Missus," she said, "him hands"; and, to prove that
they were hands, she showed me that he was holding a
biscuit in one of them as he nibbled at it.

"Perhaps he has one leg and one hand," I suggested,

saying that it was his leg he was standing on, and that his hand was the one with the biscuit in it.

That satisfied her; and she was just going off to play, when the miserable creature changed its biscuit into the other claw.

"Him twofellow hands, Missus," she said, coming back to argue it all out again. Fortunately, cocky changed the subject, by passing a few remarks about himself and the weather. Bett-Bett listened for a while, and then informed me that a white man's spirit had jumped into "Solomon Isaacs" when he was born, and that was why he could talk. Billy Muck knew, and had said so.

Before I could think of anything to say, the gramophone in the men's quarters began to play; and she and cocky went off to listen, and I had a little peace. When she came back, she told me that a "white missus" and some whitefellow bosses were in the men's rooms. I wondered whoever they could be, for "white missuses" were rather scarce out-bush; and I hurried over to the quarters to make the lady welcome. I found no one there excepting the stockmen, and they said that no travellers at all had arrived, not even men.

I called Bett-Bett and asked where she had seen the "white missus" and the travellers. She said she hadn't *seen* them, she had only *heard* them singing.

"Him there, Missus," she said, pointing to the gramophone. "I bin hear them sing-sing." Then, she wanted to know how they got in, and what they had to eat. "Which way whitefellow sit down, Missus?" she asked, peering down the funnel of the gramophone, and screwing up her comical little nose as she tried to shut one eye.

"I don't know, Bett-Bett," I said, tired of answering questions. "Come for a walkabout in the paddocks."

Off she scampered to collect the lubras; and, by the time I arrived at the gate, they were all waiting for me with their dilly-bags. I was the pupil, and they were the teachers, and my lessons were most interesting. They tried to teach me the tracks of animals, how to tell if they were new or old, where every bird built its nest, what it built it of, and how many eggs it laid, where to look for crocodile's eggs, and where the bower-bird danced. They knew the tracks of every horse on the run, and every blackfellow of the tribe; and, if they came on a stranger's track, they knew the tribe he belonged to. They tried hard to teach me this, but, try as I would, I could never see any difference, excepting in the size. They were very patient teachers, and I tried my very best; but I suppose I had not a blackfellow's sight for tiny differences, and I failed dismally. I couldn't even learn the tracks of my own lubras.

We all enjoyed the walkabouts, and generally had a good time. This afternoon, we found all sorts of queer prizes, and were coming home with them, when we came on Goggle Eye's tracks, going in our homeward direction.

Bett-Bett simply refused to go any further; and so we had to take a short-cut through the scrub. By bad luck, we came on his majesty himself, just as we came up from the creek. He and Bett-Bett shut their eyes at once, and felt their way with outstretched hand. The path was very narrow; and as they groped about I wondered what would happen if they bumped together. Perhaps debbil-debbils would have come with a whizz, and would have left nothing but a little smoke!

Chapter 5

"GOODFELLOW MISSUS"

IT was washing day, and we were delighted. So would you
have been if you had been there; for, when washing is
done by black lubras, the fun is always fast and furious.

Directly after breakfast, which was usually at sunrise,
there was a wild scramble among the bundles of soiled
clothes, followed by a go-as-you-please race to the billabong,
or water hole. Each lubra, as she ran, looked like a big
snowball with twinkling black legs; while, perched on top of
two or three of the snowballs, sat little shiny-black piccaninnies. Bett-Bett had not had many washing days, and that
accounted for her being last with the stocking-bag. As they
reached the creek, every one dropped her bundle, slipped off
her clothes, and began the day's work by taking a header into
the water.

When I came along, I threw big pieces of soap at them;
and they ducked and dived to dodge it; and, when they came
up, they all ducked and dived again to find it.

"Now," I said, sitting down in the shade of some pandanus
palms, "come and begin, and wash the clothes very clean to-
day."

"You eye, Missus," they all answered, as they scrambled
out up the banks.

"And don't play too much," I added. At least, what I really
did say was, "No more all day play-about."

"You eye, Missus," they all said again, but grinned at one
another. They knew as well as I did that, as long as the work
was well done, I would let them play over it as much as they
liked. You see, I was what white people would call a "bad
mistress"; but the blacks called me "goodfellow Missus", and
would do anything I wanted without a murmur.

They began to sort the clothes very seriously; but, before
half a minute had passed, Bett-Bett and Judy were having a

tug-of-war with a sheet, and everybody else was standing up to scream and shout. It was most exciting, particularly when Bett-Bett suddenly let go, and Judy and sheet took a somersault into the water. As soon as her head came up, every one pelted her with soap, which was the first thing that came handy. Then, of course, they all had to dive in to find it before they could go on with the washing. There is one thing a blackfellow can do perfectly, and that is to make hard work into play.

After all sorts of pranks the clothes were sorted; and, then, every one climbed along an old tree trunk that had fallen into the water. There they sat, six naked lubras in a row, and rubbed and scrubbed and soaped till the clothes looked like wet, frothy balls, and the tree trunk was as slippery as an eel.

As they scrubbed, they kept up a sort of pillow fight with sloppy balls of clothes, knocking each other off the tree, till often there were more lubras in the water than out of it. It certainly is a good plan to take your clothes off on washing day in the tropics.

When everything was washed, the rinsing began; and, if you like real fun, it's a pity you were not there.

The sheets and big things were done first. After they had been carefully spread out on top of the water, every one climbed up the banks and took flying leaps into them. Down they went to the bottom wrapped up in a sheet or table cloth, there to kick and splash till they came to the top again. The first person out of the tangle ducked the others as they came up, or else swam off up the creek with a sheet, which still had one lubra half rolled up in it, and two or three others hanging on to it.

And the babies? The little shiny-black piccaninnies? They just played and rolled over one another on the banks. Every now and then, one would roll into the water, only to swim out again, or to dogpaddle after its mother.

And what were Sue and I doing all this time? We were sitting in the warm, pleasant shade, enjoying the washing circus, and wondering why everybody wasn't drowned three or four times over. Blackfellows evidently can't drown.

When the rinsing was finished, and the clothes were "cooking", as we called boiling, the lubras put on their dresses, and came and sat down near me. They knew well enough that I should have something good for them to eat. Canned fruit or sweet biscuit were always voted "goodfellow"; but there was nothing so good as treacle—"blackfellow sugarbag", you know.

It was treacle to-day; and, as every one lay laughing, smoking and resting, the tin was passed round and round. Very thin, bony, black fingers went in, and very fat, juicy, black fingers came out, and were put into grinning, happy mouths, Sue getting a lick from Bett-Bett's, every turn.

"Do you like washing days, Bett-Bett?" I asked, as she sat waiting for another dig into the tucker.

"My word!" she grinned, dragging a crawling piccaninny from the treacle tins by its legs.

Biddy interfered at once, by putting the baby's little fists into the sticky stuff. It was her piccaninny, you see, and engaged to be married to Goggle Eye!

"Biddy," I said, as she bent forward to push the baby's treacly fingers into its open mouth, "haven't you cut your hair rather short?" I had noticed the day before how pretty and curly it was, but now it was like a convict's.

"Goggle Eye bin talk," she answered, meaning that he had told her to cut it. That was all she said, for she knew I would understand, you see; she was Goggle Eye's mother-in-law, and so all her hair or most of it belonged to him. Whenever it grew nice and long, he told her to cut it off and make him some string; and she had to obey. It was a bit of a nuisance being a mother-in-law.

I'm sure Billy Muck often wished that I was his mother-in-law, for he saw me drying my hair in the sun one day, and knew it was nice and long.

"My word, Missus!" he said, "big mob hair sit down longa you cobra," meaning, "what a lot of hair you've got on your head." Just think what lovely belts and things he would have ordered me to make, if only I had been his mother-in-law! But I wasn't; and I'm sure Billy Muck was the only person who was really sorry about it.

Bett-Bett was Jimmy's mother-in-law. Of course, she wasn't married yet, only engaged to Billy Muck; but that did not matter. She was Jimmy's mother-in-law, and, when she did grow up and have a piccaninny, it was to be his wife. In the meantime, nobody else could have her spare hair.

Common string is all right for common things, but charms and belts and special things must have hair-string, or they won't keep debbil-debbils away properly. This way of having the mother-in-law's hair divides the hair of the tribe very evenly, as every man has two or three mothers-in-law.

When the treacle was finished, Sue began to dig a hole to lie down in. As she dug she scratched up a little red and yellow worm. With a yell, all the lubras grabbed hold of the poor little dog, and nearly pulled her in pieces in their hurry to get her away. Then, they all shrieked, and jabbered, and pointed at the scraggy wriggling thing, while Sue sat just where they had thrown her, too astonished to move.

"Well," I said, "that worm won't eat us, will it?"

"Him Rainbow debbil-debbil," they shrieked, shaking with fear at Sue's narrow escape.

"Nonsense," I said; "it's only a worm."

But they insisted that it was a baby rainbow.

"Him piccaninny rainbow all right," they cried.

"Don't be so silly," I said, and bent forward to pick it up in my fingers; but they yelled their very best at this, and caught hold of my arms.

"Very well," I said; "come and tell me all about it, and what a rainbow is doing down here."

We all moved to a place of safety; and they explained that what we call hailstones are really rainbow's eggs, and that they fall on the ground and hatch into worms—I mean baby rainbows! The wise men of the tribe say it is so,—and, of course, they know everything. This is how they found out:—

Many years ago, a great number of hailstones fell, which is a very unusual thing on the Roper River; every one was afraid to touch them, for no one knew what they were; so the people looked at them in wonder until they had all burrowed into the ground—"melted", the whites call it! Now, this looked very strange; and, after a great deal of talking, one very brave old blackfellow dug a hole to see what was happening underneath. Instead of hailstones, he found brightly-coloured little creatures—worms, of course— creeping about in the wet earth. Every one looked at them, and said they were very like little rainbows, and that they must have hatched out of the hailstones, which could be nothing else but rainbow's eggs. Of course, everybody knew, before, that the grown-up rainbow is a debbil-debbil snake who lives in the Roper River, and that he kindly takes care of the fish supply for the blackfellows. He is very good, and allows you to catch as many fish as you can eat; but he can't bear to see any wasted. He gets dreadfully angry if he knows that any one has been spearing fish for fun, and leaving them to rot on the banks. I don't wonder at his anger, for, if everybody did that, soon there would be no fish left.

He and his wife often go for a stroll together in the sky. He is red and yellow in colour, and she is blue. It is while they are strolling about that they catch the guilty people. They pick them up before they can say "Jack Robinson", and carry them off to the Roper River, and feed the fish upon their bodies.

When I heard that the worm was really a baby rainbow, I felt very thankful that I had not hurt it, for it would be awful to be chased by an angry mother debbil-debbil rainbow!

After such a narrow escape, we thought that under the palm trees was not a very safe place, so we went and finished the washing, and spread everything out to dry; and then began the fun of chasing grasshoppers, lest they should settle on the clothes and eat holes in them. As the lubras darted about, here and there, the scene looked more like a Sunday-school picnic than a washing day. It certainly sounded like one.

Blacks are blacks, and whites are whites; and, as I looked from the merry black faces to the clean white clothes, I knew their way of working was best—for them, at any rate; so I kept on being a "bad mistress" and "goodfellow Missus", and we all enjoyed washing-day—all except Sue! The fun was too wet for her, and, besides, it always made her think of worms—rainbows, I mean!

My friends used to wonder why I was not lonely, a hundred miles from any white neighbours; and I used to wonder if anyone could be lonely with a perpetual circus and variety show on the premises.

Chapter 6

THE "DEBBIL-DEBBIL" DANCE

WE were going to a debbil-debbil dance. The king himself had brought the invitation to me in the garden.

"Missus," he said, "spose you come longa debbil-debbil dance, eh?"

"No, thank you, Goggle Eye," I answered. "Might it the debbil-debbils carry me off?"

He roared with delight at my joke, and explained, "This one gammon debbil-debbil."

"Oh, well," I said, "if you are only going to have gammon debbil-debbils at your party, I'll come."

"Dank you please, Missus," he said, guessing at my meaning.

Then, he asked if I would go and see the dancers being dressed for the performance; and I said I would, for I always like to see a blackfellow getting into clothes of any sort. I went in the afternoon and watched, noticing directly I arrived that two of the gentlemen had headaches. Poor Bett-Bett had to stay at home because of Goggle Eye. It took two or three men to dress one dancer properly. They laid him flat on his back to begin with, and pricked him all over with sharp stones and pieces of glass. As they sat pricking Billy Muck, they reminded me of cooks pricking sausages for frying.

When little beads of blood oozed out, they were smeared all over the man, face and all. Then tiny white cockatoo's feathers were stuck up and down and round and round him, and the blood was used as gum. They made wonderful patterns all over his body, back and front, ending up with twirli-gigs down both arms and legs. The gum stuck splendidly; if you want to find out how well blood sticks, cut your finger and tie it up with cotton wool.

The face also was covered with down, and a huge helmet,

with a long horn of emu's quills, was fixed firmly on the head.

The finishing touch was a wreath of leaves at each ankle. Ordinary leaves were not nearly good enough for a debbil-debbil dance, so special magic men, and some extra special lubras, went out-bush, and bewitched a tree with all sorts of capers, and prancings, and pointings, and magic. Then, they gathered some leaves, and carried them in for the dancers to wear. It was wise to do this, for then nothing could possibly go wrong with the corroboree.

By the time everybody was dressed, they looked truly awful; and I pleased them immensely by pretending to be frightened of these "gammon debbil-debbils".

I begged them not to carry me off; and they shouted with delight, and waved sticks at me, and danced about, and said, "Me debbil-debbil all right, me real fellow"; and tried hard to look fierce in spite of their grins. Poor old Goggle Eye was nearly bent double with laughing; for, if there is one thing a blackfellow likes better than anything else, it is a "play-about", as they call fun and nonsense.

After supper we arrived at the party—four white men and a woman! The moon had risen, and innumerable fires were flickering among the tres; and everything was ready to begin.

His majesty the king and the lords in waiting received us with a broad grin. Then they each stood on one leg and chuckled. Whenever a blackfellow has nothing better to do with his legs, he always stands on one, and lays the sole of the other foot against his knee, making his legs look exactly like the figure 4, with an extra long stem. I think our hosts chuckled because they did not know what else to do.

I thought, perhaps, that some of the old men might not be too pleased to have me at the party, and I said so to Goggle Eye. "Me bin talk," he answered, with a wave of his hand that showed that he was in every way king.

The lubras were resting near, ready to sing and beat time for the dancers. I think, in the excitement of getting ready for the party, they must have forgotten to dress themselves, for they had nothing on, excepting a few feathers and things that had been left over from the men's costumes.

181

A great big place had been cleared of all sticks and stones; and the whole tribe and their visitors stood round it, armed with spears. This particular patch of ground was near to a very sacred stone, and, unless this corroboree was danced there, it would not be much good. That was why it was so near the homestead.

The lubras began to sing a strange, weird song, and a few blackfellows sounded the bamboo trumpets; and then the dancing commenced. It was very tiring both to dancers and onlookers. Up every one lifted a leg, and down every one stamped a leg and gave a fearful yell; then Billy Muck, who was a little way off from the dancers, gave a jump and a little run — and that was the first figure!

Up went the legs again, and down went the legs again; we heard another yell; and Billy Muck gave another jump and run — and that was the second figure.

The third figure was just the same, and so were the fourth, fifth, sixth, and as many more as you liked to count.

"What name, Goggle Eye?" I asked, meaning that I wished him to explain it to me.

He said this was to teach the young men of the tribe that debbil-debbils would chase them if they did wrong. You see the dancers were supposed to be fearful debbil-debbils, and were pretending to catch Billy Muck. They kept acting this object lesson for nearly two hours, and the old men explained what it meant to the pupils; but I got very tired of it.

I amused myself with watching the lubras as they sang and swayed about, noticing, after a while, that Bett-Bett was among them, singing and swaying and having a really good all-round time. She must have crept along after us, but, as she was sitting with her back to Goggle Eye, and his eyes were fixed on the dancers, I suppose it was all right. Anyway, no debbil-debbils came along.

Suddenly there was a wild, weird shriek, quite near us. It came so unexpectedly, and was so unearthly, that I jumped and thought of Bett-Bett and Goggle Eye and debbil-debbils. Everything was so strange around us, that I believe, if they *had* been carried off, I should have looked on without any surprise.

Every one stopped singing and dancing, and Goggle Eye

whispered that it was the voice of the great sacred bullroarer, calling to say that it was time to take the young boys away into the bush. There were four or five of them at this corroboree, and they were to be taught their first real lesson to-night. After it, they would be kept away by themselves, in a special camp out-bush, and when they came back they would be treated as men.

The bullroarer is a spindle-shaped piece of sacred stone, and, when swung round and round above the head with a string, it shrieks and screams and groans. Only the wise men may touch it; and, of course, they are the only people who really understand all it says. Every man has an imitation bullroarer, which he often swings to make it speak; for this pleases the debbil-debbil spirit of the sacred bullroarer. After the voice of the debbil-debbil had spoken, a few of the very important people began to slip away to prepare for the real corroboree; for the dance was only a sort of introduction.

Goggle Eye gave us a hint to go home, and we took it; we had our revolvers with us, but it is always wise to take a blackfellow's hint, particularly when he says that a very secret, sacred corroboree is about to begin.

As we said good-night, Goggle Eye and old Jimmy presented me with two extraordinary-looking broad flat sticks with black streaks and white dots on them.

"Him goodfellow stick, that one," they explained; and it was not till some time after that I found out they had paid me the very highest compliment a blackfellow can pay a "white missus", for no ordinary woman is allowed even to look at these sticks. I often wish I had said "Dank you, please," a little more politely and gratefully for them.

A few mornings after the debbil-debbil dance, I saw Goggle Eye hide something behind an ant-bed, and then walk up to the house. When he saw me, he asked if he might go-bush for a walkabout, as he was needed at a corroboree at Duck Creek. I asked him how long he would be away, and he said, "One fellow, two fellow, big mob sleep," meaning that he would be away for a great number of nights, or sleeps, before he had finished his business.

Then he showed me a little bit of stick with notches on it, and said it was a blackfellow's letter-stick, or, as he called it, a "yabber stick". It was round, not flat like most other letters, and was an invitation to a corroboree; and there were notches on it explaining what sort of corroboree it was, and saying that it was to be held at Duck Creek. There was some other news marked on it which Goggle Eye told me; and, then, he sold it to me for some "chewbac", and I have it today; and anyone may see it who wishes. Then he sat down for a yarn, and I asked him why Jackaroo would never eat turkey, and why he always said he mustn't eat it because it was his brother.

Goggle Eye said that was quite right, and that turkeys *were* Jackaroo's brothers, for her and turkeys both had turkey spirits inside them, and, of course, no one could eat his brother. "Everybody has the spirit of some animal inside him," he said. "If you have a kangaroo spirit, you belong to the kangaroo family, or totem; and you must not eat your brothers the kangaroos. If you have a snake's or an eagle's spirit, you belong to the snake's or eagle's family, and do not eat your brothers the snakes or the eagles. Whatever spirit you may have, you belong to its family, or totem, and they are your brothers, and you do not eat them. All day likee that," said old Goggle Eye.

I asked him how each person knew which spirit was inside him, and he said that their mothers told them. You see, she knew where she had "caught" her piccaninny. If a piccaninny came to her in a snake's-spirit country, it had a snake spirit, and, if it came to her in a kangaroo's-spirit country, it had a kangaroo's spirit, and so on. It all depended on where you came from. It didn't matter what your mother and father were; your mother might have a snake's spirit; and your father might have a wallaby's spirit; but, if you came from a cockatoo's-spirit country, you had to have a cockatoo's spirit; just as peaches come from peach trees, and plums from plum trees.

Near the homestead was the kangaroo's-spirit country, and, of course, all the children who came from there had kangaroo's spirits; but those who came from the Long Reach, not a mile away, had honey-bee's spirits.

Goggle Eye said you learnt all this at corroborees. At the kangaroo corroboree, the head man of the kangaroo men dressed up, and pretended to be a kangaroo. After a little while, he suddenly changed into a man, and stood up, and looked like one, and said he really was a man now. Then he dug a little hole, and poured water into it. After this, he called a number of kangaroo-spirit men to him, and offered them the flesh of a kangaroo; but they said it was the flesh of their brother, and that they must not eat it.

The wise men then explained that this was to teach them that once, long, long ago, a big giant kangaroo had come up to the Roper River country, and changed himself into a man. When he got thirsty, he dug a hole and water flowed up into it for him to drink, and that was really how the homestead billabong came.

After a while, this kangaroo man amused himself with making spirits; but, as he was really a kangaroo spirit himself, he could only make kangaroo spirits. By and by, he noticed that some of them had got into kangaroos and some into little black children; so he called them all together, and told them that they all had kangaroo spirits, and were really brothers, and must never eat one another.

After this explanation, all the young men of the tribe understood, of course, that they must not eat their animal brothers. At honey-bee corroborees the history of the honey bees was taught, and at each animal corroboree the history of each totem, for corroborees, as I said before, were the schools of the blackfellows.

Goggle Eye, you see, was one of the wisest of the blackfellows, and, as he said this was true, perhaps it was. I know that, out-bush, we had seen portraits of the great-great-greatest grandfather of the Kangaroo men, and of the Fish and of the Iguana people, drawn on rocks and trees by the artists of the tribe.

When Goggle Eye had finished his history lesson, I gave him some sugar in a calico bag, and he tied it carefully round his neck. He said the ants couldn't get at it there. Then, I gave him a red handkerchief and some tobacco and hair pins. The blacks love hairpins; they find them so useful to dig up grubs with.

As Goggle Eye still stayed about, I said goodbye, and turned to leave him.

"Missus," he called after me, "me bin lose 'em pipe."

Something in his face made me suspicious. I went and looked behind the ant-bed to see what he had hidden, and found his pipe.

"Here you are, Goggle Eye," I said; "me bin good fellow, me bin find him."

I expected him to look ashamed of himself; but he didn't—not a little bit! He sat down, and laughed till the tears rolled down his cheeks at the joke of it all; and that made me laugh too. Of course, in the end, Goggle Eye got a new pipe, and went off "bush" with it in his mouth. As he went through the gate, he turned and waved it at me; and that was the last time I saw him looking merry-hearted and happy.

Chapter 7

"MUMMA A" AND "MUMMA B"

I HAD taught Sue some tricks — to beg, shake hands, and pretend to be "deadfellow" — and Bett-Bett was wild with delight.

"My word, Missus!" she cried excitedly, "Sue plenty savey, him close up whitefellow." Then, seizing her darling in her arms, she darted off to the humpy to show her to the lubras, singing as she ran, "Sue plenty savey; him savey, him savey!"

When they came back, I was reading, and paid no attention to them.

After a while, Bett-Bett said, "What name, Missus?"

I looked up to see her staring very hard at me, with a puzzled look on her face.

"What name, what?" I said, wondering what she meant.

She did not answer at once, but picked up a book, and held it so close to her face that it almost touched her nose; then, staring at it till her eyes nearly jumped out of her head, she said, "What name, likee this? likee this? likee this?"

I laughed at her and said, "Bett-Bett, I hope I don't look like that when I read," for she looked a fearful little object. But I saw what was puzzling her; she could not understand why I sat looking so earnestly at little black marks on paper.

I explained that books could talk like "paper yabbers", as she called letters — papers that "yabber", or talk, you know.

Then I got a little ABC book, and some paper and pencils, and told her I would teach her to read; but it was easier said than done.

We began with the capital letters. Bett-Bett repeated "A" after me, and made it on paper, and then wanted to know what it was. Was it tucker, or an animal, or somebody's name?

I said it was a mark, and was called A. "What did the

mark say?" she asked. "What name him yabber, Missus, this one A?" were the exact words she used.

You remember that, on Goggle Eye's lettersticks, marks were cut, and that every mark had a special meaning; so Bett-Bett was sure that "A" must be the name of something.

I couldn't explain it, so told her that, when she knew all the names of the letters, I would tell her what they meant; and we went on to B.

The sound reminded Bett-Bett of bees and honey. "Him sugar bag," she said, grinning at her cleverness. Then, she made it in the dust with her toe, and told Sue—"Him talk sugar bag, this one B." Sue looked wise and smelt it, and then offered to shake hands all round. And that was our first day's lesson.

Next day, we learnt a few more letters, and capital "I" was christened "This one eye," as a smutty little finger tapped Bett-Bett's eye.

A day or two afterwards, "W" was noticed on ahead.

"Missus," she cried, pointing to it, "I bin find bullocky."

"What name?" I said, wondering what was coming now.

"Bullocky," she repeated, nodding her head wisely at "W"; and, then, "him all day sit down longa bullocky."

Then, I understood her. "W" was the letter of the station brand, and she had seen it on the cattle, and remembered it.

We plodded on day after day; and, every day, Bett-Bett gave me a hint that she did not think much of the lessons.

"Me knock up longa paper yabber, Missus; him silly fellow," she kept saying.

I took no notice of her remarks, but I think the only thing either of us learnt was patience.

The capitals were bad enough, but, when we began the little letters, things got dreadfully mixed.

"Missus! this one no more 'A'," said Bett-Bett, worrying over the small "a".

I told her it was a little "a"; but she insisted that it wasn't, and, to prove it, showed me big "A", and, of course, they were not a bit alike. To try and make her understand a little better, I said that capital "A" was the mother, and little "a" the baby. This pleased her very much.

"Me savey," she said, pointing from one to the other. "This

one mumma; this one piccaninny." Then, she wanted to know the baby's name; what its mother called it. She said that piccaninnies always had different names from their mummas.

Of course, I didn't know the baby's name, and told her so. Very often, there was no answer to Bett-Bett's questions; but, somehow, she always made me feel that it was my fault, or my ignorance, that there wasn't. After this, we said: "Mumma A *and* piccaninny belonga mumma A; mumma B *and* piccaninny belonga mumma B; and so on to the very end of the alphabet, till our tongues ached.

On the page Bett-Bett was learning from, every little letter was next to its mother. Little "a" next mumma "A", and little "b" next mumma "B"; but, in the reading lessons, little letters were walking about by themselves. One day, she noticed this when she was looking through the book.

"Look, Missus!" she cried excitedly. "Piccaninny belonga mumma 'A' sit down by meself." Then, she scolded the little letter dreadfully. "You go home longa you mumma," she said, in a loud, angry voice, shaking her finger at it. But small "a" never moved; it just sat and looked at her; and Bett-Bett told me that it was "cheeky fellow longa me", meaning that it was not at all afraid of her. "My word, you badfellow all right," she went on, scolding hard; "debbil-debbil catch you dreckly." As little "a" took no notice of this awful threat, she turned back to tell "mumma A" about its naughty piccaninny. There she found that the little letter had slipped home, and was sitting quietly at its mother's knee. She was so pleased about it.

"Look, Missus," she said, coming to show me; "him goodfellow now."

"It's a very good little letter," I said, "and you're a good little lubra, and may go and help to water the garden."

She gave a piercing, ear-splitting yell of delight, and called Sue; but, before she went, asked me if the little "a" in my book was good.

I said "Yes", and hoped I was telling the truth; as far as I knew, they *were* good. I suppose Bett-Bett thought I spent hours sending naughty piccaninnies home to their mummas. Almost before I knew that she and Sue had gone, I heard shrieks from the vegetable garden, and yells of "Missus! Missus!" and Biddy and Rosey came running through the open gate. "What's the matter now?" I said, as I went to meet them, for there was always something fresh happening.

"Missus!" they panted, "Bett-Bett bin kill Rolly; him bin kill him longa quart-pot."

I waited to hear no more, but ran as fast as I could to the garden, with the lubras at my heels, hoping that Rolly was not really dead, but perhaps only stunned.

The first thing I saw was Bett-Bett and Rolly quietly watering the garden.

"You naughty lubras," I said, turning sharply to Biddy and Rosey; "what do you mean, telling such wicked stories? What name you all day gammon, eh?" for I was very angry indeed with them: they had given me a terrible fright.

To my surprise, they insisted that Bett-Bett had killed Rolly.

"Straightfellow, Missus," they said earnestly; "Bett-Bett bin kill Rolly all right." Even Rolly herself said, "Bett-Bett bin kill me, Missus! Straightfellow, me no more talk gammon."

But Bett-Bett herself said nothing; she kept on watering the garden, with one eye on the Missus. I suppose she was thinking of the paint-pot.

"You silly things," I said, feeling very puzzled, for they were in deadly earnest. "Can't you see that Rolly is not deadfellow?"

At this, everybody shouted with laughter. At last, they understood the Missus and her anger. "Me no more bin talk kill him *deadfellow*," they screamed. "Me bin talk *kill him longa quart-pot*."

So they had. I remembered now; and, as usual, it was my fault. Nobody but the Missus ever seemed to do anything wrong. I should have understood their funny pidgin English better. To "kill" only means to hit, or prick, or thump; but to put someone to death is to "kill deadfellow". Only that morning, Bett-Bett had said, when her needle pricked her finger, "My word, Missus! neenel bin kill finger belonga me."

I called Bett-Bett and asked her what she had been doing.

She said that when she got to the garden, she had found Rolly using her favourite quart-pot to sprinkle water with. She had asked for it; but Rolly would not give it up, so she had hammered her with another to make her. "Me bin long time kill him," she said, but, as Rolly wouldn't give in, Biddy and Rosey had run for me to stop the quarrel. Of course, when they saw me coming, Rolly had dropped the quart-pot and Bett-Bett had stopped "killing her", and they had both gone on with the watering.

That was all. Such a fuss about nothing! I took the leaky old quart-pot from them, and, sending them all back to their work, sat down under the banana clump.

In five minutes, they were shouting merrily, and playing practical jokes on one another; for, with a blackfellow, as soon as a quarrel is over, it is forgotten.

Watering the garden is something like washing day—plenty of fun and water, and very few clothes.

The fun began when Rosey went to fill her bucket. Judy and Biddy caught her by the heels, and sent her flying into the billabong. As she scrambled out, they "showered" her from full buckets and quart-pots, and then ran screaming and spluttering up the banks. Rosey waited her chance, and soon sent Biddy headlong into the pumpkin bed, with a bucket of water after her. Judy screamed with delight at this, only to get a full quart of water into her gaping, shouting mouth. Bett-Bett had thrown it; but, in her hurry to dodge the watermelon that Judy flung back at her, tripped and sat down in her own bucket of water, and Rolly got the watermelon in the middle of her back. It broke into a dozen pieces, and, of course, that meant a wild scramble for the red, juicy fruit; and, then, everybody sat down to enjoy it properly, and flipped the pips into each other's faces.

They were playing these pranks every night, and kept the water flying in all directions; but as it always ended by falling somewhere among the vegetables, the garden was a great success for it was always well watered. As I said before, a blackfellow sees no sense in working when play will do as well. As I sat watching them, and expecting a shower bath every minute or two, Jimmy came along, whittling a bit of stick.

"What name, Jimmy?" I asked.

"Yabber stick," he answered shortly, and squatting down near me, cut busily on.

"What name him talk?" I said, for that was the way to ask him what message he was cutting.

Jimmy spat thoughtfully on the ground and looked wise, but said nothing; and I saw I would have to flatter him a little before he would tell me much. He dearly loved to be important, and generally had to be coaxed and flattered a good deal.

"My word, Jimmy!" I said; "you plenty savey. Me no more savey yabber stick." This pleased him immensely, so I added, "I think you close up savey whitefellow paper-yabber, Jimmy."

He grinned from ear to ear with delight, and, then, taking the letter stick in one hand, and pointing at it with his pipe, began to instruct the poor ignorant Missus.

Jimmy looked very gay to-day. He had a small Union Jack flag hanging from his belt like a little apron. His dilly-bag was decorated with strips of red turkey twill and bunches of white feathers, and he had tied a little mussel shell on to the end of every bobbing curl of his head, and they danced and jingled as he talked.

"This one stick him yabber boomerang," he began, pointing to a little mark like a V drawn sideways—so 〉

I looked carefully at it; and, then, Jimmy spat once or twice before he explained that, when that mark "sat down" on a "yabber stick", it meant you were being asked for the loan of a boomerang. Then he spat again, and took a few pulls at his pipe, and looked very wise indeed.

"My word, Jimmy!" I murmured.

Jimmy grinned, and then showed me all sorts of marks which he drew in the dirt with his finger. Signs for spears, food, wet season, people's names, white men, names of places, and many other things. He ended up with "chewbac" and his own name. He was very particular that I should remember "chewbac". Then, he showed me a letter he had just received from Terrible Billy at Daly Waters. Jimmy's lubra Nellie was his mother-in-law; and this letter was to say that he was quite out of hair-string, and would Nellie kindly cut her hair and send some. All this was told in a winding line, twisting round and round the stick, and a short stroke to end with, and, then, Nellie's name, which read, "String—long—hair—Nellie". Then came some gossip—one thick ring which said "walkabout", and a mark which was Monkey's name. Now "Monkey" was a Willeroo, and always up to mischief; so it was very kind of Billy to warn Jimmy that he was having a walkabout. Perhaps he was afraid that Monkey might run off with his mother-in-law, hair and all.

Jimmy's lecture was suddenly cut short by shrieks from the lubras of—"Cheeky fellow snake sit down. Cheeky fellow snake, Missus."

Jimmy ran to the cucumber bed, all his little shells bobbing and jingling as he went, and, quick as a flash, caught the snake by the tail, and broke its back by cracking it like a stockwhip, and then flinging it from him. In case of accidents, the lubras and I had all scurried in behind the bananas. It is just as wise to be out of the way when poisonous snakes are flying through the air; for, of course, a "cheeky fellow snake" means a poisonous one.

After a good look at the horrid creature, we all went back to the house, leaving Jimmy to finish his letter. As we went, I saw that Bett-Bett was carrying the snake on the end of a long stick.

"What name, Bett-Bett?" I asked.

"Me put him longa Nellie bed," she answered, grinning and going down to the humpy. Nellie was out, and Bett-Bett arranged the snake in a very lifelike position on her bluey. Of course, in about an hour, we heard shrieks of "Cheeky fellow snake sit down longa Nellie bed". The black world flew to the rescue; and Nellie was unmercifully teased for being frightened of a "deadfellow snake"; while Bett-Bett grinned secretly and impishly.

Next morning, Nellie brought me a "yabber stick" cut all over with "chewbac" signs, and with Jimmy's name at the bottom. I now understood why he wanted me to remember this sign, for the letter read—"Jimmy wants a big mob of tobacco". I saw the old rascal grinning through the trees to see if I was understanding his joke. "Jimmy," I said, calling him up, "you're the cutest, cleverest old blackfellow that ever was born, and you ought to be king. You know exactly how to manage your Missus."

Jimmy seemed to think this was a compliment and chuckled as I threw him a couple of sticks of "chew-bac". He picked them up with his toes and passed them into his hands without bending his back. As he and Nellie walked away, I saw that she had obeyed her son-in-law and had cut her hair.

Chapter 8

A "WALKABOUT"

"GO and lay 'em egg, silly fellow you. Go and lay 'em egg, silly fellow you," shouted Bett-Bett in a sing-song voice, and she and Sue dodged between an old broody hen and the tool-house.

Bett-Bett had no patience with broody hens; she seemed to think they were wasting their time; particularly when, like this one, they would try to hatch chickens out of nails. "Come for a walkabout, Bett-Bett," I called; "I am going to the Long Reach for some water-lilies."

"You eye, Missus," she shrieked in answer, still dodging and dancing after old broody.

As I went for my hat and revolver, I heard her shrill little voice up at its highest pitch inviting every one within hearing to come with us. By the time I reached the sliprails, there were six or eight lubras, a few piccaninnies, and about twenty dogs at my heels, and I felt like a Pied Piper of Hamelin.

We had a very merry walkabout that afternoon. Everything that could, seemed to happen. Just as we crossed the creek outside the sliprails, the fun began, and Sue got into trouble. She picked up the scent of a bandicoot, and was darting off to run its tracks, when her black legs were seized by Bett-Bett, and she got a ringing box on the ears.

She deserved it, for she was actually going to run tracks away from the direction in which the animal's toes were pointing. She should have noticed at once that the scent grew stronger the other way. Good little bush dogs always do. Bett-Bett quickly put her right, and off every one scampered after her, till she stopped at a hollow log. Bett-Bett and Sue arrived first, and everybody else immediately after, only to find that the bandicoot was not at home, for there were newer tracks leading out again. Sue simply couldn't believe

195

it, and scratched wildly till stopped by another box on the ears. I was last to arrive, but came up just as the dogs scented the new tracks; and, very soon afterwards, the unfortunate bandicoot was hanging from one of the lubras' belts.

The Long Reach is a beautiful, twelve-mile-long waterhole, full of crocodiles and water lilies. It begins about three-quarters of a mile from the homestead; but we took nearly two hours to get there, for we zigzagged through the scrub, and had ever so many exciting hunts, several natural history lessons, and a peep into every nook and cranny we passed to see how birds, beasts, and insects made their nests.

Do you think if any one had seen me—a white woman with a revolver and cartridges at her belt, hunting with a mob of lubras—that they would have imagined that I was at school?

We had a strange lubra with us—one I had not seen before. I noticed that she dragged a leafy branch after her wherever she went. I asked her why she did this, and she told me that she had run away from her husband, and didn't want him to find her.

"Me knock up longa me boy," she said, "him all day krowl-krowl,"—she meant growl.

You see, he would, of course, travel about, looking at any tracks he came on, trying to find her; and so Murra-weedbee—for that was her name—dragged this branch along after her like a rake, to scratch and mix up her tracks, so that nobody could possibly recognise them. Instead of disguising herself, she disguised her footprints.

When, at last, we arrived at the Reach, the lubras went into the water to gather lilies, and Bett-Bett and I poked about in the sand after crocodiles' eggs.

She would never hunt for these eggs on the Roper River. She said the sea-going crocodiles were "cheeky fellow", and would "round you up" if you did.

Then, she told me a thrilling experience she had had once. She was scratching about on the banks of the Roper River, and found a nest of eggs. She was just gathering them up, when she heard a splash, and saw the mother crocodile swimming across the river. "My word! me race quickfellow," she said; and she looked terribly frightened as she remembered how nearly she had been caught. She had evidently just seen the mother in time. Crocodiles in the land-locked pools were "frightened fellow", she said, so it was always safe to take their eggs. They were too timid to "round you up".

She scratched around for a while, and then told me that "crocodiles all day knock up longa egg", meaning they could not be bothered with looking after them, but just left them to hatch in the sand, keeping one eye on them in case of accidents.

Bett-Bett was only eight years old, but what she didn't know about natural history was hardly worth knowing; but, then, she had the best teacher in all the world—Mother Nature. She never wearies her pupils, but punishes them pretty severely when they make mistakes. The most certain way of learning that crocodiles watch their eggs, and that sea-going crocodiles are fiercest, is to be chased by the mother. Bett-Bett certainly knew her lessons, which is more than can be said of many white children. They were only timid crocodiles in the Long Reach; and, after a long hunt in the sand, we came on a nest of eggs. Bett-Bett broke one, and, there, all ready to hatch, we saw a tiny crocodile, curled up like a clock spring. These eggs are very curious; they seem to have two distinct shells, and look exactly like a hen's egg inside a duck's egg.

The eggs we found were of no use for eating, so Bett-Bett covered them up again, keeping only one out, which she said would hatch next day. I asked her what she was going to do with it; but she only grinned impishly, and I knew she was up to some of her pranks.

As we went back to the lubras, we came on an old blackfellow, fishing in the water-hole. He was standing on a tree trunk holding a spear, poised ready to dart at the first fish that came up to breathe. I called to him, but he took no notice; and the lubras laughed, and said he was "Old No-More-Hearem", and threw stones at him.

I called to them to stop, for I was afraid he would be angry with us; but they said he was deaf and dumb, and that everyone threw stones at him when they wanted him to look round. I said this was rather painful for "No-More-Hearem";

but they seemed to think it was his own fault for being deaf and dumb. Two or three stones hit him, and he turned round. Then, they all began talking in the sign language, asking the news and answering questions. The blacks' sign language is very perfect. They have a sign for every bird, beast, fish, person, place and action. They have long talks without uttering a word. There are many times when a blackfellow must not speak, unless by signs. For instance, if he is mourning for a near relative, or has just come from a very special corroboree. Often, he must keep silent for weeks, and occasionally, for months; and it is because of this and many other reasons that the sign language is so perfect. Every one can speak it; and every one does so when hiding in the bush from enemies, to avoid the danger of their voices being heard.

It is very wonderful, but, then, the blacks are wonderful. To have any idea of how wonderful they are, you must live among them, going in and out of their camps, and having every one of them for a friend. Just living in a house that happens to be in a blackfellow's country is not living among blacks, although some people think it is.

We told old "No-More-Hearem" to come for tobacco, and, then, we all started for home. Before very long, Bett-Bett saw a bees' nest, and, shouting out, "sugar bag", as she thrust her crocodile's egg into my hand, she began climbing a tree. Everybody climbed up after her to have a look, and, then, down again for sticks, and up again for the honey, poking at it with the long sticks, and hanging on anywhere and everywhere like a troop of black monkeys. I waited below; and the dogs, thinking it might perhaps be a 'possum hunt, danced about and barked, ready to catch anything that came down. When all the honey was gathered into broad leaves, we went on home, calling in at the blacks' camp when we got there. There were a few old men at home, among them Billy Muck and an old bush blackfellow, or "myall". Billy noticed at once that I had some tobacco and matches, and began puzzling his brains to think of some way of getting a piece of tobacco without asking for it. To tease him, I gave all the others a bit, and pretended to start for home, as though I had forgotten him. Suddenly, a bright idea struck him.

"Missus," he called after me, "spose me make you blackfellow fire, eh?"

I said I would very much like to see him make a blackfellow's fire, and asked him where his matches were.

He grinned broadly at this, and showed me two pieces of stick, with a little notch cut in one. I pretended to be very ignorant, and asked what they were for.

Instead of answering, he squatted down on the ground, and, picking a few tiny pieces of dry grass, laid them in a little heap beside him; then, laying one of his sticks on the ground near the grass, he held it firmly in place with his foot, and, fixing one end of the other stick in the little notch or groove, twirled it quickly between the palms of his hands. In a few seconds, some tiny, tiny, redhot ashes, no bigger than grains of sand, were rubbed out. Billy bent over them, and blew softly till the grass took fire; then, he stood on one leg and chuckled; and stuck his fire sticks behind his ears.

It was all so quickly and cleverly done that I gave him two sticks of tobacco for payment, which pleased him immensely; but the old myall looked as though he were wondering what Billy had done to deserve so much "chewbac". Making a fire was nothing.

To see what he would do, I said, "Billy Muck, I can make a fire quicker than you;" and striking a match on my shoe, I set fire to some grass. The myall ran forward eagerly to see how it was done, so I struck another, and gave him a box for himself.

He sat down at once, and was so fascinated with his new toy that he struck off all his matches one after the other, making little grass fires all around him, till he looked like a black Joan of Arc at the stake. When they were all gone, he came and showed me the empty box, saying—

"Me bin finissem, Missus."

I gave him some more and a stick of tobacco, and then followed Bett-Bett up to the house. I found her crocodile's egg lying on the garden path, and, picking it up, hid it in the office. When she came back and found it gone, she gave one quick glance at the ground, and then walked to the office door and stopped. She was not allowed in there.

"Missus," she said, "which way you bin put him egg

belonga crocodile?"

I said, "You left it in the garden, Bett-Bett," and suggested that perhaps Sue had carried it off. "Might it Sue bin catch him, eh?"

"No more, Missus!" she said, grinning knowingly. "You bin put him longa office. Track belonga you sit down," she added, pointing at my footprints, leading from the garden to the office. I saw it was no use playing "hide the thimble" with the little black girl who followed up my tracks, and I gave her back her precious egg. Once I had tried playing "hide and seek" with the lubras; but I could never, by any chance, find *them*, and they always tracked *me* up, so it was not much fun. Their favourite way of hiding was to lie flat down in the grass, with their limbs spread out till they looked like open pairs of scissors, with grass growing between the handle and the blades. If you have ever looked for a hoop that has fallen in the grass, you will know how hard it was to find these lubras—how hard and how interesting.

When I gave Bett-Bett her egg, she took it to the broody hen, and filled her cup of happiness to the brim by letting her sit on it.

After supper, Bett-Bett threw herself down on the grass, and said, "Me tired fellow all right, Missus"; and, then, she wanted to know why white people live in houses. I could not see any connection between these two ideas till she said, "Him silly fellow likee that. Spose you tired fellow, what's the matter all day come home?" Then, I understood what was the grievance. When a blackfellow is tired, and has plenty of tucker for supper, he sees no sense in walking a long way just to sit on one particular patch of ground and call it home. When you have miles of beautiful country all your own, it is a much better plan to have your home just where you happen to be at the moment; and this can be arranged very easily, if you have nothing to carry about the world but a naked black body. When Bett-Bett lived out-bush, she told me that she and her friends would just wander about wherever they liked. If they grew tired, or the sun got too hot, they would lie down and go to sleep in the beautiful warm shade. When they woke up, very likely they would go down to the nearest waterhole, and have a bogey. If it was a pleasant waterhole, and some other blacks happened to be there, they would stay a few days until the tucker began to get scarce, and, then, all start off together to pay some friends a visit at another water-hole, taking care, as they went, to send up smoke signals to tell the tribe where they were, and whom they had met.

The smoke language is not nearly so perfect as the sign language, but still there are signals for most of the people and places in the country. Our boys could generally tell us where the stockmen were each night, and if they had met any white travellers.

"Blackfellow smoke bin talk, boy bin send him," Jimmy said once when I asked him how he knew. The stockmen's boys had evidently sent him a telegraphic smoke message. As Bett-Bett wandered about the bush, there was no danger that she would lose herself. A white child cannot possibly lose itself in *its* nursery, and neither could Bett-Bett in hers, even though it stretched for about a hundred miles.

She talked a great deal about the bush this night, and told me that debbil-debbils are very frightened of dogs, and that, if every one is very quiet, the debbil-debbils cannot find them. When she hears debbil-debbils about, she never speaks, and then they go away. Sue of course could frighten them off; but, as she is a very little dog, and debbil-debbils are very big and strong, it is just as well to take no risks. I believe that, if debbil-debbils did ever carry Sue off, Bett-Bett would insist on going too, for life without her would not be worth living.

Before I sent Bett-Bett to bed, I asked her if she would like to come a "walkabout" on horseback next time we went.

"My word, Missus!" she cried, springing to her feet, and then politely—"Dank you please, Missus!" and then called Sue to come and dream of the glories of such a walkabout.

Next morning, I heard shrieks of laughter and shouts of—"Go and lay 'em egg, silly fellow you."

I went to see what it was all about, and found Bett-Bett and the lubras doubled up with laughter at old "Broody", who seemed to be turning somersaults and catherine-wheels across the grass patch.

Bett-Bett had been right, and the crocodile's egg *had* hatched. The little curled-up creature had suddenly unwound itself, and, splintering the shell into fragments, had headed straight for the water.

Poor old Broody! we saw nothing of her for days, but, when next we *heard* her, she was announcing to all the world that she had taken Bett-Bett's advice and had "gone and laid an egg".

Bett-Bett appeared, grinning wisely, and said, "That one hen no more broody now, Missus."

I said that she might have the egg for herself, so she took it, and roasted it in the fire. Before laying it on the hot ashes, I noticed that she chipped a ring round it with her finger nails, taking great care not to pierce the skin underneath the shell.

"What name likee that, Bett-Bett?" I asked.

Carefully covering it up with ashes, she answered, "Spose *me* no more break him, *him* break meself all about."

Chapter 9

THE CORONATION "PLAY-ABOUT"

WE were camped at the Bitter Springs on the Roper River, about fifteen miles from home, and had just shut up a big mob of cattle in the yards.

We had been out-bush for a couple of weeks, riding from camp to camp, and mustering as we went. Bett-Bett was with us for her promised treat, and, as the head stockman said, was having "a wild and woolly time". Perched straddle legs on an old stock horse, with the stirrup irons wedged firmly between her little bare toes, she had had many a wild gallop after the cattle; and that, and everything else, was better than her wildest dreams of camping out.

As we rode from the yards to our camp, one of the men said, "Isn't this June? because, if it is, I reckon King Edward will be just about crowned."

We all agreed it was June right enough, but nobody seemed sure of the date; we couldn't even decide what day of the week it was. We had been out-bush so long that we had become hopelessly mixed.

"Well," said the Maluka, "we're within a week of it, and that's near enough for the Never-Never; so we'll have a 'play-about' to celebrate it. Whoop! Hallo there, boys!" he called; "come and have a bigfellow play-about." Then, remembering that some bush blacks were camped at the river, he added, "Call up your pals, and I'll shoot you a bullock for yourselves."

With yells and screechings, they obeyed, and were answered back by louder yells, as their bush friends—about twenty men, women, and children—came screaming through the trees to accept the invitation.

Some hobbled the horses, some collected firewood, others dug a big, wide, shallow hole, and lit an enormous fire in it; lubras and piccaninnies ran to hunt for stones, which were to

203

be made red hot in the fire, and everybody scampered and scuffled about, getting in one another's way, laughing and shrieking, as they played practical jokes on one another. When they heard the shot that killed the bullock, they rushed off in a wild stampede to the stockyard.

In about ten minutes, a ghastly procession came in sight, for the bullock had simply been hacked in pieces, skin and all; and every one, down to the tiniest piccaninny was carrying a red, horrible-looking joint of meat.

Billy Muck, who was to be king himself some day, had the bullock's head, and was amusing himself and everybody else by bucking and charging around, digging the horns into anyone he could catch. Bett-Bett had the tail, and was swishing about with it among the lubras and piccaninnies, greatly to their delight. In fact, the future king and queen were quite the life of the party. As the procession dodged and jumped about, it reminded me of a troop of clowns at a circus.

When it reached the fire, the meat was thrown on the ground; and, while the dogs were helping themselves to the tit-bits, the ashes and stones were scraped out; and, then, the oven was ready for the joints.

A layer of hot stones was first thrown in, then some joints of meat, then more stones and more meat, layer after layer, till the hole was full and heaped up; on top of this were poured a few quarts of water; on top again was piled earth; and, on top of everything else, a great big fire was lit.

Then, we went to our own camp to supper, and the blacks, making little fires every here and there grilled small pieces of meat to take the edge off their appetites; for it would be quite two hours before the joints were ready to eat.

As they sat, singing their strange, weird songs, the head stockman said it was a pity that we had no fireworks; but, as his Majesty would not let his mailman carry them, it was his Majesty's own fault, not ours.

"What about a poolooloomee show?" suggested the Maluka.

It was the very thing.

"Poolooloomees, boys!" we shouted; and every blackfellow sprang to his feet with a yell. Snatching tomahawks, knives, and hatchets, they rushed to the tall, white gum trees, and peeled off great sheets of bark, for they dearly loved a "poolooloomee play-about".

They dragged the bark to the fire, and, sitting down, cut it into thick strips, which were trimmed and shaped till they looked like small sized tennis racquets, or rather long-handled battledores. As these were cut, the lubras put the broad ends into the fires, leaving the handles sticking safely out. They did not blaze, for the bark was too full of sap; but they gradually changed colour till they were beautiful glowing rings of fire.

Of course, as soon as half-a-dozen were ready to send off, the blacks wanted to fire them, and the Maluka had hard work to make them wait till everybody was well supplied with poolooloomees. He managed it somehow; and it was well worth the trouble, for we had a magnificent display of fireworks.

When about two hundred of these little racquets were cut and glowing, each blackfellow drove a long, straight rod into the ground, and, holding one poolooloomee high in his right hand and a bundle of others in his left, stood looking at the Maluka, waiting for the signal.

"Let her go, Gallagher!" he shouted; and, instantly, the air was full of yells and blazing, twirling curling hoops of fire—the poolooloomee show had begun. At the word of command, every man had brought his right arm down with a peculiar, short, sharp swing, and, striking the poolooloomee handles hard against the firm upright rods, had broken off the fiery circles, and sent them whirling, and twisting, and soaring high up into the air. Quick as lightning, the handles were dropped, other poolooloomees taken from the left hand, struck off, and sent circling and sailing after the first flight, to be followed again and again by others.

It was marvellously weird and beautiful. Up went the strange fireworks, shooting like rockets through the trees, to join the brilliant cloud of poolooloomees that were floating away into the glorious tropical night. Backwards and forwards among the fires raced the lubras, looking like flitting black shadows, as they carried fresh supplies of fireworks to the men, letting no one's left hand get quite empty. The men themselves, standing full in the light of the fires, looked like shining black giants, as they worked and yelled and hallooed at their posts, surprised both at themselves and their display; and we whites sat still in wonder, amazed and admiring, sorry only that so few of the civilized world were there to see it all.

Poolooloomees are really a Daly Waters play-about; but our Roper blacks had learnt it from them, and some had learnt it very well.

As the last few poolooloomees glided out of sight, we gave a "hip, hip, hooray!" and a "tiger" for King Edward VII, and then amused ourselves by trying to fire some more.

Most of our attempts were dismal failures, the poolooloomees doing exactly what they ought not to do. All I fired tried to bury themselves in the ground; and the head stockman's spent most of their time hitting the nearest tree, and burning everybody within reach with a shower of sparks.

Altogether, we had a merry time; and the blacks cut away at bark for us, and screamed with delight at our failures; and, when one of the Maluka's rockets bounced from a tree, and dived into the head stockman's much-cherished grass-bed, their joy knew no bounds. But, when it blazed up, they rushed to the rescue and beat the fire out, looking like so many black imps, as they danced among the flames.

After that, they dug one another in the ribs with hot fire sticks, and played most foolish and painful tricks till the bullock was cooked. When the earth and fire were at last scraped away, all helped themselves to huge junks, and began tearing at them like wild beasts, dog and master eating from the same joint. I called Bett-Bett then, and we went to our camp, leaving our guests to their feast; for this part of the entertainment was not very pretty.

Long after midnight, they were still at it, singing and laughing and feasting. As I lay awake listening to them, I heard a peculiar scrunching going on inside Bett-Bett's mosquito net. I went over to see what it was, and found that she had crept back to the feast for her precious ox-tail, and that she and Sue were just finishing picking the bones.

Next morning, the bullock had completely disappeared;

and the king's loyal subjects looked as though they would burst, if only pricked with a pin!

When we reached the homestead, we found we had been a few days too soon with our demonstration; so, on the proper day, we called the blacks up, and we gave them flour, treacle, and "chewbac", for we had no bullock in the yards. Every one got an equal share; and Jimmy carried his supply in his little Union Jack apron, which was most loyal of him.

As the blacks turned to go to their camp, the men gave another "hip hooray and a tiger" for the King, and then fired a volley of revolver shots into the air as a royal salute. This was too much for our dusky friends; they thought we had suddenly gone mad, and, dropping flour and treacle-tins in all directions, fled helter-skelter into the bush, even Bett-Bett and the piccaninnies joining in the general scamper.

We shouted to them to stop, and said we were only having a play-about; but they did not wait to hear. We ran after them, but that only made matters worse. The only thing was to sit down and wait. When all was quiet, I lifted up my voice to the high sing-song pitch that the lubras had taught me would carry well and I called Bett-Bett.

Away in the distance, a thin little squeak answered. Then I called again and again; and, at last she screwed up enough courage to come back. We sent her after the others to tell them we were only in fun, and to say they had better come and collect their tucker.

For about five minutes, we heard her shrill little voice piping through the forest; and, then, Billy Muck turned up, giggling nervously. Soon after him came the station "boys", trying hard to look at ease, and pretending they had only run for fun. But it was nearly half-an-hour before everybody decided that it was really safe.

The last man in got teased unmercifully, because he had been frightened of the Missus and the Boss—the good Maluka who was every blackfellow's friend; and I thought it was very like "the pot calling the kettle black", seeing how they had run themselves.

We told them that we had shouted and fired, because that is the way that white men always have a play-about corroboree. They seemed able to see some sense in that idea, and were soon shouting with laughter at the way they had run as though it was the best joke in the world.

Bett-Bett put on great airs because she had come back first, and strutted about with her nose in the air, saying, "Me no more frightened fellow longa Missus; me all day savey Boss play-about. Me no more run long way," and so on, and so on.

As nobody had waited to see, nobody could contradict her, and she had it all her own way, and "came out on top", as the men said.

After a while, everything was gathered up again, and new pipes were given out all round to make up for the fright; and, very soon, some most indigestible-looking dampers were cooked and eaten, and everyone was happy and contented.

The King had coronation demonstrations all over his empire, and, at many of them a whole ox may have been roasted in the good old English way; but I doubt if he had a stranger or a merrier one than ours, in the very heart of the Never-Never Land.

Some weeks afterwards, we heard of the King's illness and of the postponing of the coronation, and knew that, after all, we had missed the real Coronation Day; but we had paid our homage to our King, and we were satisfied.

Chapter 10

"LOOKING OUT LILY-ROOT"

BETT-BETT and I very often went down to the billabong for an early morning bogey, and she and the lubras were always greatly amused at my bathing-gown. They called it "that one bogey dress", and said it was "silly fellow".

My swimming also amused them. They saw something very comical and unnatural in my movements, and I often caught them imitating me. They seemed to expect me to sink every moment, and never went very far from me in case of accidents.

One morning, we swam right across the billabong to the "nuzzer side", as Bett-Bett called it; and, there, I noticed a man's tracks on the bank, and asked whose they were; for, of course, I did not recognise them. To my surprise, the lubras burst into shrieks of laughter.

"Him Maluka!" they shouted in delight! "Him track belonga Maluka; him bin bogey last night."

Then, Bett-Bett screamed to the lubras on the opposite bank, "Missus no more savey track belonga Boss."

It was the best joke they had ever heard—a woman who did not know her own husband's tracks! I felt very small indeed, and, as soon as possible, went back to the house and breakfast.

We were going to have fowls for dinner, which always meant great fun for the blacks. The whole camp generally appeared with sticks and stones; and, when the cook had pointed out which fowls were to be caught, a most exciting chase took place. Off the birds went at the first alarm, followed by a shrieking, yelling crowd, flying over and under everything, and dodging round corners, till they were, at last, run down. I tried often to prevent it; but no matter how carefully the birds were shut up over night, they always managed to get out. The blacks enjoyed the chase so thoroughly that I suspect the fowls were assisted in their escape. Bett-Bett and Sue were, of course, in the worst of it this day; and, by some mishap, a stone, meant for one of the fowls, struck Sue on the front legs. She ran yelping and limping to Bett-Bett, and then, I heard shrieks of—"Missus! Missus! Sue bin break him arm. Stone bin kill him"; and they both appeared at the door. I took the poor little dog, and found it was only too true; one of her arms—as the blacks insist on calling the front legs—was hanging limp and broken. I bound it up as well as I could; and Bett-Bett cried piteously because I hurt the little creature.

When everything was made quite comfortable, she took Sue, and sat nursing and crooning over her all the morning.

In the afternoon, the Maluka and I were starting out for a ride, when Bett-Bett appeared with the lubras. They were going to travel "per boot", or on foot. Slung across Bett-Bett's back was a most ingenious sack-like affair, and from it peeped Sue's comical little face; for Bett-Bett could not bear either to leave her at home, or to see her limping about.

We were going only about three miles; and, as it was too rough and too hot to travel quickly, the lubras kept up with us easily. I noticed that Murra-weedbee was with them, and was still dragging her branch. I asked her if she had seen anything of her husband, and she said, "You eye. Him Monkey longa Willeroo."

Then, I was told that Murra-weedbee was really our Big Jack's lubra, but that Monkey had carried her off, the day that we had found Bett-Bett. Monkey had been very cruel to her, and so she had watched her chance and run back to Jack. It was a most interesting love story; and the exciting part was that Monkey was supposed to be somewhere rather near. Suspicious tracks had been seen. When we arrived at the Warloch Ponds—our destination—we found that some of the homestead blacks were there—all lubras gathering lily-roots for their husbands' supper.

When lubras go "looking out lily-root", as they call it, they take with them little wooden canoes, about two feet long, called coolamuns. They leave these floating about on top of the water while they themselves drop down to the bottom for the bulbs. As soon as their hands are full they come up again, and, putting the roots into the little vessels, disappear for more.

The Warlochs are always very beautiful ponds, all fringed round with pandanus palms, and dotted everywhere with magnificent purple water-lilies; but, this day they looked like a peep into fairyland. As I sat on my horse looking at it, I thought I had never seen anything prettier than the little, dainty rocking canoes, sailing among the blossoms, as the bobbing, curly, black heads of the lubras appeared and disappeared.

When the lubras saw us, they swam over, pushing the coolamuns before them; and, as they came nearer, I saw that in two of them were wee black piccaninnies; for a coolamun may be either a cradle or a tucker basket. There is no fear of their upsetting, for they are beautifully balanced, and even on land are very hard to overturn; besides, if the baby did scramble out, it would not matter, for most likely it would only swim about till its mother came up. I think, if I were a baby, I would like to lie in my little canoe, as it rocked and danced among the lilies.

Suddenly, Bett-Bett gave the alarm, and the air was filled with earsplitting shrieks and yells, as every one pointed to a blackfellow's tracks and said they were a Willeroo's, and that he was running quickly. Murra-weedbee pushed forward to see, and, then, giving a yell of "Monkey!" started for the homestead like an arrow from a bow, the branch bobbing and dancing and leaping behind her.

It looked as though an explosion of dynamite had taken place, for every one, seizing the nearest coolamun or tucker basket, ran helter-skelter after her. Only Bett-Bett and a poor blind lubra, "Lose-'em Eye", as she was called, stayed behind. Bett-Bett preferred white folk and revolvers when Willeroos were about; perhaps she was also thinking of poor Sue's foot.

We started for home with Bett-Bett and Lose-'em Eye between the horses for safety. At the creek, a valiant army met us, setting out to overtake and conquer Monkey. It was headed by old Jimmy, who had borrowed an old rusty revolver, and was full of courage to the finger-tips. He also had old Nellie in tow, to show where the tracks had been seen.

About sundown the valiant army returned, still thirsting for Monkey's blood; for, although they followed him a long way, his tracks were always new, and running westward. He evidently was doing a quick passage home.

After much excitement, we were, of course, told most awful stories of Willeroos, particularly of Monkey, and Murra-weedbee was the heroine of the hour.

Bett-Bett said that once she had been caught by them with some lubras and piccaninnies; and all the lubras said they remembered it well. It was a fearful tale, and a fearful experience. They were made to travel very quickly because of pursuit, and, at supper time, there was no tucker; so the Willeroos killed some of the piccaninnies and ate them, and then went to sleep. Fortunately, in the morning, some stockmen, who had been following the tracks, rode into the camp, and the Willeroos took to their heels; and, that time, the Roper River lubras escaped, Bett-Bett among them.

I asked her how it had happened that she had not been killed and eaten, and she answered with a chuckle, "Me too muchee all day bone fellow".

She had evidently not been worth eating, when fatter piccaninnies were about! "Me all day bone fellow," she repeated, holding out a thin little arm. She seemed to think she had been very clever in being thin, and she certainly had been fortunate.

Poor little mite! she had seen some fearful doings in her short life.

When I asked her if *she* had eaten any of these piccaninnies, she said that the blackfellows had not left any for her. "Blackfellows bin finissem, Missus," was all she said; and I don't believe she would have refused to have eaten her share.

She lay for a while looking up at the sky, and then changed the conversation by saying, "Missus, I think big-fellow black-fellow close up finissem that one moon."

"What?" I said, looking at the thin strip of new moon.

"I think big-fellow blackfellow close up finissem that one

moon," she repeated, jerking her voice, as she jerked her finger, towards it.

"Whatever are you talking about, Bett-Bett?" I asked.

She sat up and looked at me in surprise, and asked what did happen to the moon if a "big-fellow, big-fellow black-fellow" — a giant, I suppose — didn't cut it up to make the stars. All the lubras sat up, too, and agreed with her, saying, "Straightfellow, Missus". Even Sue joined in the conversation, but perhaps that was because some one had planted an elbow on her tail.

"Me plenty savey," said Bett-Bett, lying down again. Then, she told me that, away out east, there is a beautiful country, where a big tribe of moons live, hundreds of them. They are very silly creatures, and *will* wander about in the sky alone — you never see two moons at once, you know! Whenever a new moon wanders into the west — she called a full moon a new one — a great big giant who lives there catches it, and snips big pieces off, and makes stars with them. Some of the moons get away before he can cut them all up; but this poor moon had been "close up finissem", first thing.

"Spose me moon," said Bett-Bett, "me stay in my country; me no more silly fellow."

The suns live out east too, and were a very powerful tribe of "cheeky fellows". Every day one of them goes straight across the sky, and nobody knows what happens to him. At least, no lubra knows. Of course, the wise men know everything.

I suggested that perhaps the sun went back at night; but the lubras said, if he did, everybody would see him; and so, I suppose, they would.

Stars are very frightened of the sun. They say he is a "cheeky fellow" and will "round them up", if he finds them in the sky; so they hide all day, and towards night send two or three of the bravest of them to peep out, and see if he is really gone.

"Look, Missus," said Bett-Bett, pointing up at the sky; "littlefellow star come on now. Him look this way. Him look that way. Him talk which way sun sit down"; and it seemed, as I watched, as if they really were peeping cautiously about.

213

Suddenly, raising her voice to its very highest and shrillest pitch, she called, "Sun bin go away all right."

After she had called, a great number of stars came quickly one after the other, and she got very excited about it.

"Him bin hear me, Missus," she cried. "Straightfellow! Him bin hear me." After a long silence, Bett-Bett said, "Might it God bin make star longa your country, Missus?"

I only said, "You eye, God bin make my star." Long ago, I had given up trying to make them understand anything, excepting that God was a great, good Spirit, who was not afraid of the fiercest of debbil-debbils, and would chase them away from any one if they would ask Him. I had made them understand that much; and, after many months, they were beginning to believe it. In my first experiences with them, I had told them that God had made all things; and, of course, they had wanted to know how He made them, and what He had made them of. They assured me He had not made anything in the blackfellow's country. The wise men had an explanation of how everything there had been made; but I knew nothing of God's mysterious ways, and could explain nothing; so I decided to teach them first to believe in God Himself, and to let the other things alone.

Bett-Bett's thoughts were evidently on those early lessons, for, soon, she asked why God had not made any "bush" in the white man's country. A country without a "bush" was a constant puzzle to her. Old Goggle Eye had once gone a trip to a big town as "boy" with a mob of cattle, and had come back with the astonishing news that, in the white man's country, there was no "bush", only tracks and humpies.

Goggle Eye had gone to Western Australia in a steamer with these cattle, but had *walked home*, because, he said, the steamer had "too muchee jump-up jump-up, too muchee jump-down jump-down; me all day barcoo" (sick).

Before Bett-Bett went to bed, she once more repeated, "Blackfellow bin make this one mob star, Missus". Poor mite! she had no idea that her "mob" and my "mob" were the same "mob".

Rolly lingered behind every one, and asked if she might sleep under the veranda this night. Poor Rolly was often very ill, and then was very frightened of debbil-debbils, and liked to sleep near me. She said debbil-debbils could not come near where I was, because "Bigfellow God all day look out longa you, Missus". So, you see that, after all my trouble in teaching them, I had given them the idea that I was God's especial care.

It is very, very hard work to teach any blackfellow the truth of God's goodness and love. They have no god of any sort themselves, and they cannot imagine one.

After our Willeroo scare, we did not wander out-bush at all, for two reasons. The fear of Monkey was upon us, and Sue's foot needed rest.

Chapter 11

"NEWFELLOW PICCANINNY BOY"

ONE morning, a few weeks after our Willeroo scare, Bett-Bett came scampering up from the creek as fast as her thin little legs could carry her.

"Missus! Missus!" she shouted, "Topsy bin catch newfellow piccaninny boy, Topsy bin catch newfellow piccaninny boy;" and she sank down in a little breathless heap beside me.

Fast on her heels came some of the camp lubras bringing me an invitation to the christening party.

"You eye," they gasped, "him bin catch him all right;" and, then, they told me that Topsy, Sambo's lubra, wanted me to come and see it, and christen it with a white man's name. "Topsy bin talk, spose Missus come on, give piccaninny whitefellow name."

Of course, I went at once, taking a good supply of "chewbac" and a big red handkerchief, for we did not have a christening every day. Besides, I was curious to see this baby, for I had not yet seen a very tiny piccaninny.

Sambo met us at the creek, grinning widely with delight. We gave the proud father a new pipe and some "chewbac"; and he tried hard to grin a little wider in thanks, but found that even a blackfellow's grin has its limits. Topsy was sitting among the lubras, and looked round when she heard us approaching. On her knee was her eldest son, Bittertwine, a chubby little rascal about two years old. Beside her lay a coolamun, nearly filled with fresh green leaves and grass. As I came nearer she lifted up some of the leaves, and showed me the tiniest, tiniest atom of a baby lying sound asleep, cool, and safe from flies, in its pretty leafy cradle.

I stood for some minutes, too astonished to speak, for, instead of the shiny, jet-black piccaninny I had expected, I found one just about the colour of honey.

"What name, Topsy?" I asked at last. "Him close up whitefellow, I think."

"No more, Missus," she answered, touching the little sleeping baby lovingly. "Him blackfellow all right. Look, Missus, him blackfellow all right," she added, showing me one thin, jetblack line running right round the mouth and others round the eyes and nails.

Then, the lubras all joined in, and explained that a little black baby, when it is first born, is always of a very light golden brown, but with thin, black lines, just as this baby had. They said that, steadily and surely, these lines would widen and spread, till, in a few days, he would be like all other shiny black piccaninnies.

"All day likee that, Missus," they assured me in chorus, so I put a handful of tobacco in the baby's cradle, and spread a big red handkerchief on top. I said he was a man baby, and Mr Thunder debbil-debbil would be delighted to see he had a nice red handkerchief. The lubras laughed merrily at this, and the old men smiled on the Missus with approval.

Then, Topsy asked for a "whitefellow name" for her baby, and I said he should be called "Donald".

"Tonald!" cried Topsy. "Tonald! Him goodfellow name, that one."

Every one repeated "Tonald" after her, and then called to one another. "Missus bin talk 'Tonald' "; and the whole camp agreed it was a "goodfellow name all right". For some reason, best known to themselves, the name pleased them.

Topsy said that her baby had a kangaroo's spirit, and Jimmy was very pleased and important about it.

You see, Jimmy was head man of the kangaroo-spirit family, and it would be his duty to see that Tonald was properly brought up, for he must be taught all the laws of his totem, as well as how to throw his boomerang and use his throwing-stick. Jimmy was a sort of godfather to him; and Tonald would have to obey him even more than his own father and mother.

"By and by, me make him grow, Missus," said Jimmy, meaning that he would perform some very important ceremony to make the debbil-debbils keep away, so that Tonald could grow into a strong, wise blackfellow. It was

Jimmy's duty to do this; and a blackfellow always does his duty to his tribe.

After the christening, I passed round some "chewbac", and every one's pipe was filled, and Tonald's health was smoked. Every now and then, an old blackfellow would nod his head and chuckle.

"Tonald! Him goodfellow name, that one."

But Donald slept peacefully on; and Bittertwine sat on his mother's knee, looking from me to the piccaninny, with big, wondering eyes. Every little while, he took his mother's pipe out of her mouth, and put it in his own for a few sucks — smoking Donald's health, I suppose.

Bittertwine was a wild little black boy, or "myall", and terrified of white men; but I don't think it was the white man's fault. I fancy his mother used to tell him that the white man would catch him if he were naughty, just as some white mothers say "the black man" will catch *their* piccaninnies.

When we called on Tonald next morning, I found that Sambo was wearing his handkerchief, and that his friends had smoked his tobacco.

Topsy was very proud of her piccaninny. "Look, Missus," she exclaimed; "him close up blackfellow now." So he was; and, a day or two afterwards, he was black all over, all excepting the palms of his hands and the soles of his feet. These would be a pale grey all his life.

There was a visitor in the camp, quite a civilized blackfellow called Charlie, who was a great authority on christenings, for he had once been in a mission school. He told us that, when a white piccaninny got a name, "whitefellow chuck 'em water longa piccaninny". He had been christened himself once, and water had been "chucked" on him, and he seemed to think he knew all about it.

Charlie came up to the house a few days after the christening, and very rudely demanded a "big mob of chewbac".

I felt very angry with him for coming to me like this when he knew I was alone, so I said as quietly as I could, "Very well, I'll give you a big mob of something, Charlie"; and, before he quite knew what had happened, he was looking at my revolver, as I pointed it straight at him.

Poor Charlie, he could hardly be seen for the dust he made in his hurry to get out of revolver range. That was the first and last time I had to take my revolver to a blackfellow; but Charlie was supposed to be civilized, you see. You cannot change a blackfellow into a white man; if you try, you only make a bad, cunning, sly old blackfellow. I don't mean you can't make a blackfellow into a better blackfellow. I know that can be done, if he is kept a blackfellow, true to his blackfellow instincts.

After this, I expected that Charlie would keep out of my way, but he didn't; he now seemed to consider himself a very special friend of mine.

"My word, Missus! you cheeky fellow all right," he said next morning, when I went down to the camp, and he sat in front of a little circle of blackfellows, looking up at me in admiration.

"*My* word!" echoed the old fellows, for Charlie had told his story; and my old friends, being blackfellows, were full of reverence for any one who was a "cheeky fellow".

As we sat talking, Charlie told us that God made everything a white man has — trains and watches and horses, and that He showed him how to know miles. A blackfellow can see nothing to mark a mile, and wonders how the white man can. "Me plenty savey," said Charlie, "me savey count all about"; and he began to count his fingers. He kept getting mixed, and that meant beginning at his thumb again; and it was not till after many struggles that he managed to count to five.

"*My* word!" everybody said; and Charlie swelled with pride. You see a blackfellow only counts up to two. His arithmetic is very simple, just — "One, two, little mob, big mob"; so it was no wonder we were all amazed at Charlie.

He then told us in confidence that a little debbil-debbil "sat down" inside the telegraph wire, and ran messages "quickfellow" from one telegraph station to another. "Me savey," he said wisely; "me bin hear him talk-talk longa Daly Waters." Then, looking gravely round, he added, "Him bite all right, that one little fellow debbil-debbil."

I laughed at this; and the old men giggled nervously, for we knew that he had done what nearly every blackfellow has done—he had climbed up a telegraph pole to break off a piece of wire for a spear, and had found out that the debbil-debbil could bite when he got an electric shock! He said it didn't bite the white man because he was its master. The very fiercest dog never bites his master, you know.

Charlie knew all about that telegraph line. It was really a fence to keep the kangaroos in. That was why it was so high—too high for them to jump over. Unfortunately, the white man used up all the wire he had for the two top rails, and couldn't finish it. When the little debbil-debbil "jumped in", he made him run messages "quickfellow" for him.

"My word, whitefellow plenty savey," said Jimmy.

Billy Muck agreed with him, but said he was a "big-fellow fool" when he rounded up a big mob of cattle, and worked hard day and night only to brand them and let them go again. If Billy owned cattle, he would kill them all and invite his friends to the feast. Somehow, as I sat looking at the generous, honest, simple, unspoiled blackfellow—absolutely free from vice or care—I felt that perhaps he was right, and the white man is a "big-fellow fool" after all.

Charlie didn't like Billy's getting so much attention, and offered to count his toes; but I was tired of Charlie and his civilized ways, so called Bett-Bett and went home.

Bett-Bett was fascinated with Tonald, and asked all sorts of questions about white piccaninnies. Were they born white? Did they wear clothes? and so on.

To amuse her, I made a rag doll, and painted a face on it, and dressed it like a baby. She looked at it for a long while, feeling it carefully all over; then, she said with a chuckle, "Him gammon piccaninny I think, Missus!"

All the first day, she carried it in her arms, and Charlie told great tales of "gammon piccaninnies" that broke if they fell down.

The next day, she said that "gammon piccaninnies" were "silly fellow".

The day after that, Sue and the station pups had a tug-of-war with it, and the last we saw of it was when Sue was "going bush" with it in her mouth, and the pups in full chase after her.

Bett-Bett took no notice of the fate of her "gammon

piccaninny". She had found something much more interesting—a nest of little kittens under the raised floor of the bathroom; and, for several days, we saw very little of her, except the soles of her feet, as they stuck out from under the bathroom floor.

When the kittens were old enough, I sent Billy Muck with one of them to my next-door neighbour. With a bottle of milk and saucer under one arm, and the kitten under the other, he started for his hundred-mile walk as cheerfully as though he were just going round the corner, and, in two days reached the Katherine, his journey's end.

On his return, I asked him why he had hurried so.

"Milk close up finissem," was all he said.

Good kind old Billy Muck! He wouldn't let even a kitten suffer from hunger or thirst, if he could help it.

Chapter 12

GOGGLE EYE SUNG "DEADFELLOW"

"MISSUS!" a thin, cracked old voice whispered close to me as I sat sewing one evening. I looked up to see an old, old grey-haired blackfellow standing beside me.

"What name?" I said, feeling rather startled; and, then, something in his face make me look more closely at him, and I saw that it was Goggle Eye; but oh, such a worn old scarecrow! There was hardly a trace of the merry, laughing rogue, who had gone off, a few weeks before, with his bag of sugar tied round his neck.

"Poor old Goggle Eye!" I said, "whatever has happened?"

"Blackfellow bin sing me deadfellow longa bush," he croaked in a hoarse whisper. "Flour-bag bin come on quickfellow long me cobra," he added, pointing to his grey old head, with its thickly-sprinkled "flour-bag", as he called the white hairs.

I knew what this "singing" meant. He had been cursed by the magic men of the tribe. They had bewitched him by singing magic, and pointing death-bones at him, and he would die. Nothing that I could do would save him.

He looked so weak and worn that I gave him some brandy, and he lay down under the veranda. As he lay there, he told me that Tommy Dod, a blackfellow, had carried him thirty miles on his back to bring him in to me and the homestead. Tommy Dod was his younger blood-brother, and it was his duty to help the poor old fellow.

I called Tommy and told him to make a bark humpy at the camp. He did this, and then carried Goggle Eye up to it, and lit his fire. Then, we rolled him up in a blanket and gave him some food: and, very soon, the poor, tired old king was asleep.

In the morning, I took him some arrowroot, and persuaded him to eat it all, telling him that it often killed blackfellow's magic. I knew that, if only I could make him believe this, I might cure him. After he had finished, I sat down in the camp; and Billy Muck, Jimmy, Tommy Dod, and Goggle Eye told me all sorts of wonderful tales about "singing magic" and "bone-pointing".

There are many ways of killing by magic; and, if a blackfellow wants to get rid of an enemy, it is a much safer way than spearing, because he will not run any chance of being hurt himself, unless some one finds out who did the bone-pointing; when, of course, he would be "sung" in turn by way of revenge.

The way of killing by bone-pointing is this:— The blackfellow takes a sharp-pointed bone—the Roper blacks prefer a kangaroo's, but some tribes say that a dead man's bone is best; this bone is stuck in the ground, and the would-be murderer bends over it, and "sings magic" into it.

Supposing that he was going to make Goggle Eye die by magic, this is what he would sing:—

"Kill Goggle Eye, kill Goggle Eye, make him deadfellow;
Pull away his fat, make him bone fellow;
Shut him up throat, shut him up throat;
Break him out heart, break him out heart;
Kill him deadfellow, kill him deadfellow;
Spose him eat fish, poison him with it;
Spose him eat bird, poison him with it."

And he would keep on singing, till he had sung or cursed everything he could think of; but he would not try to "sing water", for nobody can do that.

Any one can "sing magic", even lubras, but, of course, the wise old magic men do it best. It never fails with them, particularly if they "sing" and point one of the "special death-bones", or "sacred stones", of the tribe. Generally, a blackfellow goes away quite by himself when he is "singing magic", but, very occasionally, a few men join together, as they did in the case of Goggle Eye.

When enough magic has been "sung" into the bone, it is taken away to the camp, and very secretly pointed at the unconscious victim. The magic spirit of the bone runs into the man who is pointed at, and gradually kills him.

Everything must be done secretly, for, if the man's

relatives had any idea who had done the bone-pointing, they would go and "sing" *him* in revenge. You must be particularly careful that there are no willy-waggletails, or jenning-gherries, about, for these little mischief makers would go and tell the cockatoos, who, in their turn, would make a dream about it, and carry it to the bewitched man when he was asleep, to let him know who had "sung" him.

Cockatoos make all dreams, and carry them to the sleeper in the night. If you are lying awake, you may often hear them moving in the dark, for they are very restless birds. The best time to point bones is at night, for, then, all jenning-gherries are asleep.

Of course the man who has been "sung" must be told somehow, or he will not get a fright and die. There are many ways of managing this. One very good way is to put the bone where he will be sure to find it, in his dilly bag, or near his fire, or through the handle of his spear. There are many ways of telling him without letting him know who has "sung" him; but the man who leaves the bone about must, of course, be very careful to destroy his own tracks.

Have you ever heard of faith healing? Well, dying from bone pointing is faith dying! Goggle Eye, after he had found the bones lying about, knew exactly what was going to happen to him—and, of course, it did. His throat became very sore, and he grew so thin and weak that he could barely stand.

A man can be cured by magic men charming the "bone" away again; but Goggle Eye was old, and, what was worse, he was getting very cross, and too fond of ordering people about; so the blackfellows thought that it would be the best plan not to cure him, and a few more sneaked away into the bush, and "sang" some more "bones", and pointed them at him to make quite sure about his dying.

It was fearfully cruel. Poor old Goggle Eye suffered so dreadfully, and the only friend he had—excepting the Missus—was Tommy Dod! Nobody else would do anything for him, because they were afraid of the curse coming to them. It couldn't touch Tommy, because he was his blood-brother, and had to do all he could to help.

Old Jimmy and Billy Muck said they would like to help,

but that, if they made Goggle Eye's fire for him, their own would never burn again. Nobody could even carry his food to him. To make matters worse, Tommy Dod had to go "bush" on some private business—perhaps he was singing some of his own enemies dead—and, then, I had to do everything myself.

Day after day, I took his food to him, and made his fire, but I soon saw it was too late. He ate anything that I brought him, and ordered me about generally, and growled at me for not putting enough sugar in his tea—he didn't want sugar in his tea, what he preferred was a little tea in his sugar!

Sometimes, a glimpse of the merry old rogue would peep out from the gaunt old skeleton. One day, I was on my hands and knees at his fire, blowing hard at it.

"My word, Missus," he laughed merrily, "you close up blow him all away;" and he showed me the proper way to blow, and chuckled to himself at my clumsy attempts, for a blackfellow can make a fire better than any one else.

It sounds very grand being a lady-in-waiting to a king, but it was really very smelly and disagreeable. His humpy was, in fact, only a sheet of bark leaning against a fallen tree, and I had to crawl about on my hands and knees and everything was dreadfully close and stuffy. But I had plenty of Eau de Cologne, and used it freely. One day, when Bett-Bett smelt it, as I was sprinkling it over my dress, she screwed up her little black nose, and, after half a dozen very audible sniffs, said, "My word, Missus! That one goodfellow stink all right!"

I said I was glad she liked it; and, as Goggle Eye also remarked on it, I always used plenty of this "goodfellow" stink before I visited him.

At last, Tommy Dod came back, and I had not so much to do. One evening, when I went up with some arrowroot, all the blacks in the camp were sitting round in a circle, looking at Goggle Eye. They had taken away the sheet of bark so as to see him better, and were talking about him, and wondering when he would die, and if debbil-debbils would take him away.

"I think him die tonight, Missus," said Billy Muck cheerfully, as I came up. "I think him die fowl sing out."

Goggle Eye gave a little glad cry when he saw me.

"Missus," he called weakly; and I went to him, and gave him a little brandy and arrowroot.

"Be quiet!" I said angrily, as the old men began talking about him again. They looked surprised, but obeyed, wondering, I think, why I objected to such an interesting topic of conversation.

Soon the poor old fellow asked me if I would tell my "Big-Fellow God" to chase away the debbil-debbils. I was very touched, and did exactly as he wished in queer pidgin English. Then Goggle Eye was happy and contented, and the strange prayer was answered, for he was no longer afraid of his fearsome debbil-debbils.

Soon after supper, he fell asleep, and I left him, and never saw my strange old friend again. Billy Muck was right, and, at "fowl sing out", or cockcrow, Ebimel Wooloomool, King of Dullinarrinarr, died and with him died many strange, weird old legends, and a good big slice of the history of the blacks of the Never-Never.

Billy Muck, the Rainmaker, was now king, and I suppose that Bett-Bett was queen consort. But the tribe will never be afraid of the new king, for he is neither cute nor clever, and I don't think the wise men will take much notice of him. He is head man, of course, and knows all his corroborees; but he is only a kind, simple-hearted old blackfellow, and will never be the absolute monarch that Goggle Eye was.

They buried the poor old king in a very shallow grave, just where he had died. They laid his spears and his pipe, and all that belonged to him, on the top of his grave, covering them over with a sheet of paper-bark, which was kept in place with a few large stones. After that, they built his bark humpy over him again, and then went away, leaving him all alone in the deserted camp; for a camp is always deserted after a death. Their new camp was two or three hundred yards away; and never again would any one willingly enter the old one.

South of the Roper River, dead men are always put away in the branches of a tree for a long time before burial, but I never heard of this being done at the Roper. I know Goggle Eye was buried at once; and there was a big "cry-cry" in the camp. Everyone ran about, and pretended to cut themselves with knives, but I noticed that it was nearly all pretence. I don't believe that any of them cared as much as I did.

Next day, Tommy Dod started on a journey to try and find out, by different magic signs, who had "sung" his brother, so that he could "sing" them in revenge. That was his duty, you know. As far as I could find out, somebody was always looking for somebody else in order to "sing" him. If Tommy found the murderer, he would "sing" him; and, if the murderer died, his relatives would all "sing" Tommy, and, then, Tommy's relatives would "sing" the murderer's relatives; and that is how it goes on, till the wonder is that anybody is left alive.

Nobody ever mentioned Goggle Eye's name again. It didn't matter, but it was just as well not to do so, because, if he heard his name, he might think some one was calling him, and come to see.

When they needed to speak of him, they gave his name in the sign language. To do this, they crooked up all their fingers, till their hand looked like a bird's claw, and, then, suddenly jerked it forward, and that meant, "Ebimel Wooloomool Neckberrie," or "Goggle Eye the Deadfellow!"

Chapter 13

BETT-BETT IS "BUSH HUNGRY"

FOR some days Bett-Bett had wandered about in an aimless, listless way, doing nothing and saying nothing, but just looking out-bush with big, dreamy eyes.

She did not know what had happened to her; but I, who had seen this many times in her people, knew.

She was homesick — "bush hungry" — hungry for her own ways and her own people; for the bush talks, and the camps, and the long, long wanderings from place to place, for the fear of debbil-debbils, for anything that would make her a little blackfellow girl once more, for anything — if only she could shake off the white man for a little while, and do nothing but live.

We whites sometimes grow very weary and "bush hungry" when we are taken away to the towns; but we can never even guess at the pain of a blackfellow's longing for his own people and his beloved "bush".

Poor little Bett-Bett! as I watched her, I knew that, sooner or later, I must let her go, for there was no other cure for her. If I tried to keep her, she would only run away or be ill.

At last, she came to me, saying, "Missus! me sick-fellow, I think," and sat down at my feet.

I talked to her quietly for a little while about her people and their long walkabouts; for, the sooner she went, the quicker she would be cured.

All at once, she knew what she needed.

"Missus," she cried, springing to her feet, all life and energy again, "Missus, me want walkabout. No more longa you, Missus, longa blackfellow."

That was all — and I only asked, "How long, Bett-Bett?"

"Me no more savey, Missus," she answered, her eyes burning like stars. She could not tell. She only knew that she must stay till she was cured.

Next morning at sun-up she went. She took nothing with her but the little bag made from her "shimmy shirt" string, for in that was her most precious treasures. She stuffed all her clothes into her box, wearing only a gaily-striped handkerchief wound round her middle. Even that would soon be gone, for she was going to be just a little blackfellow girl for a while.

Sue didn't like the look of things at all. She sat down and whined miserably, trying to say that the homestead was quite good enough for her, as long as Bett-Bett was in it. Poor little Sue! It was really only her body that was so miserably ugly, for her comical little face was brimful of beautiful love and devotion for her little mistress.

I went as far as the camp with them, where Bett-Bett was to meet her friends. Then, I stood and watched this tiny black princess of the Never-Never, with her faithful speckled subject at her heels, fade away into her wonderful, lonely palace. Once, Sue sat down and whined; and Bett-Bett, looking round, saw me still watching her. She ran back, and, without speaking, thrust a little pearl mussel shell, one of her most treasured belongings, into my hand; then, scampering after her friends, disappeared into the forest.

I walked back to the homestead, feeling strangely lonely, for I had grown accustomed to the little black shadow that was always chattering at my heels; but, when I looked at the little pearl shell, as it lay in my hand, I knew that, in a little while, Bett-Bett would need her Missus, and come back bright and happy again.

AUTHOR'S AFTERWORD

THERE is little more to tell. Just that old, old story—that sad refrain of the Kaffir woman that we British-born can conquer anything but Death.

All unaware, that scourge of the Wet crept back to the homestead, and the great Shadow, closing in on us, flung wide those gates of Death once more, and turning, before passing through, beckoned to our Maluka to follow. But at those open gates the Maluka lingered a little while with those who were fighting so fiercely and impotently to close them—lingering to teach us out of his own great faith that "Behind all Shadows, standeth God". And then the gates gently closing, a woman stood alone in that little home that had been wrestled, so merrily, out of the very heart of Nature.

That is all the world need know. All else lies deep in the silent hearts of the men of the Never-Never—in those great, silent hearts that came in to the woman at her need; came in at the Dandy's call, and went out to her, and shut her in from all the dangers and terrors that beset her, quietly mourning their own loss the while. And as those great hearts mourned, ever and anon a long-drawn-out sobbing cry went up from the camp as the tribe mourned for their beloved dead—their dead and ours—our Maluka, "the best Boss that ever a man struck".

PUBLISHER'S AFTERWORD

THE scourge of the Wet — malarial dysentery — that Mrs
Aeneas Gunn describes in her Afterword, killed her
husband on 16 March 1903. After the Maluka's death a new
manager was appointed to run the Elsey Station and the
Missus had to leave. On returning to Melbourne she went to
live with her father at her former home in Hawthorn. Shortly
afterwards, during a visit to relatives and friends in
Adelaide, whom she delighted with stories about the
endearing but mischievous Bett-Bett and her dog Sue, she
was persuaded to write a book about the Aboriginal child. In
1905 *The Little Black Princess* was published and in the
following year Mrs Gunn began writing her second book,
We of the Never-Never. This memorable account of her life in
the North was finally published in 1908 after the manuscript
had been rejected by no fewer than six publishers!

Mrs Gunn planned to write two more books: one about
Aboriginal lore retold by John Terrick, a son of one of the
last of Victoria's Aboriginal chiefs, and the other to be set
against the Dandenongs. Although she began the painstaking task of collecting facts and background material for
the books, she was so heavily involved in work for the
Returned Servicemen's League that she was unable to
complete the research.

More and more of her time was devoted to caring for
disabled soldiers and their wives and families. During World
War I she packed parcels, wrote innumerable letters and
bore both good and bad tidings to relatives. After the war she
acted as an unofficial liaison between the Repatriation
Department and those needing its help. In this work the
talents which had helped her as an author — her ability to
research thoroughly and to express her ideas
clearly — enabled her to deal successfully with the

servicemen's complicated problems. And the devotion she showed to their cause, a devotion earlier evident in her care of the Aboriginal Goggle Eye, was honoured by many welfare associations. In 1939 Mrs Gunn was awarded an OBE "in recognition of her services to Australian Literature and to the disabled soldiers and their dependents of two world wars". In her later years this amazing woman remained actively interested in welfare work.

After an extremely full and long life Mrs Gunn died on 9 June 1961, a few days after her ninety-first birthday. Although she had stayed in touch with her friends in the North, she never revisited the land of the Never-Never. But, as she wrote in the Prelude of her classic about that land, "we who have lived in it, and loved it, and left it, know that our hearts can Never-Never rest away from it".